The Library Reference Series

LIBRARIANSHIP AND LIBRARY RESOURCES

The Library Reference Series

Lee Ash
General Editor

THE DEVELOPMENT OF
REFERENCE SERVICES

Through Academic Traditions,
Public Library Practice
and
Special Librarianship

By
SAMUEL ROTHSTEIN

(ACRL Monographs Number 14)

GREGG PRESS

Boston 1972

Library of Congress Cataloging in Publication Data

Rothstein, Samuel, 1921-
    The development of reference services through
academic traditions, public library practice, and
special librarianship.

    (Library reference series)
    Reprint of the 1955 ed., which was issued as no. 14
of ACRL monographs.
    Bibliography: p. 111-124.
    1. Reference services (Libraries) I. Title.
II.   Series: ACRL monographs, no. 14.
[Z711.R645 1972]   025.5'2   72-10127
ISBN 0-8398-1776-2

THE DEVELOPMENT OF
REFERENCE SERVICES

ACRL MONOGRAPHS

ACRL MONOGRAPHS are published by the ASSOCIATION OF COLLEGE AND REFERENCE LIBRARIES (ACRL) at whatever intervals demand warrants, supplementing the Association's journal COLLEGE AND RE-SEARCH LIBRARIES. The ACRL is a division of the AMERICAN LIBRARY ASSOCIATION, and the Editorial Board of ACRL MONOGRAPHS collaborates with the Editorial Committee and the Publishing Department of the parent organization.

ACRL MONOGRAPHS are original contributions covering all aspects of collegiate and research librarianship. In general, they consist of items too lengthy for publication in COLLEGE AND RESEARCH LIBRARIES and particularly suited for presentation as separates because of the nature of their content. Sometimes they include symposia or proceedings of various professional groups. Every effort is made to present material that will be of interest to all the sections of ACRL, whether or not prepared by ACRL members. On occasion, particular issues will carry appropriate matter to wider audiences of professional librarians.

The EDITORIAL BOARD consists of the EDITOR, *David K. Maxfield*, University of Illinois Library, Chicago Undergraduate Division, and four ASSOCIATE EDITORS, *Frances B. Jenkins*, University of Illinois Library School, *Rolland E. Stevens*, Ohio State University Library, *Fritz Veit*, Chicago Teachers College and Wilson Junior College, and *Howard W. Winger*, Graduate Library School, University of Chicago. *Maurice F. Tauber*, Editor of COLLEGE AND RESEARCH LIBRARIES and *Lawrence S. Thompson*, Editor of the ACRL MICROCARD SERIES, serve as EDITORIAL CONSULTANTS. *Cynthia Spigelman* is EDITORIAL ASSISTANT.

Manuscript contributions will be welcomed from anyone, and will be edited in accordance with the same standards as apply to COLLEGE AND RESEARCH LIBRARIES. Unless specifically indicated in the preliminary pages of particular issues, the views expressed are those of individual authors, and not those of the Association of College and Reference Libraries. Manuscripts should be addressed only to the Editor, c/o University of Illinois Library, Chicago Undergraduate Division, Chicago 11, Illinois. All issues are indexed in LIBRARY LITERATURE and have individual Library of Congress printed catalog cards.

THE PRICE OF THIS 14th ISSUE IS $2.75 (paper); $3.25 (cloth)

For list of titles in print and information about placing orders see back flyleaf.

THE DEVELOPMENT OF

REFERENCE SERVICES

through

ACADEMIC TRADITIONS, PUBLIC LIBRARY

PRACTICE AND SPECIAL

LIBRARIANSHIP

by

SAMUEL ROTHSTEIN

Assistant Librarian

University of British Columbia

ACRL MONOGRAPHS

Number 14

Chicago:

ASSOCIATION OF COLLEGE AND REFERENCE LIBRARIES

June, 1955

LIBRARY OF CONGRESS CATALOG CARD NUMBERS

All ACRL MONOGRAPHS are cataloged by the Library of Congress, and printed catalog cards are available for the series, as well as for each separate number in the series.

The card number for the ACRL MONOGRAPHS series is 52-4228.

The card numbers for the separate ACRL MONOGRAPHS issued to date are as follows:

No. 14: 55-9938

No. 13: 55-9607

No. 12: 55-8476

No. 11: (53-2932)

No. 10: (53-2932)

No. 9: 53-12097

No. 8: 53-2697

No. 7: 53-2695

No. 6: 53-2698

No. 5: 53-2696

No. 4: (53-2932)

No. 3: 52-4225

No. 2: 52-4227

No. 1: 52-4226

LITHOPRINTED IN THE UNITED STATES OF AMERICA BY
CUSHING-MALLOY, INC., ANN ARBOR, MICHIGAN, 1955

TABLE OF CONTENTS

TABLE OF CONTENTS (Continued)

PREFACE

This study was submitted in partial fulfillment of the requirements for the degree of Doctor of Philosophy in Library Science in the Graduate College of the University of Illinois, 1954.

Though the responsibility for this work is mine alone, in many ways it has been a cooperative undertaking. I am glad to have this opportunity to record my appreciation for the advice, information, and encouragement which have done so much to enable me to carry the study to completion.

My greatest debt is to Dr. Leslie Whittaker Dunlap, who has variously acted as supervisor, class instructor, adviser, and critic in the long process of library experience, course work, research, and writing that has culminated in this dissertation. The initial idea for the study arose out of my course with him; its development has taken its shape largely out of our many subsequent discussions. He has always managed to combine searching criticism with the warmest personal encouragement. I am deeply grateful.

My thanks also go out to the other four members of my committee — Dr. Thomas E. Benner, Dr. Robert B. Downs, Dr. Rose B. Phelps, and Professor Ernest J. Reece — who were kind enough to read the lengthy initial draft; their suggestions and criticisms helped me avoid many errors. Dr. Harold Lancour also favored me with a thorough reading of the first draft.

A number of librarians have, by personal interviews and by making materials available, given me important information on the development of reference services in their institutions. I wish to express my thanks for help of this kind given to me by Dr. Burton W. Adkinson, Mr. David C. Mearns, and Mr. Thomas S. Shaw of the Library of Congress; Mr. Charles Mixer and Miss Constance Winchell of the Columbia University Library; Mr. Archibald P. De Weese, Mr. Barron F. Franz, and Mr. James G. Tobin of the New York Public Library; Mr. Herman H. Henkle of the John Crerar Library; Mr. Charles M. Mohrhardt of the Detroit Public Library; Mr. B. Bowman and Mrs. Gertrude Woodward of the Newberry Library; Miss Estelle Brodman of the Armed Forces Medical Library; and Dr. Otto Kinkeldey, formerly librarian of the Cornell University Library. Mr. Stephen Stackpole of the Carnegie Corporation of New York generously placed at my disposal the Corporation's files on the "research librarianships."

The staff of the University of Illinois Library and Library School has been consistently indulgent in meeting the many requests entailed by this dissertation. I owe particular thanks to Miss Helen Stewart and her girls at the Loan Desk, who renewed my many overdues without a grumble; to Mr. T. E. Ratcliffe and his assistants in the Reference Department, who supplied me with inter-library loans and many facts; and to Miss Donna Finger and Miss Billie Hurst of the Library School Library.

In its long months "in process," this study has come to intrude on the lives of many people. To my friends Frances and Leonard Blackman, Joan and Bill Taylor, Jean and Jack Sumner, Marie Dunlap, John Boll, Eleanor Blum, Walf Erickson, Wesley Simonton, and Rick Farley, who have patiently suffered through many a long monologue, this word of thanks is well warranted. I am especially indebted to Frances Blackman, who typed both the draft and final copy at the cost of so many late hours. She showed me what assistance really means.

Most of the time I spent on this dissertation and on the course work that preceded it, I was the recipient of a grant from the Carnegie Corporation of New York. To the Corporation — and particularly to Mr. Stephen Stackpole, the executive assistant of its British Dominions and Colonies Program, and to Dr. Norman MacKenzie, president of the University of British Columbia, who was largely instrumental in my receiving this generous aid, — I again express my thanks.

To my wife Miriam, who has done most of all — well, she gets a page of her own.

For their most welcome assistance in correcting proof, I owe sincere thanks to my brother, Aser Rothstein, and to Neal Harlow. I also wish to express my appreciation for the interest and advice of Mr. David K. Maxfield, editor of A C R L MONOGRAPHS, and for the work of Mrs. Cynthia Spigelman in seeing the manuscript through the press.

                                                                      Samuel Rothstein

Vancouver, B.C.: June 15, 1955

FOR MIRIAM

INTRODUCTION

Modern American library history has received only sporadic attention as a subject for investigation. Though we have now accumulated an adequate supply of source materials to draw upon in the form of annual reports, service studies, biographical accounts, and chronicles of individual libraries, no one has yet fashioned out of these materials a critical history of American librarianship. To paraphrase Leo LaMontagne, we have salvaged remnants from the past, but we have yet to convert them into history.[1]

The lack has cost the profession dearly. Even a casual survey of the literature of librarianship reveals the shocking degree of duplication and naiveté that stem from an insufficient awareness of previous efforts.

There is clearly room and need for a series of evaluative studies of the development of American library services which could eventually be put together to form the desired definitive history of American librarianship. The present dissertation is intended as a contribution toward that end. It undertakes to furnish the historical background for one of the continuing problems of American librarianship — the provision of reference services in research libraries.

Definitions

Reference services in research libraries exist for, and are conditioned by, the needs and purposes of research. The task of definition must accordingly begin with the examination of the meaning of "research."

As a "popular" word, "research" has lent itself to a wide variety of usage. "Research" backs up the glittering claims of cosmetics advertisements, and students complacently label their exercises as "research papers." As if by way of rebuttal to popular usage, within the academic field proper there has been a recent tendency, mainly on the part of workers in the natural sciences, to identify "research" with the experimental method. Neither usage is acceptable here. While it is manifestly inappropriate to dignify as "research" every casual attempt at investigation, it is also a misconception of the scientific method to refuse to admit under the rubric of research serious inquiries that rely on methods other than those pre-eminently useful in the natural sciences. As Shryock points out, "the continued attempt to define 'research' or 'science' in terms of a particular method or result is confusing, since historically the methods and results have changed in any given field without changing what is more essential — the objective."[2]

There yet remains room for a logically defensible intermediate ground between these poles, as is evidenced in the position adopted by such competent judges as Frederic Ogg and the National Resources Committee. Thus Ogg, writing from the point of view of the humanists and social scientists, has defined research as

> any investigative effort — in library, laboratory, field or shop — which has for its object an increase of the sum total of human knowledge, either by additions to the stock of actual present knowledge or by the discovery of new bases of knowledge... Research may or may not come to success; it may or may not add anything to what is already

[1]Leo LaMontagne, "Historical Background of Classification," in *The Subject Analysis of Library Materials,* edited by Maurice F. Tauber (New York: School of Library Service, Columbia University, 1953), p. 27.

[2]Richard H. Shryock, *American Medical Research Past and Present* (New York: The Commonwealth Fund, 1947), p. 8.

known. It is sufficient that its objective be new knowledge, or at least a new mode or orientation of knowledge. [3]

The National Resources Committee was at some pains to distinguish serious investigations from routine testing operations. Its definition reflects the Committee's orientation toward the sciences, but otherwise displays the requisite amplitude.

> "Research" has been defined to comprise investigations in both the natural and social sciences, and their applications, including the collection, compilation and analysis of statistical, mapping and other data that will probably result in new knowledge of wider usefulness than aid in one administrative decision applying to a single case. [4]

From these definitions, combining breadth of view and precision, the distinguishing features of research are seen to lie in the facts that it rests upon a serious, careful inquiry, and that its object is the extension or revision of knowledge. These two criteria accordingly form the basis of the writer's own definition, which reduces research to these essentials: *Research is a critical and exhaustive inquiry directed toward the extension or modification of knowledge.*

The *research library* is, as the name suggests, an agency designed to be of service in research. In its simplest and purest form it might be plausibly defined, as in the words of Conyers Read, to be "an institution designed to assist those engaged in extending the boundaries of knowledge." [5]

The realities of the situation demand, however, some modification of Read's definition. As actually constituted, research libraries are complex institutions serving a variety of purposes. The university library looks to the needs of undergraduates as well as to those of the faculty. The large public library is legitimately as concerned with the promotion of recreational reading as with its service to scholarship. On the other hand, no library, even the meanest, is wholly remote from research, for the vagaries of scholarship may lead the researcher to find assistance in the most unlikely sources. A more precise definition of the research library would therefore describe it as a library which assumes as one of its *primary* functions the supply of materials and assistance to persons making critical and exhaustive investigations with the aim of extending knowledge.

This definition eliminates from consideration in the present study school libraries, all but a handful of college and public libraries, and many university libraries whose collections are so meager as to make their service to research only casual and intermittent. The libraries admissible to the category of research library under the above definition would include the larger university libraries, the libraries of historical and learned societies, special libraries serving research workers in government and in industry, and a small number of outstanding public and state libraries.

Without attempting here an elaborate classification of the various types of research library, [6] we may usefully distinguish two main categories — the special library devoted to the intensive cultivation of a small area of knowledge and closely limited to the service of a specified group of research

---

[3] Frederic Austin Ogg, *Research in the Humanistic and Social Sciences; Report of a Survey Conducted for the American Council of Learned Societies* (New York: The Century Company, 1928), p. 13.

[4] U. S. National Resources Committee, Science Committee, *Research – a National Resource* (Washington: Government Printing Office, 1938-41), I, 62.

[5] University of Pennsylvania Library, *Changing Patterns of Scholarship and the Future of Research Libraries; a Symposium in Celebration of the 200th Anniversary of the Establishment of the University of Pennsylvania Library* (Philadelphia: University of Pennsylvania Press, 1951), p. 98.

[6] Cf. Ogg, *op. cit.*, p. 363. Ogg distinguishes no less than ten different types of research libraries — university libraries, public libraries, the Library of Congress, libraries of learned societies, historical libraries, state libraries, government department libraries, legislative reference libraries, and "special libraries." As he himself admits, this scheme (and for that matter, probably any other) involves a good deal of overlapping, since historical libraries are often libraries of learned societies, and all but the first three types might well be called "special libraries." An elaborate scheme should also make a place for the endowed reference libraries, such as the Huntington Library and the Newberry Library; nearly all of these are also "special" in terms of their coverage and clientele.

workers, and the general research library, which undertakes coverage of a wide range of knowledge. The general research library — the Library of Congress, the New York Public Library and the University of Illinois Library are representative examples — usually serves a variety of functions, and its clientele is likely to be heterogeneous. Both factors affect its service to research.

Reference work, like research, is an intangible, a process which is susceptible to, and has been the subject of, a variety of definitions. The earliest came from William B. Child. Speaking before the New York Library Club in 1891, he said: "By reference work is meant simply the assistance given by a librarian to readers in acquainting them with the intricacies of the catalogue, in answering questions, and, in short, doing anything and everything in his power to facilitate access to the resources of the library in his charge."[7]

Alice Kroeger's *Guide to the Study and Use of Reference Books* declared reference work to be "that branch of administration which deals with the assistance given to readers in their use of the resources of the library."[8]

For William Warner Bishop, writing in 1915, reference work was "the service rendered by a librarian *in aid* of some sort of study. It is not the study itself — that is done by the reader.... The help given to a reader engaged in research of any sort is what we mean by reference work."[9]

Wyer's textbook on *Reference Work* (1930) simplified the definition to "sympathetic and informed personal aid in interpreting library collections for study and research."[10] However, Margaret Hutchins, in her *Introduction to Reference Work*, found Wyer's statement inadequate and expanded her own definition to include not only "the direct, personal aid within a library to persons in search of information for whatever purpose," but also "various library activities especially aimed at making information as easily available as possible."[11]

A recent definition is that supplied by Lucy Edwards: "Reference work is not only, as the phrase suggests, the use of books on the premises, as against borrowing them for home reading, but an individual and a personal service to each reader, to enable him to obtain the information he requires with the greatest ease, and the least possible delay."[12]

Through these statements, culled from sixty years of library literature, there runs a common thread in the general agreement that the essential feature of reference work is the *personal assistance given by the librarian to individual readers in pursuit of information*. It is significant also that these definitions do not say anything about reference books or reference rooms, the implication being that these do not constitute integral components in the process of reference work but rather only equipment for its performance.

In defining reference *service*, however, it is necessary to go beyond these definitions of reference *work*. For reference service implies not only the personal assistance given by librarians to individual readers in pursuit of information but also a definite recognition on the part of the library of its responsibility to do so, and a specific organization for that purpose.

The criteria by which reference service is distinguished in the present study may then be summarized as follows:

---

[7] William B. Child, "Reference Work at the Columbia College Library," *Library Journal*, XVI (October, 1891), 298.

[8] Alice Bertha Kroeger, *Guide to the Study and Use of Reference Books: a Manual for Librarians, Teachers and Students* ... (Boston: Houghton, Mifflin Co., 1902), p. 3.

[9] William Warner Bishop, "The Theory of Reference Work," *Bulletin of the American Library Association*, IX (July, 1915), 134.

[10] James Ingersoll Wyer, *Reference Work: a Text-book for Students of Library Work and Librarians* (Chicago: American Library Association, 1930), p. 4.

[11] Margaret Hutchins, *Introduction to Reference Work* (Chicago: American Library Association, 1944), p. 10.

[12] Lucy I. Edwards, "Reference Work in Municipal Libraries," in *The Reference Librarian in University, Municipal and Specialised Libraries*, edited by James D. Stewart (London: Grafton, 1951), p. 55.

(1)   the provision by librarians of personal assistance to individual readers in pursuit
       of information.

(2)   the recognition by the library that such assistance is an indispensable means of
       fulfilling the duties of the library as an educational institution, and the assumption
       of a definite responsibility to provide it.

(3)   the existence of a specific administrative unit to furnish such assistance, com-
       prised of personnel specially equipped in the techniques of reference work.

Scope

This study is limited to research libraries in the United States and deals almost entirely with
the developments of the period 1875-1940. The beginning date has been selected on the basis of the
writer's earlier study, which has shown that, apart from a few inconsequential antecedents, the
very notion of reference service goes back no further than 1875.[13] The terminal date, 1940, has
been selected on purely pragmatic grounds as being the latest date for which reasonably complete
documentary evidence is already at hand. However, a few of the more obvious developments of the
last dozen years are examined briefly in the last chapter in order to bring the story up to date.

The activities studied are those comprised in the term "reference service," which, as the pre-
ceding section has shown, is taken to mean the organized provision by libraries of personal assistance to individual readers in pursuit of information. For most libraries, since 1900 at least, this
function has been delegated to a specifically titled "reference department." It should be made clear,
however, that the study of reference service cannot be limited to the study of the activities of reference departments. Reference departments may engage in a number of activities, such as maintaining records of government publications, which cannot be construed as "personal assistance." On
the other hand, some forms of personal assistance, such as the provision of inter-library loans,
may not be a reference department responsibility. We cannot therefore merely equate reference
service with reference department activities.

Two other questions arise in connection with the scope of the present study. Research libraries
customarily offer assistance to readers through a number of channels, notably through the catalog,
shelf-list, and classification of books on the shelves. These are important media of assistance and
constitute perhaps the most useful tools for reference service. However, like reference books and
reference rooms, these are not integral elements in the process of reference work. As equipment
of the reference worker, they influence the performance of reference work but they are not part of
it. Accordingly, they do not form part of this study.

The last question concerns the clientele served. The main object of the dissertation is to describe the growth and development of reference services to research workers. The special research library, as previously indicated, limits its services almost exclusively to research workers
and thus offers no particular difficulty. The general research library serves various types of users
and does not always organize its services by type of reader. In such cases the approach selected
has been to concentrate on the reference services to research but not to ignore the services to
other types of readers with which these are intermingled.

Sources

As a historical study, the present inquiry is primarily dependent upon documentary evidence.
The main source has been the published reports of the institutions and of their libraries. Unfortunately, reference services by their very nature are not easily described, and as a result many of

---

[13]Samuel Rothstein, "The Development of the Concept of Reference Service in American Libraries, 1850-1900," *Library Quarterly*, XXIII (January, 1953), 3-4.

the reports offer only scanty data on reference activities. A further difficulty has been that practically none of the industrial research libraries issue reports; for these institutions the main source of primary materials has been the descriptions of their operations that have appeared in such journals as *Special Libraries*.

Other published primary materials which have been utilized for this study have been the records of conferences and reports of surveys. These have been supplemented where possible by unpublished data derived from manuscript reports of reference departments, and from interviews with library directors and reference workers.

Secondary materials have included the numerous articles that have appeared in the various library journals, and the histories of individual research libraries, such as those available for the Library of Congress, the New York Public Library, and the University of Chicago Library.

Chapter I

THE CONTEXT FOR REFERENCE SERVICE: THE RISE OF RESEARCH
AND RESEARCH LIBRARIES, 1850-1900

American Scholarship at the Mid-Century

Arthur Bestor has called the changes that took place in the organization of American intellectual
life in the latter half of the nineteenth century a "fundamental transformation" and an "intellectual
revolution."[1] At the mid-century these changes were hardly yet apparent. The universities remained still faithful to the traditional prescribed curriculum of liberal arts and religion inherited
from the colonial era and to the stultifying textbook-cum-recitation method of instruction.[2]

The study of natural science, which promised a more liberal approach to scholarly investigation,
had not yet been able to make its influence felt in the university. Under pressure to bring under
their aegis the growing body of scientific knowledge, the universities had finally permitted the sciences entry but only through the back door. Unwilling to accord to the newer disciplines the prestige of a full-fledged partnership with the traditional subjects, the colleges adopted the expedient
of admitting the natural sciences as separate "schools." The Lawrence Scientific School (established in 1842) and the Sheffield Scientific School (founded in 1847), attached to Harvard and Yale
respectively, had only the minimal and most grudgingly accorded connection with their parent institutions.[3]

Under these discouraging circumstances natural science studies could not aspire to high levels
of scholarship. Where instruction was offered it was elementary in character; graduate work and
laboratories were still all but unknown.[4]

If the university environment of the mid-century proved bleak for the nurture of scholarship,
the non-academic world offered equally meager sustenance. Though the general scientific societies
inherited from the eighteenth century continued to maintain their existence, their activities demonstrated little more than a continued interest in the promotion of learning in the polite tradition of
the Enlightenment.

The historical societies were more numerous and active; Dunlap has listed sixty-five founded
before 1860.[5] However, as Dunlap points out, the motives for the establishment of the historical
societies were by no means all related to the cultivation of scholarly interests. Patriotism, civic
and state pride, respect for ancestors, the self-interest of founders, and the desire to emulate the
example of societies already in existence all played their part.[6] An undiscriminating zeal for collection diverted many societies into the profitless piling up of relics, minerals, natural history
specimens and curiosities of dubious value.[7] Even where the attention remained firmly centered

---

[1] Arthur B. Bestor, Jr., "The Transformation of American Scholarship, 1875-1917," *Library Quarterly*, XXIII (July, 1953),
165.

[2] Cf. Andrew Dickson White, *Autobiography of Andrew Dickson White* (New York: The Century Co., 1905), I, 26, 28, 255.
White, later president of Cornell University, recalled that in his student years at Yale (1850-54), all independent investigation
was stifled in the interest of rote recitation of prescribed subject matter.

[3] Andrew Dickson White, "Scientific and Industrial Education in the United States," *Popular Science Monthly*, V (June, 1874),
171.

[4] U. S. National Resources Committee, Science Committee, *Research—a National Resource* (Washington: Government
Printing Office, 1938-41), II, 20.

[5] Leslie Whittaker Dunlap, *American Historical Societies, 1790-1860* (Madison, Wisconsin: Privately Printed, 1944), p. vii.

[6] *Ibid.*, pp. 10-13.

[7] *Ibid.*, pp. 73-76.

on the authentic materials of historical scholarship, few societies were able to advance from the collection of materials to the active exploitation of them in publications of significance.[8]

The federal government could offer little more in the way of encouragement for the organization of research. Though the censuses and such scientific bureaus as the Coast and Geodetic Survey had made a beginning in the collection of scientific data, attention and support remained limited to the severely practical, with little regard for the long-range utility of basic research. A more significant venture was the establishment of the Smithsonian Institution in 1846, but this indeed was something of a lucky stroke, prompted by the unexpected bequest of the Englishman, James Smithson. It was hardly a conclusive demonstration of any national interest in scientific investigation.

From this review of American scholarship at the mid-century there emerge two central and related facts. The first is that research activity — the extension of knowledge by scholarly inquiry — was insignificant in quantity and character, and the ideal of research all but unknown. The second is that the structure of American intellectual life did not yet provide organized arrangements for the promotion, training, and support of scholarship. What scholarship existed at the mid-century was the scholarship of the gifted amateur. Bestor points out that in the field of history, for example, the most prominent writers, such as Prescott, Bancroft, Motley, and Parkman, had practically no institutional connections.[9] Their training was the product of independent reading and study abroad. While engaged in scholarly investigations they supported themselves out of private funds. They themselves gathered the bulk of the materials needed or paid for the trips necessary to consult them. The mid-century scholar functioned largely in independence from his colleagues, doing for himself the spadework which his chosen theme required. And when he published his results, these made their appearance through the channels of the regular commercial publication agencies, unassisted by special subsidies. Research was still an avocation — if occasionally a full-time one — and not yet a profession.

The Transformation of American Scholarship, 1850-1900

Though no particular significance can be attached to the dates 1850 and 1900, which themselves mark only convenient lines of demarcation, it seems clear that the period defined by these limits witnessed a fundamental change in the structure of American scholarship. The introduction of the natural sciences, even as subjects of low prestige, heralded the break-up of the tightly-closed and narrowly circumscribed curricula that had kept the universities hostile to the spirit of free investigation. The needs of a national economy that was becoming rapidly industrialized gave scientific studies an obvious importance which was soon reflected in their rapid rise in the academic hierarchy. The federal government recognized and encouraged the new status of scientific studies by the passage of the Morrill Land Grant Act in 1862, which provided federal subsidies for higher education in science, technology and agriculture.

Other subjects were also successful in winning academic acceptance. Chairs in history were created at Columbia and at Michigan in 1857. Modern languages, first established as an elective subject at Harvard through the efforts of Ticknor, began to vie in prestige with the classical languages. Cornell University was founded in 1868 with the avowed purpose of teaching any subject that seemed desirable to the faculty and students. With the inauguration of the free elective system at Harvard under President Eliot, the way became open for a hitherto unprecedented degree of specialization in studies.

A potent influence for change came from without in the form of ideas and methods imported from the German university. The nineteenth century had seen the German universities become centers for advanced scholarship. Their high prestige and elaborate facilities, especially

---

[8]U. S. Bureau of Education, *Public Libraries in the United States of America: Their History, Condition and Management,* Special Report, Part I (Washington: Government Printing Office, 1876), p. 313.

[9]Bestor, *op. cit.,* p. 166.

laboratories, attracted many foreign students, amongst them Americans who wanted something more than their own modest institutions could offer.

From Germany the returning scholars brought back the use of the lecture and the seminar as teaching devices more appropriate for the pursuit of higher education than the cramping textbook and recitation method hitherto enthroned by tradition. More important, they brought back the idea that the pursuit of truth per se and the extension of knowledge through research were the highest functions and responsibilities of the university.[10]

The ideas imported from the German university found their fullest realization in Johns Hopkins University, founded in 1876. Without attempting an exact adherence to the German model, Daniel Coit Gilman and his associates were able to incorporate its ruling ideas into their new institution. As Gilman's biographer described it, "the graduate work was carried on in its main lines upon the model of the German universities; . . . the keynote of the German system was also the keynote of Mr. Gilman's conception of the university that was to be."[11] This "keynote" was research, for Johns Hopkins University was to be "a university permeated by the spirit of the universities of Germany, with research as the center, the heart, of the whole organism."[12]

The example of Johns Hopkins University was, in its turn, a magistral influence in turning the course of the American university toward graduate work and research, and in making their symbols — the graduate school and the Ph.D. degree — characteristic features of American higher education. At the 1902 ceremonies celebrating the twenty-fifth anniversary of the founding of Johns Hopkins University, the nation's leading educators joined in acknowledging its leadership in the university research movement. [13]

Actually, however, Johns Hopkins University was more important in the development of American research for what it represented than for what it directly brought about. As the first American university to give full-fledged and deliberate recognition to research as a dominant concern of higher education, its contribution was distinctive and conspicuous. But the trend was already apparent before the opening of Johns Hopkins University in 1876. Yale and Harvard established graduate schools as early as 1847 and 1872 respectively. Harvard granted its first Ph.D. degree in 1873, and the University of Michigan did likewise in 1876.

Similar reservations must apply to any attempt to equate the development of American graduate education with the deliberate adaptation to another setting of the ruling ideas of the German university. W. Stull Holt's study of the correspondence of Herbert B. Adams has shown that the German influence on American scholarship was not as intimate nor as far-reaching as has been commonly supposed. [14]

All this suggests that the transformation of American scholarship in this period resulted from no simple acceptance of any single idea but was the complex product of a number of elements, indigenous and foreign. Bestor has characterized it as "a far larger process of assimilation."[15] The broadening of the curriculum to include scientific, technical and professional education, the

_____

[10]Charles Franklin Thwing, *The American and the German University; One Hundred Years of History* (New York: The Macmillan Company, 1928), pp. 19, 130.

[11]Fabian Franklin, *The Life of Daniel Coit Gilman* (New York: Dodd, Mead and Company, 1910), p. 196.

[12]*Ibid.*, p. 227.

[13]Johns Hopkins University, . . . *Celebration of the Twenty-fifth Anniversary of the Founding of the University and Inauguration of Ira Remsen, L.L.D. as President of the University, February Twenty-first and Twenty-second, 1902* (Baltimore: The Johns Hopkins Press, 1902), pp. 39-40, 62. Woodrow Wilson called Johns Hopkins "the first . . . in which the efficiency and value of research as an educational instrument were exemplified in the training of many investigators. . . ." (p. 39).

[14]Though Adams was a graduate of a German university and was teaching at Johns Hopkins, the most important intermediary of German influence, he maintained very little correspondence with German fellow-historians, and his admiration for German scholarship was by no means unqualified. Herbert Baxter Adams, *Historical Scholarship in the United States, 1876-1901; as Revealed in the Correspondence of Herbert Baxter Adams,* edited by W. Stull Holt ("The Johns Hopkins Studies in Historical and Political Science," Series LVI, Number 4. [Baltimore: The Johns Hopkins Press, 1938]), p. 11.

[15]Bestor, *op. cit.*, p. 169.

introduction of the graduate school as the agency for the training of scholars, the acceptance of research as a university function on a coordinate basis with teaching — all these were elements in the process. The new university of 1875 brought them together into one institution.[16]

In fact, the very essence of the movement was that scholarship became institutionalized.[17] Where the earlier scholars had worked independently, relying only on their own resources, the new university provided a center of concentration. It offered scholars the means of training, a subsidy for their investigations, the association of colleagues and media for the dissemination of their researches. The American college of the mid-century gave room only to teachers; the new American university made a place for the scholar and, in so doing, made of scholarship a profession.

With the professionalization of scholarship came the customary results of professionalization — the disappearance of the amateur and the increase of specialization. The professional scholars controlled the channels of training and the major means of communication. Only the properly trained student with the requisite set of academic credentials could hope to win the university position that assured support for his research; only the professors had effective access to the learned journals published by their institutions and edited by their associates. "Research," concluded Robert Binkley, "ceased to be an honored sport and became an exclusive profession."[18]

The rise of the university, which made possible a career in scholarship, also led to a sharp increase in the number of research workers. Inevitably there followed a splintering of learning into smaller segments and an attendant specialization in scholarship. Its effects were visible in the formation of national societies dedicated to the advancement of particular subjects. The American Philological Association (founded in 1869), the Archaeological Institute of America (1879), the Modern Language Association (1883), the American Historical Association (1884), the American Economic Association (1885) were typical examples of the many learned societies, representing smaller divisions of knowledge, which in this period came to supersede in prominence the older general scholarly associations.[19]

A by-product of specialization was a change in the characteristic form of publication, most easily visible in the field of history. Where the mid-century historians — a Bancroft or a Parkman — had taken whole centuries and continents for their themes and brought forth their results as multi-volume histories, the newer specialists carefully exploited their smaller areas in monographs and articles. The sub-division of topics in turn made for a greater emphasis on documentation. The monograph did not afford room for large-scale generalizations. It was meant primarily as an exploration in depth, an objective ascertainment of all the facts on a particular small topic, in which every statement had to be supported by relevant documents.

None of these processes of professionalization and specialization of research achieved full development overnight, but their progress was surprisingly rapid. In 1875 the very word "research" was, according to Daniel Coit Gilman, a new term in the academic vocabulary. Since that time, he noted graphically, "the conception of 'research' ... spread throughout our land from peak to peak like the signal fires described by the Greek dramatists."[20]

The sharp increase of interest in research helped carry the conception outside the academic walls. For the first time research began to be an active factor in the operation of industrial enterprises. Hitherto, industrialists had relied on the abundance of natural resources and the protection of the tariff as the chief means of maintaining profits. With growing competition and the depletion

---

[16]*Ibid.*, pp. 169-70.

[17]*Ibid.*

[18]Robert C. Binkley, "New Tools for Men of Letters," in *Selected Papers of Robert C. Binkley*, edited with a biographical sketch by Max H. Fisch (Cambridge: Harvard University Press, 1948), p. 191.

[19]Merle Curti, *The Growth of American Thought* (2d ed.; New York: Harper and Brothers Publishers, 1951), pp. 580-93.

[20]Daniel Coit Gilman, "Research — a Speech Delivered at the Convocation of the University of Chicago, June, 1903," in his *The Launching of a University* (New York: Dodd, Mead and Company, 1906), pp. 242-43.

of natural resources facing it, industry began to question the efficiency of its processes and to look to applied science research for new approaches to its problems.[21]

The same realization that research could have important practical value gave impetus to the expansion of the work of scientific investigation sponsored by the federal government. The Department of Agriculture, from its establishment in 1864, quickly became an important producer and sponsor of research in a wide variety of fields. The Smithsonian Institution under Joseph Henry and Samuel Langley achieved a position of leadership in basic research. New agencies for research such as the Bureau of Mines, the National Bureau of Standards and the National Institutes of Health added significant contributions in applied science.

However, the research activities of industry and government represented emergent tendencies rather than fully-realized movements. Up to the end of the nineteenth century research continued to find its chief base in the universities, where it was recognized as one of their primary responsibilities. Daniel Coit Gilman described this sense of obligation with dramatic emphasis:

> The third function of a university is to extend the bounds of human knowledge. Call it research, call it investigation, call it scientific inquiry, call it the seeking for truth — never has the obligation been so strong as it is now to penetrate the arcana of the world in which we dwell, to discover new facts, to measure old phenomena, and to educe principles and laws that were written in the beginning, but have never yet been read by mortal eye.[22]

By accepting research as one of its basic functions, the university assured the means of support for the productive scholar and made possible the emergence of a new class — the professional scholar working within an institution and dependent upon institutional arrangements for the prosecution of his studies.

The Demands of the New Scholarship upon the Library

The nineteenth century converted scholarship from an amateur's avocation to a full-time profession. Inevitably the needs and working habits of professionalized and institution-centered scholarship differed vastly from those of the independent investigators of the earlier period. With the change in methods there came also a basic re-orientation of scholars' attitudes to the library.

A principal feature of the change in attitude was a vastly increased regard for the importance of libraries to the progress of scholarship. The roots of the change probably went back as far as American students' first contact with the impressive collections of the German university libraries. George Ticknor, a pioneer in the establishment of the idea of research in America, wrote to his friend Stephen Higginson from Göttingen in May, 1816:

> I cannot, however, shut my eyes on the fact, that one very important and principal cause of the difference between our University [i.e. Harvard] and the one here is the different value we affix to a good library, and the different ideas we have of what a good library is . . . what is worse than the absolute poverty of our collections of books is the relative inconsequence in which we keep them. We found new professorships and build new colleges in abundance, but we buy no books; and yet it is to me the most obvious thing in the world that it would promote the cause of learning and the reputation of the University ten times more to give six thousand dollars a year to the Library than to found three professorships, . . . We have not yet learnt that the Library is not only the first convenience of the University, but that it is the very first necessity, — that it is the

---

[21] U. S. National Resources Committee, Science Committee, *op. cit.*, II, 24-28.

[22] Daniel Coit Gilman, "Higher Education in the United States," in his *University Problems in the United States* (New York: The Century Company, 1898), p. 296.

light and the spirit, — and that all other considerations must yield to the prevalent one of increasing and opening it on the most liberal terms to *all* who are disposed to make use of it.[23]

Ticknor's contemporaries and successors in attendance at the German universities echoed his appreciation of the worth of the library in university studies. Of the first generation of American scholars in Germany, Edward Everett, George Bancroft, and Joseph Green Cogswell all were influential builders or donors of libraries. In the next generation, Henry Philip Tappan was an energetic promoter of library interests at the University of Michigan. He personally solicited funds for the University's library from the citizens of Ann Arbor; his son John became the University's first regular librarian.[24] At about the same time, Francis Lieber, a German émigré and first occupant of the chair of history at Columbia College, was writing to his friend General Halleck: "We cannot do in our days without large public libraries, and libraries are quite as necessary as hospitals or armies. Libraries are the bridges over which Civilization travels from generation to generation and from country to country."[25]

Herbert Baxter Adams typified the group of German-trained historians who helped establish the idea of scientific historical research in the generation after 1875. For him "the most important factor in the constitution of an historical department is the proper adjustment of relations with the college or university library... The promotion of historical study in any college or university is absolutely dependent upon the use of books."[26]

However, like the research movement itself, the appreciation of libraries was not confined to the German-trained scholars. Yale University was relatively remote from German influence in the nineteenth century, yet the reports of President Dwight came to echo the same sentiment. "The Library is, in a most important sense, the center of the University life," he wrote in 1893; "The place where it is located is the place towards which teachers and students alike must turn, in order to find the means of pursuing their investigations."[27]

By the end of the century such assertions were so numerous as to make the statements "the library is the heart of the university" and "the library is the center of the university" only commonplaces. When President Benjamin Ide Wheeler announced on his accession to office at the University of California, "Give me a library and I'll build a university about it,"[28] he could claim credit only for the forcefulness of the expression; the idea was already in the public domain.

A realistic appraisal of all these encomiums about the importance of the library would conclude that they reflected not so much foreign influence or philosophical appreciation of the place of books in the progress of scholarship as the increasing dependence of the scholar upon the library. The amateur scholar of the earlier era worked more or less completely on his own so far as book resources were concerned. It was taken for granted that the accumulation of a large private library was the necessary and customary procedure of the scholar. At best he could expect that the materials he required, if already collected, would be scattered among numerous institutions, with perhaps the most important of them reposing in libraries and archives abroad.

---

[23] As quoted by Thomas Wentworth Higginson, "Göttingen and Harvard Eighty Years Ago," *Harvard Graduates Magazine,* VI (September, 1897), 6.

[24] Charles M. Perry, *Henry Philip Tappan, Philosopher and University President* (Ann Arbor: University of Michigan Press, 1933), pp. 232-34.

[25] Francis Lieber, *The Life and Letters of Francis Lieber,* edited by Thomas Sergeant Perry (Boston: James R. Osgood and Company, 1882), p. 361.

[26] Herbert Baxter Adams, *The Study of History in American Colleges and Universities* (U. S. Bureau of Education "Circulars of Information," No. 2; [Washington: Government Printing Office, 1887]), p. 43.

[27] Yale University, *Report of the President...for the Year Ending December 31, 1893,* p. 80.

[28] Quoted by Benjamin Kurtz, *Joseph Cummings Rowell, 1853-1938* (Berkeley: Printed by the University of California Press, 1940), p. 42.

The biographical accounts of the amateur scholars offer ample evidence as to their all but complete independence of institutional libraries. Ticknor's *History of Spanish Literature* was based on his own collection of some thirteen thousand volumes. Hubert Howe Bancroft's autobiography is largely the story of the formation of his outstanding private library.[29] George Bancroft estimated that his "expenses of various kinds in collecting materials, MSS, and books, in journeys, time employed in researches, writing, copyists, money paid for examination, etc., etc., might be put without exaggeration at fifty or even seventy-five thousand dollars."[30]

Wealth was then the normal pre-requisite for scholarship in the days of the amateur. The men of the new professional group usually had no such private resources to draw upon. If they were able to consult and utilize the materials necessary for their research, it was because of the existence of the institutional library. A number of other factors joined in increasing the dependence of the scholar upon the library. The mounting flood of publications attendant upon the increase of knowledge was rapidly making even the largest of private libraries insufficient for thorough research. At the same time a more rigorous conception of research was demanding a more exhaustive investigation of sources. Thus, in the field of history, the idea of "scientific history" popularized by Von Ranke emphasized the careful collection of facts — facts which could be taken as established only when supported by an imposing array of documentary evidence.[31]

If all these factors made the scholars much more dependent upon the library, a reciprocal influence made the library in its turn subject to a whole series of demands from the scholars. Of these the first, the strongest, and the most common was the pressure for more materials. The cry for more books ran through the whole period of the transformation of scholarship. Struik has noted the demand of the European-trained scientists of the 1860 decade for the specialized journals with which they had become familiar abroad.[32] Herbert Baxter Adams attributed the growth of the University of Michigan's collections to "the intelligent demands made by the faculties, by the students, and by the administration."[33] The reports of President Eliot at Harvard and President Dwight at Yale persistently hammered at the need for greater library resources. At the end of the century the demand had lost none of its urgency. Charles Mills Gayley pressed for the acquisition by the University of California of the Bancroft Library in the full confidence that he and his fellow scholars had and would continue to have "no greater need than that of materials and sources with which to develop investigation and first-hand scholarship."[34]

Closely related to the demand for increased resources was the desire for easier access to the materials. If the institutional library was to serve him in place of a private collection, the professional scholar wanted the same unrestricted approach to the books he needed that his amateur predecessor had enjoyed in his personal library. This claim was reinforced by the exigencies of the newer teaching methods. The distinctive feature of the seminar was the first-hand investigation of the original materials by the students under the close supervision of the professor. Preferably this process would take place in the library itself, where the group could discuss the students' work within easy reach of the materials cited. Thus Henry Adams, in casting aside the textbook method in favor of having his students go directly to the original sources, criticized the existing library

[29] Hubert Howe Bancroft, *Literary Industries*, Vol XXXIX, *The Works of Hubert Howe Bancroft* (San Francisco: The History Company, Publishers, 1890), *passim*.

[30] M. A. DeWolfe Howe, *The Life and Letters of George Bancroft* (New York: Charles Scribner's Sons, 1908), II, 261.

[31] W. Stull Holt, "The Idea of Scientific History in America," *Journal of the History of Ideas*, I (June, 1940), 358-62. For a description of the "scientific historian" as "slave to documentation," see Dixon Ryan Fox's account of the working methods of Herbert Osgood. (Dixon Ryan Fox, *Herbert Levi Osgood, an American Scholar* [New York: Columbia University Press, 1924], p. 47.

[32] Dirk J. Struik, *Yankee Science in the Making* (Boston: Little, Brown and Company, 1948), p. 342.

[33] Adams, *The Study of History . . .*, *op. cit.*, p. 120.

[34] Manuscript letter of December 1, 1898, in the Bancroft Library, quoted by John Walton Caughey, *Hubert Howe Bancroft, Historian of the West* (Berkeley: University of California Press, 1946), p. 357.

policy at Harvard of keeping books all but locked up in the alcoves, and demanded greater accessibility to materials for his students.[35]

President Gilman took up the same theme in many of his annual reports. For example, he expressed his satisfaction at the growing tendency of the Johns Hopkins library system to develop in the direction of departmental collections, for he thought no measure likely to be of more assistance to the research men than "placing those books which are most likely to be needed, or which specially bear upon the work, within easy reach of the worker's hand."[36]

With repetition the idea of easier access to materials became crystallized in the catchphrase that the library should be the "laboratory" of the humanist and social scientist, usually uttered with a corollary statement that the library should no longer be a "store-house of books."[37] The concept of the library as a laboratory implied its use as a tool for investigations. As a tool it could be most effective when it furnished not only the required materials but also the means of obtaining a subject approach to the particular topics of interest. The need of a subject approach to library materials gained added intensity from the very growth of collections so vigorously advocated by the scholars. A small collection required only the broad classification appropriate to a personal library; with a many-fold expansion of resources a more minutely organized arrangement of the books was needed, if the much desired free access to materials was to produce anything other than confusion. In the same way, the catalog had to become more than a simple record of holdings, for it became increasingly apparent that no scholar could hope to know all the literature of potential value, especially on subjects outside his immediate specialty.

These circumstances motivated the scholars to press for some form of subject approach to knowledge. Herbert Adams' review of the facilities for the study of history in American colleges led him to complain that in many college libraries searching for material on a given topic was like looking for a needle in a haystack. By way of contrast he held up for commendation Melvil Dewey's newly re-organized library at Columbia, where the object was to "organize so thoroughly its literary resources in any given field like history or political science that they can be speedily massed upon a given point with the precision and certainty of a Prussian army corps in the execution of a military manoeuvre."[38] Hubert Howe Bancroft had a subject index compiled for his large personal library at a cost of $35,000; "by this or other similar means alone can the contents of any large library be utilized; and the larger the collection the more necessity for such an index," he maintained.[39]

Such statements were, however, fewer in number and much less explicit than the demands for more materials and easier access to them. There was evidently some feeling that the library had to be organized so as to provide a subject approach to knowledge, but the details of organization do not seem to have concerned the scholars. Evidence on this point is lacking, but it may be plausibly surmised that the research men considered matters of classification and subject cataloging technical problems that could be safely left to the librarians.

Evidently for most scholars, the overwhelming preoccupation with the accumulation of materials cast a shadow of indifference over all library matters other than the acquisitions function. Certainly this was true for problems of library staffing and service. In general the scholars, if one may judge by the absence of comments in memoirs and biographies, felt relatively little need or concern for reference services. Such statements as did appear came only late in the century.

---

[35]In a letter of 1875, addressed to the Harvard Corporation; quoted by Robert W. Lovett, "The Undergraduate and the Harvard Library, 1877-1937," *Harvard Library Bulletin*, I (Spring, 1947), 223.

[36]Johns Hopkins University, *Seventh Annual Report of the President . . . 1882*, pp. 56-57. See also in this connection Johns Hopkins University, *Fourth Annual Report of the President . . . 1879*, p. 18.

[37]Adams, *The Study of History . . . , op. cit.*, p. 46.

[38]*Ibid.*, p. 84.

[39]Bancroft, *op. cit.*, pp. 241, 243.

A related theme — teaching the use of books and libraries — did arouse some considerable interest. President Barnard of Columbia devoted considerable attention to the topic, arguing that instruction in the use of library materials was a task as important as that performed by the professors in the regular academic departments. He concluded with some fervor that "it has seemed more and more important to careful observers to give such instruction and aid to undergraduates as shall enable them in all their after lives to do their individual work more readily and more successfully."[40] Herbert Baxter Adams, who was familiar with the instruction given at Columbia and at Cornell, thought that "such a course of general bibliographical information, given to students by the librarian of their college or university, cannot be too highly commended."[41]

The same two scholars were those most explicit in voicing a demand for reference work proper. In the same report in which he advocated a program of instruction in "practical bibliography," Barnard argued that in the interest of educational progress the Columbia library "must be put in charge of a librarian, himself well acquainted with books and their uses, and experienced in guiding inquirers in bibliographical researches."[42] Adams thought that a "great public library, like a great railway station, must have a bureau of information, . . . "[43]

Both Adams and Barnard seem to have had in mind assistance for the undergraduate and the neophyte in learning rather than aid for the mature scholar. Adams did indeed have words of commendation for the more specialized assistance that George Baker was providing in the library of the School of Political Science at Columbia, but even here he was probably thinking of the seminar students rather than of their instructors.[44]

In the absence of explicit statements from the scholars themselves, it is impossible to define precisely their attitude toward the idea of personal assistance by the librarian in their own researches, but a statement from Hubert Howe Bancroft affords a good clue to their reasoning.

> Often have I heard authors say that beyond keeping the books in order, and bringing such as were required, with some copying, or possibly some searching now and then, no one could render them any assistance. They would not feel safe in trusting any one with the manipulation of facts on which was to rest their reputation for veracity and accuracy.[45]

The scholar of the late nineteenth century was familiar with the idea of reference work and some, at least, approved of such library assistance for their students. Few yet thought of it as important for their own researches.

The Rise of the Research Library

By definition the research library is a service agency for scholarship. Its establishment and development have therefore, not surprisingly, followed closely along the lines marked out by the development of learning in America.

At the mid-century the research library could hardly have been said to exist. Some efforts in purposeful collection had already been made by the historical societies, notably by the American Antiquarian Society and the New York Historical Society, but such zeal was by no means the rule. Most historical societies' collecting was as lukewarm and as haphazard as their other contributions

---

[40] Columbia College, *Annual Report of the President . . . May 7, 1883*, p. 45.

[41] Adams, *The Study of History . . . , op. cit.*, pp. 167-68.

[42] Columbia College, *op. cit.*, p. 44.

[43] Herbert Baxter Adams, *Public Libraries and Popular Education* ("Home Education Bulletin," No. 31; [Albany: University of the State of New York, 1900]), p. 89.

[44] Adams, *The Study of History . . . , op. cit.*, pp. 82-83.

[45] Bancroft, *op. cit.*, p. 565.

to learning. As late as 1876 the government report on *Public Libraries in the United States of America* credited only thirteen of the then extant societies with collections numbering more than 10,000 volumes.[46]

The small achievement of the historical societies in the development of libraries was matched by the general paucity of American library resources at this time, both in turn reflecting the low level of scholarship in the country as a whole. William Fletcher alleged that in 1850 the entire library resources of the United States aggregated only a million volumes.[47] In the same year an article in the *North American Review* gave the following illuminating table of holdings for the largest libraries in the United States:[48]

Harvard College, including the Law and Divinity Schools	72,000 volumes
Philadelphia and Loganian Library	60,000 volumes
Boston Athenaeum	50,000 volumes
Library of Congress	50,000 volumes
New York Society Library	32,000 volumes
Mercantile Library (New York)	32,000 volumes
Georgetown College (D. C.)	25,000 volumes
Brown University	24,000 volumes
New York State Library	24,000 volumes
Yale College	21,000 volumes

Provisions for use were equally negligible. W. N. Carlton has collected some examples, now amusing, of the way in which narrowly conceived and rigorously applied regulations made college book collections all but unusable.[49] Thus the Amherst College Library up to 1852 was open only once a week for the withdrawal of books and provided no facilities for reading on the premises. At Brown University in 1843 no undergraduate could take a book off the shelves without the special permission of the librarian. A Maryland college did not permit any lending at all — the practice had indeed formerly existed, but it was discontinued because of abuse of the privilege!

It would be unfair to see in such regulations mere ineptitude; in part at least they reflected only a prudent concern for the protection of books at a time when these were few and esteemed precious. But they also reflected the well-nigh complete divorce of the college library from the ordinary process of scholarship. The student used his textbooks; the professor, if anything more than a teacher, his personal collection. President Hadley of Yale recalled a conversation which seemed to typify the attitude which imposed a separation between the scholar and the college library:

> One of the professors of the old school — and, I might add, one of the more enlightened professors of the old school — said to me only a few years ago, "I conceive that the chief educational use of a university library is to lend an occasional book to a professor who does not happen to have the book in his own library." He regarded the university library as a sort of museum; the actual laboratories where the work was done were the special libraries of the professors.[50]

---

[46] U. S. Bureau of Education, *op. cit.*, pp. 375-77.

[47] William Isaac Fletcher, *Public Libraries in America* (Boston: Roberts Brothers, 1894), p. 115.

[48] [George Livermore], *Remarks on Public Libraries;* reprinted from the *North American Review,* July, 1850 (Cambridge: Printed by Bolles and Houghton, 1850), p. 17.

[49] W. N. Carlton, "College Libraries in the Mid-Nineteenth Century," *Library Journal,* XXXII (November, 1907), 483-84.

[50] Arthur Twining Hadley, "The Library in the University," *Public Libraries,* XIV (April, 1909), 116.

An even more revealing glimpse of the college library in the old order is offered by the exchange of correspondence between Gilman, then librarian at Yale, and President Woolsey. When Gilman complained at the administration's lack of support for the library — he was paying his sole assistant out of his own salary and had himself to stoke the small stove that was the single source of heat for the building — Woolsey sent this astonishing reply: "In regard to your leaving your place my thoughts have shaped themselves thus: the place does not possess that importance which a man of active mind would naturally seek; and the college cannot, now or hereafter, while its circumstances remain as they are, give it greater prominence."[51]

While restrictive regulations and the grip of tradition were keeping university libraries all but moribund, a new tool for scholarship was being forged outside the academic community — the public library. The public library in its present form may be said to date from the founding of the Boston Public Library in 1852. As with most social institutions, the motivation behind its establishment and development was complex. The detailed studies of Ditzion and Thompson indicate that the desire for popular education, a naive faith in the efficacy of "good" reading in the preservation of virtue, civic pride, and sheer imitation all played their part in the creation of the public library.[52]

But, as Shera makes clear, the interest of scholars, especially the historians, in finding a viable basis for the preservation and servicing of the materials of research was a compelling and perhaps decisive motive.[53] Certainly, in the larger cities at least, the public library collections from the outset included material of a character manifestly intended only for scholarly use. The Everett collection of documents in the Boston Public Library, the "Green Library" in the Worcester Free Library, and the comprehensive collection of bibliographies brought together by Joseph Green Cogswell for the Astor Library were cases in point.

Evidence for the belief that at this time the public library was more quick to respond to the needs of scholarship than the university library is given in the statistics of library holdings compiled by Rhees. His figures for 1857-1858 showed that less than a decade after their founding the Astor Library and the Boston Public Library had accumulated 80,000 and 70,000 volumes respectively. The comparison with the college library holdings of the same date is illuminating. After more than two centuries of operation, the Harvard College Library had brought together only 74,000 volumes, and Yale, after a century and a half of existence, only 36,000 volumes. Other academic institutions had fared even worse. Rhees credited the Brown University Library with only 29,500 volumes, Columbia with 18,000, Princeton with 11,000, and Pennsylvania with 5,000![54]

As the research movement gathered strength, its impact on the library began to make itself more clearly and widely felt. Library reports from the seventies on indicated a clear recognition of responsibility for service to research. Librarian Homes described the New York State Library as "one for historical and scientific research chiefly."[55] The Lenox Library proclaimed in 1883 that the use of the library "will be hereafter enlarged and extended, to promote research."[56] Raymond Davis of the University of Michigan Library claimed that "the especial purpose for which the University Library exists is *the increase of knowledge.*"[57] Daniel Coit Gilman, speaking at the opening of the new Princeton University Library building in 1898, summed up the progress of a half-

---

[51] Quoted in Franklin, *op. cit.,* p. 78.

[52] Sidney Herbert Ditzion, *Arsenals of a Democratic Culture; a Social History of the American Public Library Movement in New England and the Middle States from 1850 to 1900* (Chicago: American Library Association, 1947), pp. 190-93; C. Seymour Thompson, *The Evolution of the American Public Library* (Washington: Scarecrow Press, 1952), *passim.*

[53] Jesse Hauk Shera, *Foundations of the Public Library; the Origins of the Public Library Movement in New England, 1629-1855* (Chicago: University of Chicago Press, 1949), pp. 206-13.

[54] William J. Rhees, *Manual of Public Libraries, Institutions and Societies in the United States and British Provinces of North America* (Philadelphia: J. B. Lippincott and Co., 1859), pp. 585-651.

[55] New York State Library, *Sixty-first Annual Report...for the Year 1878,* p. 23.

[56] Lenox Library, *Fourteenth Annual Report...for the Year 1883,* p. 5.

[57] University of Michigan Library, *Librarian's Report for the Year Ending Sept. 30, 1888,* p. 6.

century: "Finally, libraries are now recognized as places of research, ... This marks a great advance quite in accord with the dominant spirit of inquiry and investigation." [58]

In thus aligning themselves with the research movement, the university and reference libraries undertook, more or less consciously, to fulfill the demands of the scholars. The most urgent of these demands, as previously noted, was for larger book resources, and the librarians gave to the work of acquisitions the first claim on their attention and energy. Almost every librarian of the period felt that his library's major responsibility and hope for distinction lay in the large-scale amassment of materials. Justin Winsor, librarian at Harvard, thought that no single American library had yet come close to satisfying the book requirements of the specialist in any given field, and that the only hope that any would ever do so lay in broad, almost indiscriminate collecting.[59] Of Joseph Rowell, librarian of the University of California, his biographer wrote: "He had always vastly preferred an increase in accessions to an increase in staff assistance. He had repeatedly doubled his own tasks in order repeatedly to double the accessions."[60] Raymond Davis summed up his career at the University of Michigan Library in a single revealing sentence. "If I were asked to characterize in a few words my work as librarian my answer would be ready: *A struggle for books.*"[61]

The result of this conjunction of scholars' demands and librarians' activity was a pronounced increase in the dimensions of American library resources. At the outset of the period American library holdings appeared insignificant in comparison with the riches of European libraries. A generation later the New World could almost rival the Old, if not yet in the intrinsic value of its resources, at least in the number of volumes held. Table I (p. 18) sets forth the record of book holdings for a number of prominent libraries in 1876 and in 1891.

The theme of collection and its corollary theme of building needs indisputably dominated the attention of the librarians. They relegated to the background all but a few pressing problems of internal administration. Of these easily the most important were those connected with cataloging and classification, and the "use of books," both in turn reflecting the larger aim of converting the library from a "storehouse of books" into a "laboratory for scholarship."

Neither problem was entirely new or peculiarly the product of the research movement pressures. Librarians since the day of Callimachus had recognized that the arrangement, display, and use of the materials in their charge were responsibilities inherent in their professional position, regardless of the type of library. But the demands of the scholars for a subject approach to knowledge lent a certain added urgency to these responsibilities for the managers of libraries that presumed to exist for the prosecution of research. For example, John Burgess, a leader in the research movement at Columbia, recalled how he pressed the college administration for the appointment of a librarian who could make the literature of his subject more readily available through subject cataloging and close classification.[62]

As a result of such pressures, when Dewey came to Columbia, a principal feature of his "revolution" in the library's administration was the re-organization of the cataloging and classification procedures. A similar absorption with the catalog was evident in Winsor's reports at Harvard, in Billings' administration of the Surgeon-General's Library, in Rowell's management of the University of California Library. The work of cataloging was customarily the first to receive the recognition of formal departmental status. A safe guess would be that insofar as a librarian was then recognized as a professional worker, such recognition was based primarily on his technical qualifications in cataloging.

---

[58] Daniel Coit Gilman, "Books and Politics," in his *The Launching of a University, op. cit.,* p. 197.

[59] Justin Winsor, "An Address," in *Public Exercises on the Completion of the Library Building of the University of Michigan, December 12, 1883* (Ann Arbor: Published by the University, 1884), pp. 30-36.

[60] Kurtz, *op. cit.,* p. 52.

[61] University of Michigan Library, *Annual Report of the Librarian for 1905-1906,* p. 55.

[62] John William Burgess, *Reminiscences of an American Scholar: the Beginnings of Columbia University* (New York: Columbia University Press, 1934), pp. 216-19.

TABLE I

RESEARCH LIBRARY HOLDINGS IN 1875 AND IN 1891

Library	Number of Volumes 1876[a]	Number of Volumes 1891[b]
Brown University Library	45,000	71,000
California University Library	13,600	42,287
Cornell University Library	10,000	111,007
Columbia University Library	33,590	135,000
Harvard University Library	227,650	292,000
Michigan University Library	28,400	77,705
Pennsylvania University Library	25,573	100,000
Princeton University Library	41,500	84,221
Yale University Library	114,200	185,000
Astor Library	152,446	238,946
Detroit Public Library	22,882	108,720
Cleveland Public Library	24,000	66,920
Boston Public Library	299,869	556,283
Grosvenor Library	18,000	35,000
Library of Congress	300,000	659,843
Surgeon-General's Library	40,000	104,300

[a]Source: U. S. Bureau of Education, *Public Libraries in the United States of America: Their History, Condition and Management*, Special Report, Part I (Washington: Government Printing Office, 1876), pp. 762-773.

[b]Source: U. S. Bureau of Education, *Statistics of Public Libraries in the United States and Canada*, by Weston Flint, statistician of the Bureau of Education ("Circular of Information," No. 7; [Washington: Government Printing Office, 1893]), pp. 22-203. The basis of computation was not the same as in the 1876 statistics, so the two sets of data are not wholly comparable. However, the general impression conveyed by the comparison — that of rapid growth in library holdings — is undoubtedly reliable enough.

The proper form for the required guide to the library's resources was a matter of lively controversy. By the end of the century, however, the arguments over printed versus card catalog, classed versus dictionary arrangement, broad versus close classification, had been more or less decided. Only the card catalog could keep abreast of a rapidly growing collection, while specific subject headings and close classification seemed to provide the best approach to the minute subjects wanted by the specialist scholars. Though nothing like uniformity or full satisfaction on these matters was achieved then (or even yet), the task of constructing the technical apparatus of the research library had been accomplished in its essentials by 1900.

The other great problem of internal administration — the "use of the library" — was solved with less controversy. The increased dependence of the scholar upon the institutional library clearly called for longer hours of opening and easy access to materials. Though independent reference libraries such as the Astor, the Lenox and the Reynolds continued to oppose circulation of their books on the grounds that such service dispersed materials and increased costs, the university libraries, with the scholars actually on their doorstep, could not and did not resist. Harvard, which had provided forty-eight hours of service per week in 1876, was open eighty-two hours a week in 1896; Yale increased its hours of service from thirty-six to seventy-two in the same period.[63] Columbia changed even more radically. The library gave twelve hours of weekly service in 1876; in 1888 Dewey offered prospective library school students the inducement that "for 14 hours daily there is opportunity for work."[64]

The same liberal policy of "service" was bringing the university library user much freer access to his materials than he had heretofore enjoyed. When Justin Winsor came to Harvard in 1877, Henry Adams had already been petitioning for permission to have his seminar students given direct access to the shelves.[65] Winsor thoroughly approved of the seminar method and its library implication — use not storage. In his first report he proclaimed his advocacy of a liberal lending policy:

> Books may be accumulated and guarded, and the result is sometimes called a library; but if books are made to help and spur men on in their own daily work, the library becomes a vital influence; the prison is turned into a workshop.[66]

In subsequent reports and articles Winsor expanded his idea into a full-fledged "doctrine of use," summed up in the dictum "A book is never so valuable as when it is in use." In his own institution he admitted advanced students to the stacks, extended the reserve book collections and threw open the reference collection to all comers.[67]

The new doctrine rapidly gained adherents. It became generally accepted that reference books should be available on open shelves.[68] Even the conservative reference libraries, which clung to the policy that their books ought not to leave the building, assiduously collected statistics of within-the-building circulation that would demonstrate "the use of the library." The Lenox Library, for example, which had been heretofore quite content to be a museum of typographical rarities, hopefully noted in its 1884 report an increasing use of its materials by scholars and promised measures for its encouragement.[69]

The ideas of service had important implications for reference service as well, but these were not fully realized in most research libraries in the nineteenth century. The detailed account of the genesis of the concept of reference service and of its development as a research library function is reserved for the next chapter. It may, however, be said at this time that reference service was never seen as more than a secondary responsibility in the nineteenth century research library.

The development of research and the professionalization of scholarship made the research library a necessity. They also brought to it demands for a large-scale expansion of holdings, for improved physical facilities, for freer access to books, and for an apparatus that would provide a subject approach to materials. The librarians in their turn put these first things first and gave their chief attention to the problems of acquisitions, cataloging and classification, and circulation. Their achievement was considerable. At the mid-century, roughly speaking, America was practically without research libraries. Fifty years later its libraries could claim collections of some magnitude, a well-developed system of catalogs and shelf arrangements, and a policy of administration that sought to make them indispensable tools for scholarship. The foundations had been laid for the organization of an expert personal service.

[63] Kenneth J. Brough, *Scholar's Workshop; Evolving Conceptions of Library Service* (Urbana: University of Illinois Press, 1953), p. 112.

[64] Columbia University, School of Library Service, *School of Library Economy, Columbia College, 1887-1889: Documents for a History* (New York: School of Library Service, Columbia University, 1937), p. 109.

[65] *Supra*, pp. 12-13.

[66] Harvard College Library, ["Report of the Library"] in *Fifty-second Annual Report of the President...1876-77*, p. 109.

[67] Lovett, *op. cit.*, pp. 223-227.

[68] Louis Kaplan, *The Growth of Reference Service in the United States from 1876 to 1893* ("ACRL Monographs," No. 2; Chicago: Association of College and Reference Libraries, 1952), p. 5.

[69] Lenox Library, *Fifteenth Annual Report...for the Year 1884*, p. 5.

Chapter II

THE GENESIS OF REFERENCE SERVICE: 1875-1895

The basic element in reference service — helping readers — is so simple that it seems reasonable to believe that as long as there have been libraries, librarians must have occasionally furnished some sort of personal aid to their clientele. The beginnings of reference service are lost in antiquity.

Examples of personal assistance can be thus found even in the earlier pages of America's library history. At the Congressional Library in the 1820's, Watterston was "called upon for facts, dates, acts, official communications and even lines of poetry."[1] William Alfred Jones, librarian of Columbia College in the 1850's went on record as considering personal assistance to readers desirable and proposed plans for supplying lists of references.[2] Even Sibley of Harvard, enshrined in library legend as the very personification of "custodial librarianship," was "the very soul of courtesy,"[3] and a source of "ready and efficient aid."[4]

Such instances of helpfulness were not uncommon, but the amassing of examples would be pointless. Courtesy and occasional personal assistance did not in themselves constitute reference service. It was only when such assistance was recognized as a basic function of the library and translated from casual help into a deliberate program of aid that reference service came into being.

No such conception of organized reference work had been formulated before the third quarter of the nineteenth century. The proceedings of the Librarians' Conference of 1853, which constitute a cross-section of library opinion in the middle of the century, practically ignore reference work.[5] Though the agenda of the conference included many topics, reference work was not among them. The then current notions of the scope of library activities may be seen from the contents suggested for inclusion in a manual on library practice. The manual was to embody "the most important information upon the chief points" in the administration of a library, these being organization and finance, buildings and shelf arrangement, cataloging, and book selection.[6]

The exhaustive *Report on Public Libraries in the United States* (1876), which fairly represents the theory and practice of the next generation of American librarianship, showed no greater cognizance of reference work. The term itself was not used at all, and the whole subject of help to readers received only the most casual mention.[7]

Speculation as to why the idea of reference work, which now seems so obvious, took so little

---

[1] This description, written by Watterston himself, appeared in the *Washington City Chronicle*, July 11, 1829. It is quoted in William Dawson Johnston, *History of the Library of Congress; Volume I: 1800-1864* (Washington: Government Printing Office, 1904), p. 181.

[2] William Alfred Jones, "Statement of Librarian," in *Statements, Opinions and Testimony Taken by the Committee of Inquiry Appointed by the Trustees of Columbia College* (New York: John W. Amerman, Printer, 1857), p. 5; quoted in Kenneth J. Brough, *Scholar's Workshop; Evolving Conceptions of Library Service* (Urbana: University of Illinois Press, 1953), p. 146.

[3] Andrew P. Peabody, *Harvard Reminiscences* (Boston: Ticknor and Company, 1888), p. 153.

[4] William Coolidge Lane, "The Harvard College Library, 1877-1928," in *The Development of Harvard University . . . 1869 1929;* edited by Samuel Eliot Morison (Cambridge: Harvard University Press, 1930), p. 608.

[5] George Burwell Utley, *The Librarians' Conference of 1853: a Chapter in American Library History*, edited by Gilbert H. Doane (Chicago: American Library Association, 1951), pp. 131-76.

[6] *Ibid.*, p. 156.

[7] An article by A. R. Spofford did advocate the establishment of an open-shelf collection of reference books, but his idea was that readers could thus help themselves without distracting the librarians from other duties. (Ainsworth Rand Spofford, "Works of Reference," in U. S. Bureau of Education, *Public Libraries in the United States of America: Their History, Condition and Management,* Special Report, Part I [Washington: Government Printing Office, 1876]), p. 688.

hold on the library thought of the day finds its best answer in an analysis of the prevailing library context. As indicated in the previous chapter, the transformation of scholarship, which was eventually to revitalize the library, had not yet had time to work its effects. The college library was still very much on the periphery of the college. Meagerly supported, open only a few hours a week, its management relegated to part-time and untrained personnel, the college library was only beginning to emerge from the situation when it was, in Canfield's phrase, "almost an aside in education . . . to be almost entirely omitted without making a serious change in the sense."[8]

The fact was that both faculty and students had little occasion to make any formidable demands on the library or its staff. The idea of research had as yet made small inroads on the American university; scholars who had hardly begun to look to the library for their materials were not likely to seek assistance there. The demands by students must have been even more modest. With their reading horizons effectively limited by the traditional reliance on the textbook, their contacts with the library were rarely more than the casual encounters motivated by occasional curiosity. It was not until a new spirit and method had changed the character of American higher education and transformed the library into a tool for scholarship that the concept of reference service could hope to find a fertile field in the university library.

For their part, the librarians themselves were still fettered by traditional regulations which placed an overriding emphasis on custodial responsibilities. The chief duty of the college librarian under such constricting legislation was to preserve from harm the books entrusted to his care. Cast in the role of the keeper of the books, he was naturally disposed to regard the needs of the reader with indifference, if not hostility.

In the case of the public library, the reasons for the delay in the genesis of reference service were probably more practical than ideological. The period from 1850 to 1875 saw the public library movement at the very beginning of its active development, and the most pressing problems to be faced were those of organization and finance. Collections were small and staff members few. There were scant bibliographical resources to draw upon, and few librarians, other than perhaps the busy chief himself, qualified to offer any real assistance.

However, these difficulties were transitory rather than inherent. Public libraries, unlike college libraries, were not burdened by regulations committing them to the narrow limits of service implicit in the custodial concept of librarianship. On the contrary, public librarians had to face from the beginning the task of justifying the expenditure of city funds by demonstrating the values to be derived from their institutions. These values they appraised in terms of volume of use and number of services. Public librarians had therefore a definite incentive to look for new ways in which to demonstrate the utility of their institutions. Thus it is not surprising that the first real steps toward the inauguration of reference service should have come from the public library. Logically too, it came from institutions such as the Worcester Public Library and the Boston Public Library, securely established by two decades of experience, with staffs and resources strong enough to enable their chiefs to look beyond the day-to-day problems of circulation, maintenance and finance.

"Access to Librarians"

The first explicit proposal for a *program* of personal assistance to readers, as distinguished from the occasional aid described in the previous section, was made by a public librarian. In a paper read at the historic 1876 conference of librarians, Samuel Swett Green of the Worcester Free Public Library argued for "The Desirableness of Establishing Personal Intercourse and Relations Between Librarians and Readers in Popular Libraries."[9]

Green's proposal was modest enough. His central thesis was that the people who frequented a

---

[8] James Hulme Canfield, "The College Library," *Outlook*, LXXI (May, 1902), 248.

[9] Samuel Swett Green, "Personal Relations between Librarians and Readers," *Library Journal*, I (October, 1876), 74-81. The longer title was used for the original reading of the paper at the 1876 conference.

popular library generally lacked the knowledge to be able to select the books they required. It was not enough to send such readers to the catalog, for they would be unskilled in its use and in any case they would not have the discrimination to find the materials best suited to their limited capacities. For such readers personal assistance by the librarian was essential. Accordingly the librarian should make himself "accessible," and by his cordiality and greater knowledge of materials ensure a greater degree of satisfaction for his clientele.

In the elaboration of his argument Green displayed mixed motives. As much as anything else he was concerned with the effectiveness of personal assistance as a means of elevating the fiction reading tastes of the people.[10] There was also a generous measure of practical self-seeking on behalf of the library. By stressing cordiality and the willingness to be of general service, Green hoped to increase the popularity of his library with the people who used and *supported* it. To his colleagues at the 1876 conference Green spelled out the practical benefits librarians might expect to derive from a program of personal assistance.

> The more freely a librarian mingles with readers, and the greater the amount of assistance he renders them, the more intense does the conviction of citizens, also, become, that the library is a useful institution, and the more willing do they grow to grant money in larger and larger sums to be used in buying books and employing additional assistants.[11]

It seems clear therefore that what Green was sponsoring was not a new theory of library service but a new technique. The very phrase "desirableness of personal intercourse" indicated the still tentative nature of his approach. Personal assistance was seen to be mainly useful as a means of creating a better impression on the library's clientele. The provision of an information service was not yet regarded as a central responsibility of the library, and its contribution to the role of the library as an educational instrument was no more than vaguely forecast.

Nevertheless, in showing that a program of personal assistance could stimulate library use and support, Green had made a significant step forward to the establishment of reference service. He himself was confident that he had made a new and distinctive contribution,[12] and his "new method" drew favorable comment from newspapers in Boston and New York, which contrasted the hospitality of the Worcester Free Public Library with the "unaccomodating spirit" in the libraries of their own cities.[13]

Green's thesis received general approval from his colleagues at the 1876 conference. When he repeated his arguments in favor of "access to librarians" at the London conference of English and American librarians in 1877, he met, however, with objections that, repeated later in one form or another, were to act as braking forces on the "reference work idea" for a generation. Harrison of the London Library was openly skeptical of the value of answering the frivolous questions that might be expected from the users of a popular library and implied that scholarly readers would not have inquiries the librarian could answer.[14] Charles Ammi Cutter's objection was more obliquely presented. Specifically, he proposed an alternative method: reliance on catalogs and book lists, by means of which questioners might find their own answers with no trouble to the librarian.[15]

Even these criticisms questioned the practicability rather than the desirability of "access to librarians." Whether derivative from Green or not, the points which he advocated came to be echoed in the library literature of the 1870's and the early 1880's, though not always with his

[10] *Ibid.*, p. 79.

[11] *Ibid.*, p. 81.

[12] Samuel Swett Green, *The Public Library Movement in the United States, 1853-1893* (Boston: Boston Book Co., 1913), p. 13.

[13] According to Green's citations, *ibid.*, p. 305.

[14] "Proceedings of the Conference of Librarians, London, October...1877...Sixth Sitting," *Library Journal*, II (November-December, 1877), 278.

[15] *Ibid.*

confidence and enthusiasm. At the Boston Public Library the librarian of the Lower Hall still thought that a "considerable class of persons" would "prefer that the fullest information of what is to be had shall be set before them, and be their own assistants,"[16] but reported that "within the last year an advance has been made in the establishment of closer relations with the public in this Hall, and there have been many evidences that where this personal assistance is rendered in an unobtrusive manner, it is cordially met and often gratefully recognized."[17] By 1882, even the conservative W. F. Poole, one of the old guard of the profession, was stating somewhat pontifically the new doctrine of "accessibility:" "To aid inquirers . . . is one of the most pleasant duties of my position. My office door is always open, and anybody seeking for information is encouraged to come to me directly and without formality."[18]

The College Library and the Doctrine of Use

Green's paper was directed specifically at the popular library, but his ideas won the attention and support of college librarians as well. In the general discussion that followed the reading of the paper at the 1876 conference, Professor Otis Robinson of the University of Rochester expressed his agreement with Green's point of view and pointed out the desirability of introducing the "new method" in the college library:

> A librarian should be much more than a keeper of books; he should be an educator . . . . The relation which Mr. Green has presented ought especially to be established between a college librarian and the student readers. No such librarian is fit for his place unless he holds himself to some degree responsible for the library education of the students . . . . It is his province to direct very much of their general reading; and especially in their investigation of subjects, he should be their guide and friend.[19]

At the London conference held the following year, Reuben Guild of Brown University spoke in support of Green's position on "access to librarians" and claimed to have himself instituted a liberal program of "access both to the librarian and to the shelves" at Brown.[20]

Too much should not be made of Green's direct influence. Green had provided a useful example, but Robinson and Guild were agreeing with rather than following Green. Actually the crux of the problem for the academic library lay in Robinson's statement that "a librarian should be much more than a keeper of books; he should be an educator." To make possible the introduction of reference work in the college library a basic shift in orientation was first necessary, and the roots of this change from "sanctum" to "workshop" stemmed from the transformation in scholarship rather than from any direct personal influence.

The previous chapter has already described the factors that entered into the large-scale transformation of scholarship and their effects in turn upon the academic library. It is sufficient to repeat at this point that the combined influence of these factors made for a new approach to the academic library and a new concept of its possibilities for higher education.

Justin Winsor's administration of the Harvard College Library illustrates how the changing climate in the academic library helped prepare the way for the introduction of reference service. A scholar himself, Winsor was heartily in accord with the educational philosophy that sought to make the college library the workshop for scholarship.[21] He brought about a complete change in

---

[16] Boston Public Library, *Twenty-ninth Annual Report . . . 1881*, p. 41.

[17] *Ibid.*

[18] "Libraries and the Public," *Library Journal*, VII (July-August, 1882), 201.

[19] "Librarians and Readers," *Library Journal*, I (November, 1876), 123-24.

[20] "Proceedings . . . 1877 . . . Sixth Sitting," *op. cit.*, p. 278.

[21] *Supra*, p. 19.

atmosphere, with service to readers as characteristic of the new order as zealous protection of materials had been of the old. As Henry Ware, a contemporary, described the change:

> A new life and spirit seem to pervade the place; and it is safe to say that a public library does not exist to which readers are more cordially welcomed, or more intelligently and courteously aided in their researches, than the library of Harvard College under its present enlightened and modern management.[22]

Winsor's reports indicated some of the ways in which he strove to extend the "aid in researches" to which Ware alluded. He instituted an ingenious system of "notes and queries," — his name for a row of spindles on which inquirers could place slips of paper bearing their questions. The slip having been hung up on the spindle, it would wait there until anyone who possessed the necessary curiosity and knowledge supplied the answer.[23]

A more ambitious venture was the preparation of lists of references in anticipation of the students' essays, themes and "forensics" (debates).[24] Winsor also advocated teaching the use of books and libraries to the undergraduates, arguing that such instruction would do much to promote the use of the library.

> It is a librarian's luxury when a man comes to him who knows how to master a book and to dominate a library. If our colleges would pay more attention to the methods by which a subject is deftly attacked, and would teach the true use of encyclopedic and bibliographical helps, they would do much to make the library more serviceable.[25]

It was never quite clear, however, whether Winsor meant such instruction to be furnished by the faculty or by the library staff. His own reports did not describe any such program in his library, and it is probable that Winsor did not develop the idea.

It is evident that the Harvard Library, under the influence of Winsor's new philosophy of "service," was certainly offering some forms of assistance to readers. Such assistance was, however, clearly quite unorganized and informal, and it never achieved the prestige of departmental status, as the work of cataloging, ordering, circulation and shelf arrangement had already done. There is good reason to believe that Winsor's advocacy of reference lists and group instruction may have led him to minimize the necessity or even the utility of *individual* assistance. For example, though he was something of an authority on reference books and two of his lists of such works were published, he gave no indication in either compilation that the librarian might be expected to provide personal assistance to the readers using the books.[26]

A further explanation of Winsor's relative indifference to reference work is suggested by his strong belief in the efficacy of the subject catalog. Cutter had already properly pointed out that the subject catalog constituted the most important tool for the library's information service.[27] Winsor went somewhat further and intimated that the subject catalog was self-sufficient and rendered the personal services of the library staff no longer necessary!

---

[22] Henry Ware, "The Harvard College Library. No. 2," *Harvard Register*, II (October, 1880), 202. The wording of Ware's statement supports the inference that, insofar as the new policy in academic library administration was the product of the librarians' own efforts, it owed much to the example of the public library.

[23] Harvard College Library, ["Report of the Librarian"], in *Annual Reports of the President and Treasurer of Harvard College, 1877-78,* p. 113.

[24] Harvard College Library, ["Report of the Librarian"], in *Annual Reports of the President and Treasurer of Harvard College, 1879-80,* pp. 111-12.

[25] Justin Winsor, "The Development of the Library; Address at the Dedication of the Orrington Lunt Library, Northwestern University, Evanston, Illinois," *Library Journal*, XIX (November, 1894), 374.

[26] American Social Science Association, *Free Public Libraries; Suggestions on Their Foundation and Administration, with a Selected List of Books* (Boston: Riverside Press, 1871) — Winsor wrote the section on reference books; Justin Winsor, "A List of the Most Useful Reference Books," *Harvard University Bulletin*, II (April, 1882), 341-43.

[27] Charles Ammi Cutter, "The Cataloguer's Work," *Nation*, XXIV (February 8, 1877), 86-88.

> There is no factor in the efficiency of a library equal to the Catalogue. It used to be the
> librarian. Van den Weyer in 1849, in his remarks before the Royal Commission at the
> British Museum, when some librarians were raising all sorts of objections against the
> preparation of even Author's Catalogues, met them very squarely when he told them,
> that the librarians who undervalued catalogues were aiming to make themselves per-
> sonally indispensable. It was a telling blow at the traditional librarian and it was the
> truth. The race is not yet dead; and I could name one or two in this country.[28]

These facts indicate that the new concept of the library as the "laboratory" of the college was
not in itself synonymous with that of reference service. Nevertheless, the "doctrine of use" was a
necessary preliminary to full development of the idea of reference work. Displacing the previously
held view that the college librarian had little to do with readers, it focused the attention of librarians
upon the needs of their clientele and led them to look for new means of meeting those needs.

"Aid to Readers"

The educational role which had, in a sense, been imposed upon the college librarians by the new
trends in higher education was eagerly assumed by the public librarians. From cordiality and willingness to assist readers it was only a short leap to a recognition of the responsibility to do so;
from a more or less condescending interest in improving the reading tastes of the people, it was an
easy transition to the idea that the proper function of the public library was to seek all means for
maximum usefulness to its clientele. It was, of course, an idea that had been implicit in the very
founding of public libraries, but it did not assume its full proportions until the growing professionalization of librarianship in the seventies and eighties led librarians to identify themselves as
active workers for the service of the public. Melvil Dewey proudly called it the "modern library
idea:"

> So came into prominence what we fondly term the "modern library idea." The old
> school librarian was a jailer who guarded his books, often from being read.... The
> modern librarian is active, not passive. He is as glad to welcome a reader as the
> earnest merchant a customer.... He magnifies his office, and recognizes in his pro-
> fession an opportunity for usefulness to his fellows inferior to none.[29]

Thus the eighties saw many public librarians already keenly conscious of the library's opportunities
as an educational institution and alert to meet the needs of readers. Increasingly committed to a
program of "aid to readers," they found a useful tool in the new technique of personal assistance
described by Green.

Green's own library greatly developed and amplified its service to readers. The work was now
being carried on, not just through the intermittent help of the chief himself, but by assistants specifically assigned to the task. Green's reports consistently emphasized the educational value of
this service, and he took pride in the fact that the Worcester methods were winning general approval and imitation. "It is pleasant to note that the methods in vogue in this library have approved
themselves to the judgment of managers of libraries in other places and that they are being adopted
in many cities and large towns and in smaller communities."[30]

The most important of the libraries to which Green alluded was the Boston Public Library, then
the largest institution of its kind in the country. The Boston Public Library began, like the Worcester Public Library, by making no clear-cut distinction between the themes of "information service"

---

[28]Justin Winsor, "An Address" in University of Michigan Library, *Public Exercises on the Completion of the Library
Building of the University of Michigan, December 12, 1883* (Ann Arbor: Published by the University, 1884), p. 38.

[29]Dewey's address was given at the Brooklyn Library. It was printed in Brooklyn Library, *Twenty-seventh Annual Report
...Presented March 26, 1885*, pp. 9-10.

[30]Worcester Free Public Library, *Twenty-fourth Annual Report...for the Year Ending November 30, 1885*, p. 11.

and "improvement in reading tastes." The work of assistance centered in the Lower Hall, which was that portion of the building containing the popular books available for home use. The service there was obviously designed to aid the less knowledgeable type of reader, unused to the management of the library apparatus and vague as to his own information requirements. The duties of the attendants in charge of this service consisted mainly in showing readers how to use the catalog, giving suggestions in cases of doubt as to which book was wanted, recommending programs of reading, and advising parents and teachers on the reading requirements of children.[31] Begun on a part-time basis as part of the other duties of the loan desk attendants, the work of assistance rapidly grew to the point where it warranted a full-time position by 1883.[32]

A broadly representative view of the rapid expansion of reference work (though it was not yet so called) in American libraries was furnished by the series of reports submitted to the American Library Association under the heading of "Aids and Guides." The 1883 report, compiled by William Foster, gave most of its attention to the usual lists, bulletins and catalogs. But it also indicated the growing acceptance of a new type of "aid" — personal assistance. Foster commented: "It is certainly one of the most gratifying evidences of the gradual lifting of the level of library work that never before has there been anything like the degree of personal assistance reported from the various libraries all over the country."[33]

For his 1886 report on the same topic of "aids to readers," Frederick Crunden of the St. Louis Public Library collected data from 108 libraries. He found a growing sentiment in favor of the provision of personal assistance by the librarian as the most effective form of aid to the reader.

> Among the most acceptable and effective methods for assisting readers to the best books and sources of information, fifty-three librarians report "personal help." Many of them believe this to be the most important of all "aids;" and on this point again your reporter is glad to record his vote with the majority. His own opinion is entirely in accord with the sentiment expressed in a number of the reports, that nothing can take the place of "an intelligent and obliging assistant at the desk."[34]

Crunden's own enthusiasm for personal assistance led him to exaggerate somewhat the extent of the advances made. Indeed, on the evidence of his own statistics, a numerical "majority" in favor of such aid was yet to be achieved. Moreover, the very inclusion of personal assistance among indexes, bulletins, catalogs, and mechanical devices in the category of "aids to readers" indicated that it was still regarded as of no real difference in kind, but only as another desirable technique or contrivance.

Even as an "aid," scholarly libraries were still inclined to doubt the practicability and value of personal assistance, offering it intermittently, if at all. The antithesis in points of view was clearly brought out by the experience at the Boston Public Library. Though in the Lower Hall (the "popular library") the work of assistance warranted a full-time position, in Bates Hall (catering to the more scholarly class of readers) there was a strong disposition to limit personal aid by librarians, in deference to the supposed ability and desire of the more learned readers to minister to their wants by themselves. When the Examining Committee suggested in 1887 that there should be in Bates Hall a "person whose sole duty it would be to answer questions of all sorts, and to direct inquirers in their search for information,"[35] the recommendation received the stiff reply from the Trustees that it was hardly practicable in that it would require the transfer of personnel from other and

---

[31]"Library Economy and History," *Library Journal,* VII (May, 1882), 88-89.

[32]Boston Public Library, *Thirty-second Annual Report...1884,* pp. 14-15.

[33]William E. Foster, "Report on Aids and Guides to Readers, 1883," *Library Journal,* VIII (Buffalo Conference Number, 1883), 241.

[34]Frederick M. Crunden, "Report on Aids and Guides, August '83 to June, '85," *Library Journal,* XI (Milwaukee Conference Number, 1886), 310.

[35]Boston Public Library, *Thirty-fifth [Annual] Report...1887,* p. 18.

more important work.[36] Similarly John Schwartz, writing as late as 1889, still took it for granted that personal assistance would be suitable only for small libraries, and then only when other means of satisfying readers were lacking.[37]

It is all but certain that most university and reference libraries followed policies closer to Schwartz' views than to Crunden's. An analysis of the library reports for the eighties brings forward little evidence that the scholarly libraries had accepted the work of personal assistance as anything more than a casual and intermittent part of library duties. The reports of the Lenox and Astor Libraries, the major research collections in New York City, ignored the subject completely, though problems of acquisitions and cataloging received consistent and detailed description. It is a fair inference that the provision of information to readers formed no regular part of the staff duties.

The inference is equally justifiable in the case of the Library of Congress under Spofford's administration. W. Dawson Johnston's memorial address paid ample tribute to Spofford's personal zeal and courtesy in dealing with the questions referred to him by the members of Congress.[38] Yet Spofford's own reports made no mention of reference work. Admittedly these were so skimpy as to afford no more than negative evidence, but it is safe to conclude that reference work under Spofford was a one-man show, the by-product of his own amazing memory and scholarly accomplishments and quite incidental to his other duties.

Melvil Dewey and Reference Work at Columbia

While most academic and reference libraries were still hesitating over the value of individual assistance as a useful technique for aiding readers, at least one had attained a much more advanced position. Under Dewey's dynamic and positive leadership, the Columbia College Library had already recognized that such assistance was more than just another aid or subsidiary activity, that the personal help given to individual readers was a necessary and integral part of the library's educational function.

It would be difficult to ascertain precisely to what extent Dewey's enlarged concept of reference work stemmed from outside influences, but undoubtedly these had a large share in the formation of his ideas. As secretary of the American Library Association, manager of the Library Bureau and editor of the *Library Journal,* Dewey had been in the very forefront of the public library movement and was indisputably well-acquainted with the pioneer efforts of the public librarians in developing the concept of reference work. There is some direct evidence to indicate that he was consciously aiming at adapting the principles first enunciated by the public librarians to the college library situation. Thus, in the address which he gave to the Brooklyn Library trustees in 1885, Dewey outlined the progress which the "modern library idea" had made in public libraries and then, in reference to his own work at Columbia, stated: "We are trying to work out the modern library idea in a university library."[39]

Whatever his debt to his predecessors, Dewey, with his characteristic *élan,* went well ahead of them in the specific and fully developed concept of reference service which he formulated during his stay at Columbia College. For Dewey there was no longer any question of reference work being

[36]Boston Public Library, *Thirty-sixth Annual Report...1888,* p. 6.

[37]John Schwartz, "The Librarian an Educator — Mr. John Schwartz Replies to Mr. Cohen," *Library Journal,* XIV (January-February, 1889), 5.

[38]W. Dawson Johnston, "Dr. Spofford and the Library of Congress, 1860-97," in *Ainsworth Rand Spofford 1825-1908: a Memorial Meeting...* (New York: Printed for the District of Columbia Library Association by the Webster Press, 1909), pp. 31-32.

[39]Brooklyn Library, *op. cit.,* p. 10. Undoubtedly Dewey also owed much to the support and encouragement of the Columbia faculty. Columbia College was exceptional in that there was a clear-cut demand from at least some of the faculty members for improvements in internal library administration as well as the more usual demand for more materials. (Cf. the statements of Barnard and Burgess, *Supra,* pp. 14, 17). Nicholas Murray Butler recalled that there was a whole group of younger faculty members who supported what he called the "Barnard-Burgess-Dewey revolution" in library administration. (*Across the Busy Years; Recollections and Reflections* [New York: Charles Scribner's Sons, 1939], I, 95).

considered peripheral to the activity of the library. He recognized that the educational function of the library involved a responsibility for interpreting the resources to the user and that it was necessary to assign personnel specifically to the task of interpretation. In his first *Circular of Information* at Columbia (1884), Dewey gave, under the rubric of "aids to readers," the following explicit statement of the library's responsibilities for reference service.

> The Library is not content to accumulate and safely store many thousands of volumes. Nor is it sufficient to have carefully classified and fully catalogued its treasures. With the limited time at the command of students and investigators, and the immense amount of material with which the individual must often deal, the aid of some one fully acquainted with the resources of the library, able to discriminate between the sources of information, and adjust them to the manifold needs of readers, and at hand to impart the desired help, becomes imperatively necessary. Where to find and how to get at the fullest and readiest answer to his questions, is the student's practical want....

> To meet this proper demand, the Library offers students the best bibliographies, cyclopaedias, dictionaries, and other works of reference, and aims to induce them by example, by discriminating counsel, and by direct training, to know these books, to use them intelligently, and to acquire the habit of hunting down a needed fact.,...

> What are the best books on the subject, in what order, and how to take them up, are points on which the undergraduate student most often needs light. Students working up subjects for theses, prize essays, orations, debates, etc. find this feature of the Library organization of the greatest utility, and it is the first and paramount duty of the Reference Librarian to give such help.[40]

Dewey did not fail to put these principles into practice. The roster of library staff members included in his first annual report listed George Baker and William G. Baker as members of the "reference department." The former was "in special charge of law, political science and history;" the latter "in special charge of sciences, arts, and serials."[41] It is clear that the term "reference department" here really meant organized personal assistance, for in answer to Crunden's questionnaire of 1885, Columbia reported that "it keeps two reference librarians specially to aid inquirers."[42] By 1886 Dewey could report that the work of the new department was growing constantly in extent and usefulness, and he added the significant comment that "we esteem this perhaps the most important single department."[43]

Reference Service

By showing that personal assistance was central, not peripheral, to library service and that the most effective way of providing it was to assign personnel specifically to that task, Dewey supplied the essential last links in the development of the concept of reference service. The new concept rapidly gained other adherents in the next decade. Where Crunden's study had shown that many still had reservations on these points, the library literature of the subsequent ten years gave clear evidence that "desirability" had crystallized into necessity and responsibility, and that casual, intermittent help was being replaced by specific administrative organization. "It is in precisely this direction [i.e. answering questions] that the library does its best work and becomes a means of real help to the students," stated the librarian of the Cambridge Public Library in 1886.[44] William E.

---

[40] *Circular of Information, 1884, Columbia College Library and School of Library Economy*, pp. 15-16; reprinted in Columbia University School of Library Service, *School of Library Economy, Columbia College, 1887-1889: Documents for a History* (New York: School of Library Service, Columbia University, 1937), pp. 31-32.

[41] Columbia College Library, *First Annual Report of the Chief Librarian, May 31, 1884*. p. 6.

[42] Crunden, *op. cit.*, p. 316.

[43] Columbia College Library, *Second and Third Annual Reports of the Chief Librarian, June 30, 1886*, p. 39.

[44] "Library Economy and History — Reports," *Library Journal*, XI (May, 1886), 147.

Foster supplied the added and telling argument that it would really be an economy of time to concentrate the work of answering questions in the hands of special assistants, for otherwise it would interfere with routine operations of the library staff.[45]

As the new, unified conception gained wide acceptance and became securely established in the practice of American librarianship, the term "reference work" began to replace the older, vaguer terms "aid to readers" and "assistance to readers." In 1891 it appeared for the first time in the index to the *Library Journal*. In the same year the first article on reference work specifically so titled was published.[46] The article consisted of a series of papers on the nature and methods of reference work at the Brooklyn Library, the Pratt Institute Library, and the Columbia College Library. The tone of the papers was uniformly matter-of-fact, not exhortatory; in these libraries, at least, reference work was a practice, not an aspiration.

The 1894 meeting of the Massachusetts Library Club was devoted to discussion of the same topic. There was a general agreement among the speakers that "there is no place so large and none so small, but what reference work can be done."[47] Adelaide Hasse's article of 1895 indicated that special training courses for reference workers were being given by many libraries.[48] From 1896 on, reference work occupied a regular place on the programs of the American Library Association conferences.

By that time specialized reference workers were to be found in at least a dozen of the larger public libraries. However, only a few academic and reference libraries could boast of similar advances. Columbia continued its leadership and achieved a further degree of specialization in reference service in that its reference department was subdivided along subject lines. Herbert Baxter Adams had high commendation for the specialized assistance provided for the students in the Columbia College School of Political Science. "The librarian there serves as an efficient mediator between men and books. Like the person whose duty it is in our great railway stations to answer the questions of perplexed travelers, Mr. George D. Baker . . . informs every inquirer where to go for what he wants."[49]

Other scholarly libraries which appointed specialized reference workers in the decade after 1885 were the New York State Library and Cornell University Library. The establishment of a reference department at the former institution followed directly upon Melvil Dewey's appointment as chief librarian in 1888. Only one member of the staff (D. V. R. Johnston) was assigned solely to reference work, but the archivist and the "sub-librarians" for education, law and legislation undoubtedly spent at least part of their time in supplying information to readers and correspondents.[50]

At Cornell University an interest in some phases of reference work had been demonstrated as early as 1886, when the then acting librarian, George Harris, gave a course of lectures on "bibliography." In 1891, the opening of a new building and an increase in staff made possible "the establishment of the long desired Reference Library . . . with the appointment of an assistant librarian to take charge of this library, assist students in the use of the catalogue, and in their researches, and to give such information as may be needed to facilitate the use of books."[51]

---

[45] William E. Foster, "The Information Desk at the Providence Public Library," *Library Journal,* XVI (September, 1891), 271-72. Foster did much to pioneer the development of reference service. His reports at the Providence Public Library offer an exceptionally detailed and closely reasoned account of the evolution of reference service in a particular public library. For a résumé of this evolution, see the present author's paper "The Development of the Concept of Reference Service in American Libraries, 1850-1900," *Library Quarterly,* XXIII (January, 1953), 13-15.

[46] "Reference Work in Libraries," *Library Journal,* XVI (October, 1891), 297-300.

[47] "Massachusetts Library Club," *Library Journal,* XIX (November, 1894), 382.

[48] Adelaide R. Hasse, "The Training of Library Employees — IV," *Library Journal,* XX (September, 1895), 303-04.

[49] Herbert Baxter Adams, *Seminary Libraries and Historical Extension* ("Johns Hopkins University Studies in Historical and Political Science," Fifth Series, XI [Baltimore: 1887]), 17.

[50] New York State Library, *Seventy-third Annual Report . . . for the Year Ending September 30, 1890,* pp. 35-38; *Seventy-fourth Annual Report . . . for the Year Ending Sept. 30, 1891, passim.*

[51] Cornell University Library, *Report of the Librarian . . .* [1891-92], p. 1.

The above statement is noteworthy in that it reveals clearly the rather limited scope of reference services even in those college libraries which had come so far as to employ librarians specifically for that task. Interpreting the catalog and assisting undergraduate students were the chief responsibilities of the reference worker in the American college of the 1890's, with only an occasional hint as yet that such assistance might be pertinent to more advanced researches.

At most other academic and reference libraries the service was still on a part-time basis, where indeed it was offered at all. At Harvard the staff roster still did not list anyone with title of reference librarian. Thomas Kiernan, the Superintendent of Circulation, did give valuable assistance in inquiries,[52] but in addition to his reference duties, he presided over the delivery desk, supervised conduct in the reading room and had charge of the library's binding.[53] Despite his personal gifts, the reference service at Harvard must have been extremely limited.

At the Library of Congress the public services had simply been marking time, as the lack of space and of staff prevented the Library from doing much more than receiving and storing its new acquisitions. Whatever reference service was offered was largely a matter of Spofford's supplying information from his own intimate knowledge of the collections.[54] With the new building promising a solution for the most pressing problem of space, Spofford began to give attention to the improvement of the public service departments of the Library.[55]

But Spofford's statements even at this time never made it clear that he had in mind the organization of a full-fledged reference department. This supposition is borne out by the fact that the Library, as late as 1896, still did not have a single full-time reference worker. David Hutcheson, who bore the resplendent title of "chief of the library service," officially functioned as Spofford's "representative to supply books and information and to answer all inquiries that are needful to be answered." Actually he spent a large part of his time in cataloging.[56]

Of the other major research libraries of the period — Yale University Library, the Lenox Library, the Astor Library, the Newberry Library, the University of Chicago Library — it can only be stated that their reports made no mention of reference services. It is a fair inference that if assistance was in fact being provided, as it probably was, it was being done only on an informal and part-time basis.

An unusually comprehensive and detailed picture of contemporary opinion on the administration of research libraries was supplied by the testimony given at the hearings held by the U. S. Congress's Joint Committee on the Library of Congress in November and December of 1896. The immediate purpose of the investigation was to inquire into the condition of the Library of Congress and to bring out recommendations for its reorganization, but, since the witnesses included the most eminent librarians of the day, in a broader sense the testimony was representative of the needs and policies of American research libraries in general.

The great majority of the opinions held that the Congressional Library's first need was for more and better cataloging.[57] Underlying this recommendation was evidently a strong faith in the value of the dictionary catalog as *the* preeminent tool for revealing the library's resources on a given subject. Some of the statements in support of the subject catalog went so far as to indicate an

[52] Frank Carney, "The Harvard Library under Justin Winsor," *Harvard Library Notes,* Number 29 (March, 1939), 245-52; W. C. L. [William Coolidge Lane], "Thomas J. Kiernan," *Library Journal,* XXXIX (September, 1914), 691.

[53] Carney, *op. cit.,* p. 249.

[54] David C. Mearns, *The Story up to Now; the Library of Congress, 1800-1946* (Washington: 1947); reprinted from the *Annual Report of the Librarian of Congress for . . . 1946,* p. 125.

[55] U. S. Library of Congress, *Annual Report of the Librarian of Congress . . . during the Calendar Year 1891,* Senate Misc. Doc., No. 151, 52d Cong., 1st Sess. (Washington: Government Printing Office, 1892), p. 5; *Special Report of the Librarian of Congress,* Senate Doc. No. 7, 54th Cong., 1st Sess. [1895], pp. 11-13.

[56] U. S. Congress, Joint Committee on the Library of Congress, *Report under S.C.R. 26, Relative to the Condition, Organization and Management of the Library of Congress; with Hearings; March 3, 1897,* Senate Report 1573, 54th Cong., 2d Sess. 1897, p. 37.

[57] Cf. the statements by Dewey and Putnam, *ibid.,* pp. 143, 228.

almost naive belief in the subject-catalog's self-sufficiency, implying that the properly made catalog would almost automatically and with a minimum of effort supply the answer to any inquiry. Thus W. H. Brett testified that "you could find in a properly made catalogue *everything* the library has on the subject, no matter what it is."[58]

William Fletcher, of the Amherst College Library, had no such faith. In a strongly-worded dissent he proclaimed his doubts as to the feasibility and desirability of involved analytical cataloging, predicting that with the increasing size of collections such a system would break down of its own weight. Instead he recommended "the employment of a sufficient number of intelligent and trained assistant librarians, at whose hands whatever the library has of catalogue or bibliographic apparatus will be readily placed at the service of readers and always supplemented by quick-witted intelligence."[59]

Brett's views and those of Fletcher represented the extremes; most of the other opinions fell somewhere in between. Probably a fair statement of the consensus position would have been that reference service was supplementary to the subject guides furnished by the catalog and would have to be postponed or placed on a minimal basis until the library was in good mechanical order.[60] This position would have been in conformity with most of the reference work actually being done at the time, which strongly stressed the interpretation of the catalog. For instance, as Herbert Putnam described reference work in his own Boston Public Library, it had "three attendants constantly in charge of the card catalogue interpreting feature. We have three other attendants at different points in the Hall who are answering readers."[61]

The hearings also produced several glowing prophecies for the future. Dewey looked forward to a vast expansion of bibliographic work — the preparation of trustworthy lists of references and guides to subjects. Spofford and his staff had done practically nothing in this direction, he stated, largely owing to the inadequate quarters and the lack of personnel. The new library should do "one hundred-fold more." He foresaw the day when every library and every scholar in the country would feel free to call upon the Library of Congress for information on a subject or the location of a book.[62] W. T. Harris, Commissioner of Education, had in mind the employment of a whole corps of subject specialists at the Library of Congress, a group of experts who would not only select the materials for their departments but be competent to furnish information on a scale going well beyond the simple answering of factual inquiries and the indication of possible sources.[63]

Such expectations went well beyond contemporary practice and form the subject-matter of succeeding chapters, rather than that of the present. In this first stage in the development of reference services progress had been considerably more modest. Even so, the history of reference services could show a number of important steps already taken. The first step had been the statement of the desirability of personal assistance, reflected in practice by the willingness to offer guidance to individual readers, though this help was rather casual and intermittent. The next stage was distinguished by the recognition of a felt need for a *program* of personal assistance, if only to supplement the other means of meeting the needs of readers. More and more libraries were then offering personal help as a useful adjunct to the other "aids to readers." With the growing concern over the library's role as an educational institution, personal assistance came to be seen, not as peripheral, but as central in the library's responsibilities, a service which would require personnel with special training and expressly assigned to the task of interpreting the library's resources. As personal assistance came to be recognized as an important feature of library service, it acquired a distinctive name — "reference work" — and departmental status.

---

[58] *Ibid.*, pp. 264-65 (Emphasis by the present writer).

[59] *Ibid.*, pp. 232-33.

[60] Cf. George Baker's testimony; *ibid.*, p. 213.

[61] *Ibid.*, p. 197.

[62] *Ibid.*, p. 148.

[63] *Ibid.*, p. 254.

In this progression the public libraries consistently took the lead, impelled no doubt by the sound practical motives that first inspired Green to see the "desirableness of personal intercourse between librarians and readers." The university and reference libraries, while following essentially the same course, were generally slowed down by a number of braking forces stemming from the background factors described in the previous chapter. The university library had first to overcome the inertia of the custodial tradition. The transformation of scholarship gave the university library a greatly expanded role in the academic process. At the same time it brought vigorous demands for augmented collections and improved physical facilities. The problems of acquisitions and accommodation unquestionably had first priority on university librarians' attention throughout this period and quite overshadowed matters of internal administration other than cataloging.

The development of subject cataloging in its turn had important implications for reference service. At first its success carried with it the idea that proper mechanical organization could in itself largely achieve the requisite subject approach. To some extent this idea persisted throughout the period under review, but most commonly it came to be felt that the complexity of the catalog itself called for assistance by the librarian in its use. Interpreting the catalog to the presumably befuddled reader became the most common task of the reference librarian.

This duty was also in keeping with the prevalent notion that personal assistance was a method suitable primarily for the uninitiated library user. Where assistance was provided in the academic library it went customarily to the undergraduate student and was often undertaken with the aim of teaching the use of books. Again, such practice corresponded rather closely to the demands of the scholars, who had voiced a certain interest in the bibliographic instruction of the students, but who seldom expressed a clear-cut demand for reference services in their own researches. The statements of Adams, Harris, Burgess and Hubert Howe Bancroft were, however, already harbingers of a demand for the more specialized reference services for which Dewey had provided the prototype.

Thanks to these braking forces, the reference service picture showed rather large variations, from the New York State Library, which was well on its way to subject specialization, to such institutions as Yale and the Lenox Library where it had not yet made any perceptible impress. In general the large public libraries had already given reference service departmental status, but the university libraries had not. Nearly all research libraries had however grown to the point of recognizing reference service as a regular library function. The start had been made.

Chapter III

REFERENCE SERVICE IN THE GENERAL RESEARCH LIBRARIES, 1896-1916:
GROWTH AND ORGANIZATION

The twenty years following Green's ground-breaking paper of 1876 constituted the pioneer period in the development of reference service. Vague and heterogeneous ideas had crystallized into a unified conception, and a marginal activity had become a recognized and specialized function. The next two decades were a period of consolidation and development, translating the ideas explored in the previous generation into organizational forms and standard patterns of practice.

The Growth of Reference Services in Public Libraries

The public libraries had been amongst the most active in promoting reference service in the pioneer period of its history, and in general they maintained their momentum in the next twenty years. In a relatively straight-forward course of expansion and intensification of reference service, the public libraries came to give the work cf assistance departmental status, added steadily to their staff of reference librarians, extended the hours of service to evenings and Sundays, undertook to supply assistance by mail and telephone, and brought the service closer to the consumer by a system of branch library reference service.

Most of the larger public libraries were employing specialized reference workers by the end of the nineteenth century, and from this point their usual course was to give formal recognition to the importance of reference service by making it a separate department. The achievement of departmental status also reflected the fact that there was a steady growth in the volume and diversity of reference services in public libraries. While this growth was not susceptible to confirmation by direct measurement, it was clearly implied by the increase in the number of reference librarians. In a progression typical of most metropolitan libraries, the reference staff of the Detroit Public Library doubled in numbers in the space of a dozen years.[1]

The increase in staff was in part dictated by the extension of the number of outlets for reference service. Within the main library buildings, service by telephone and correspondence came to supplement the regular across-the-desk facilities, and after 1900 reference service was generally available in branch libraries as well.[2]

Reference work in the branches was aimed chiefly at the needs of adults studying in the evening schools, members of study clubs, and high school students. While this branch service was limited to assistance of an elementary kind, it had several important implications for the development of reference service to research as well. For one, the extension of reference service to library agencies which had hitherto been concerned only with the supply of popular books for home reading was indicative of the high esteem which the function was beginning to command in library thinking. An annual report of the Boston Public Library claimed that "the reference work of the branches and reading rooms is perhaps their most important function."[3] While this claim was not supported by any conclusive evidence, the fact that it was made at all was significant. More and more the reference service of the public library was coming to exemplify and justify its pretentions to serious educational influence in the community.

---

[1] In 1902 the Detroit Public Library had three reference librarians; in 1913-14, six. (*Thirty-Eighth Annual Report...for the Year 1902*, p. [6]; *Forty-ninth Annual Report...for the Fiscal Year 1913-14*, p. 27).

[2] Cf. Cleveland Public Library, *Forty-first Annual Report, for the Year 1909*, p. 33.

[3] Boston Public Library, *Fifty-fifth Annual Report...1906-1907*, p. 44.

33

In a more immediate sense the reference work in the branches affected services to research by bringing about a more clearly realized differentiation in level of service. With the branches taking care of much of the simpler reference work, the main libraries were more free to become the centers for scholarly activity. The distinction was made evident in a statement of the Detroit Public Library. "The central library should, fundamentally, present the complete and well rounded reference library where the ripened scholar may continue his learned investigations for the benefit of mankind, but the branch library is properly supplemental to our grammar and high schools, especially for those denied the privilege of higher education."[4] Probably this statement represented a plan for the future rather than the situation which then existed, but by 1913 a number of public library reports attested to the fact that there was already a significant increase in the use of the central buildings for research.[5]

The Growth of Reference Services in University Libraries

From the outset the university libraries had been slower than the public libraries in accepting the necessity for reference service. By and large the relative position remained unchanged through the two decades between 1896 and World War I.

With the exception of Cornell and Columbia, the private universities were still without reference librarians specifically so titled in 1896, and only slowly came round to making organizational changes to that end. Yale did not appoint a reference librarian until 1900.[6] Even then, the position was only a part-time one and remained such throughout the period presently under review. Clearly, reference service was a minor activity in the Yale University Library until after the first World War.

Very much the same situation prevailed at Cornell, Chicago and Harvard. At Cornell, Willard Austen, the only staff member described as having reference duties, administered the "Reference Library" as a part-time responsibility. His assistance to readers was confined to lectures on bibliography and occasional instruction in the use of the library tools.[7] The reference service there was obviously little changed from the rather simple and rudimentary form in which it was first begun in 1891.

At both Chicago and Harvard, the high degree of decentralization stood in the way of the formation of strong central library reference services. During the initial decade of the Library's existence, reference work at Chicago was limited to the provision of general reference books, along with such occasional assistance as could be furnished by the associate librarian herself.[8] In his reorganization of the library following Mrs. Dixson's resignation, Librarian Burton established a "readers' department" which was responsible for both circulation and reference service. The new plan provided one full-time librarian for assistance in the reference room and additional assistants to help in the use of the catalog.[9] However, the departmental libraries, which loomed so large in the general picture of library service at Chicago, did not employ full time reference personnel, the attendants in charge being expected to carry on such work along with their other duties.[10] Since none of these attendants had had previous library training or experience, it is fair to assume that the service available could only have been severely limited.

---

[4]Detroit Public Library, *Forty-fifth Annual Report...for the Year 1909*, p. 7.

[5]Cf. Cleveland Public Library, *Fortieth Annual Report, for the Year 1908*, p. 31; Boston Public Library, *Sixty-first Annual Report...1912-1913*, p. 15.

[6]Yale University Library, *Report of the Librarian...January, 1899--July, 1900*, p. 10.

[7]Cornell University Library, *Librarian's Report, 1907-1908*, p. 6.

[8]Charles Haynes McMullen, "The Administration of the University of Chicago Libraries, 1892-1928," (Unpublished Ph.D. dissertation, University of Chicago, 1949), p. 51.

[9]*Ibid.*, pp. 142, 146.

[10]*Ibid.*, p. 143.

For most of the period under review, Harvard's main library, like Chicago's, provided personal assistance only as a part-time function of the circulation department, with Thomas Kiernan, Superintendent of Circulation, continuing, as previously, to carry most of the load.[11] Though Kiernan's services drew warm praise from his superiors, the feeling grew that more assistance was required, especially in the face of Harvard's unusually cumbersome catalogs.[12]

The pressure for additional assistance gained support from the results of a survey of the Harvard library system conducted by two graduate students of the Harvard Business School in 1914. The surveyors recommended the organization of a reference department to provide the help needed by the students.[13] This recommendation may have been responsible for the transformation of the Circulation Department into the Reference and Circulation Department, organized in 1915 under the supervision of Walter Briggs, formerly reference librarian of the Brooklyn Public Library.[14] While the change in nomenclature seemed to indicate a greater interest in reference service at Harvard, the reports themselves gave little evidence of any marked alteration in the volume or nature of service in the main library. Briggs himself simply took over all the responsibilities formerly held by Kiernan, most of them quite unrelated to reference service, and none of his subordinates gave full time to reference work.

The foregoing review of developments in the chief private universities indicates that in most of these institutions reference service was only beginning to be recognized as a distinct function warranting its own full-time personnel. This generalization does not apply to Columbia University. As inheritors of the tradition established by Dewey and Baker, Librarians Canfield and Johnston vigorously supported the promotion of reference service. Canfield pressed strongly for the inauguration of an expanded service that would provide reference specialists for all the subject divisions of the university. "It is hoped that this is the beginning of a full corps of reference librarians; including at least one thoroughly competent, well-trained, experienced man for each of the great divisions of the library."[15] While he did not realize this goal, he achieved enough to be able to take pride in the valued performance of his staff.[16] Canfield found special satisfaction in the fact that service was not restricted to undergraduates, but was of real help to research personnel both within and without the university.[17]

Canfield's successor, W. Dawson Johnston, shared similar views of the necessity for increased personal service. Johnston's first report advocated the adoption of a system of departmental libraries staffed by subject specialists,[18] and this remained a major theme through the entire period of his administration.

Johnston made a good start towards his goal of a highly qualified reference staff by his appointments in 1911-12 and 1912-13, recruiting men of the caliber of J. David Thompson, Alfred Robert and Dr. H. V. Arny for the positions of law librarian, medical librarian and pharmacy librarian respectively. He also managed to secure full-time appointments of qualified personnel for the School of Philosophy, the School of Political Science, the School of Applied Science, and the School of Journalism.

---

[11]Harvard College Library, *Report of Archibald Cary Coolidge . . . Including the Seventeenth Report of William Coolidge Lane, Librarian . . . 1914*, reprinted, with additions, from the *Report of the President of Harvard University for 1913-14;* p. 3.

[12]Harvard College Library, *Twelfth Report of William Coolidge Lane, Librarian . . . 1909*, reprinted, with additions, from the *Report of the President of Harvard University for 1908-09;* p. 7.

[13]Robert W. Lovett, "The Undergraduate and the Harvard Library, 1877-1937," *Harvard Library Bulletin*, I (Spring, 1947), 233-34.

[14]Harvard College Library, *Report of Archibald Cary Coolidge . . . Including the Eighteenth Report of William Coolidge Lane, Librarian, 1915*, reprinted, with additions, from the *Report of the President of Harvard University for 1914-15;* p. 26.

[15]Columbia University Library, "Report of the Librarian for the Academic Year Ending June 30, 1900," in *Eleventh Annual Report of President Low to the Trustees, October 1, 1900*, p. 343.

[16]Columbia University Library, "Report of the Librarian . . . ," in *Annual Reports of the President and Treasurer . . . for the Year Ending June 30, 1903*, p. 207.

[17]*Ibid.*, pp. 195, 203.

[18]Columbia University Library, "Report of the Librarian . . . ," in *Annual Reports of the President and Treasurer . . . for the Year Ending June 30, 1910*, p. 246.

After this auspicious beginning, the ambitious program for reference service at Columbia came to an abrupt halt when Johnston resigned, apparently under faculty pressure, in 1913.[19] The subsequent appointment of Dean Lockwood, a professor of classics, as Acting Librarian represented the assumption of control by the faculty, and in a sense the repudiation of Johnston's policies. At any rate, the annual reports said little more of these large plans for an expanded reference service, the inference being that they remained in abeyance.

The setback in the development of reference services at Columbia illustrated the common difficulty experienced in attempting to impose new functions on old, intrenched organizations. Though Columbia itself had probably gone farther than any other university, private or state, in accepting the idea of personal assistance as a library responsibility, as a group the older private universities undoubtedly were slower in making a place for reference service than were the state universities.

As relative newcomers on the academic scene, the state university libraries had the advantage of commencing their active operations as research institutions at a time when the idea and the techniques of reference work were becoming widely accepted. Where the older institutions tended to make personal assistance an extra and part-time function of existing departments, the state universities ordinarily proceeded rather rapidly toward the creation of full-fledged reference departments. Thus, at the University of Illinois Library, the formal organization of a reference department followed only three years after the appointment of the first full-time staff member.[20]

Significantly, the organization of the department at Illinois was coincident with the appointment of the Library's first professionally trained chief librarian and with the opening of a new building, both of these factors often serving elsewhere as well to trigger the inception of reference work on a separate departmental basis. At the University of California, reference service had already been accepted in principle and was being offered on a part-time basis before 1911, but the actual creation of a reference department had to be deferred until the construction of the Doe Library provided adequate physical facilities.[21] Similarly, the reports of the University of Michigan Library, while containing occasional allusions to reference work in Davis' administration, indicated that the service did not really get off the ground until after the appointment of Theodore Wesley Koch as chief librarian in 1905. In the same way, the arrival of James Thayer Gerould (1906) proved to be a turning point in the progress of reference service at the University of Minnesota.

In terms of increase in reference personnel, the history of the Reference Department at the University of Illinois again provides a typical example of the situation in state university libraries. From 1897 to 1908-09 the Library had one full-time professionally trained reference librarian and the part-time service of assistants from other departments, as well as a number of student assistants. From 1908-09 there were two full-time reference librarians, and from 1913 on never less than three.[22]

While reference service became an established function in the main libraries of the state universities, personal assistance was seldom yet provided in the departmental libraries there. Many of the departmental libraries were quite independent of the central library administration. They usually consisted of little more than office collections available for occasional consultation, provisions for service being wholly negligible. Even where, as at the University of California, the departmental libraries were officially under the administration of the chief librarian, the supervision was usually only nominal. The so-called "departmental librarians" were in almost all cases no more

[19]Kenneth James Brough, *Scholar's Workshop; Evolving Conceptions of Library Service* (Urbana: University of Illinois Press, 1953), pp. 45-47.

[20]Madeline Cord Thompson, "The History of the Reference Department of the University of Illinois Library," (Unpublished M.S. thesis, University of Illinois, 1942), p. 8.

[21]University of California Library, *University Library*, reprint from the *Annual Report of the President of the University, 1912-13*; p. 10.

[22]Thompson, *op. cit.*, pp. 63-75.

than clerks who gave most of their time to non-library duties, and were quite incompetent to afford skilled assistance to readers.[23]

Taken together, the foregoing accounts of the position of reference service in university libraries suggest that the usual development was one of only halting progress. A substantial advance had indeed been made. By 1915 reference work was ordinarily accepted as a necessary service of the university library and in many cases was invested with the prestige of departmental status. In relatively few cases, however, had the university libraries yet put into practice the secondary specialization of reference work by subject fields that was so important for service to research workers.

Some of the hindrances in the way of expansion of reference service in the university libraries have already been suggested. Lack of funds, inadequate physical facilities, and inability to obtain administrative supervision over the departmental libraries were perennial practical problems which effectively limited the horizons of even those most ardently in favor of augmenting service.

Another factor inhibiting the development of reference service was the continued emphasis on acquisitions, especially on the part of the scholars themselves. This point was brought out most clearly at Columbia, when Lockwood became librarian. Since Lockwood represented the faculty point of view in library management, his ideas probably could be considered typical of the wishes of the Columbia faculty, and to a certain degree of faculty members in general. For him the main issue in library administration was clearly acquisitions. Lockwood's initial report stated bluntly: "During my incumbency I have laid chief stress upon the acquisition of books.... In a university library nothing can take the place of books. We must strain every nerve to keep pace with the growing output of the world's scholarly literature."[24]

The scholars' emphasis on collections tended to lead the professional librarians themselves into equating library excellence with extent of holdings, and brought on what amounted to a race in acquisitions. A commonplace in the reports of the university libraries was the request for larger book funds, a request often buttressed by statistics showing the more rapid growth of other universities' collections.[25] Many of these exhortations were plainly no more than calculated tactics for securing interest and support for the library, but there was undoubtedly a very real rivalry among the various institutions, and it tended to focus attention on the area most susceptible to publicity and claims of superiority – the increase in accessions.

Another continuing difficulty was the librarians' lack of status in the university community. W. Dawson Johnston complained that the traditional view of librarianship as a quasi-clerical function still persisted, to the detriment of the organization of an expert and extensive service. Referring to the "naive conceptions of what the duties of a library assistant are, and...the equally mischievous conceptions of what his duties should be," Johnston concluded that, in so far as these ideas persisted, "the expert service which should be given in a large library must be lacking and the duties of the library staff must remain largely clerical in character."[26]

Johnston's charges were unintentionally confirmed by President Nicholas Murray Butler. When the latter sought to justify the appointment of a faculty member to take charge of the Columbia libraries, he intimated that professional librarians in general were only technicians who could not really understand and serve scholars' requirements.[27] The same suspicion of librarians'

[23] University of California Library, *University Library*, reprint from the *Annual Report of the President of the University, 1915-16;* p. 11.

[24] Columbia University Library, "Report of the Acting Librarian...," in *Annual Reports of the President and Treasurer... for the Year Ending June 30, 1916,* p. 343.

[25] Cf. University of Minnesota Library, "The University Library," in *The President's Report for the Year 1915-16,* p. 157; University of Wisconsin Library, "Report of the Librarian," in *Biennial Report of the Board of Regents for the Years 1914-15 and 1915-16,* p. 284.

[26] Columbia University Library, "Report of the Librarian...," in *Annual Reports of the President and Treasurer...for the Year Ending June 30, 1913,* p. 282.

[27] Columbia University, *Annual Reports of the President and Treasurer...for the Year Ending June 30, 1916,* p. 24.

capabilities seems to have lain behind the appointment of faculty members Coolidge, Burton and Schwab as chief librarians at Harvard, Chicago, and Yale respectively.

How far such suspicions applied to reference librarians in particular is not clear. While there is no record of any overt faculty opposition to the inauguration of reference service in university libraries, there is also no indication that the faculty members looked with favor upon the idea of librarians using materials on their behalf. A safe inference might be that faculty members accepted the idea that the library staff should provide personal assistance, but regarded such aid as pre-eminently suitable for students, not for mature scholars.

The Growth of Reference Services in the "Reference Libraries"

Most of the difficulties that stood in the way of expansion of reference services in the university libraries stemmed from reasons peculiar to the university library situation, such as the divergent views of faculty and librarians on the proper management of libraries. These difficulties did not apply to the "reference libraries," which were more or less autonomous. Their rate of progress was, accordingly, considerably more rapid. Of course, the reference libraries were no more free from the practical problems of inadequate physical facilities and limited funds than libraries of any other type, (the reference services of the New York Public Library limped along until the opening of the new building in 1911), but such impediments were incidental rather than intrinsic.

Where external conditions were favorable, the development of reference services in such libraries was remarkable. The John Crerar Library, from the outset of its operations in 1896, numbered a full-time reference librarian among its staff.[28] By 1900 the volume of reference work was large enough to warrant the employment of two reference librarians, both with Ph.D. degrees.[29] The uniformly high caliber of these and subsequent members of the reference staff warrants the belief that the John Crerar Library consistently set a high valuation on the importance of reference service.[30]

Only a decade after its opening, the John Crerar Library embarked on a program of secondary specialization by subject, with the appointment of a medical reference librarian.[31] In pursuing this policy the John Crerar Library was only following what was already a clearly discernable pattern in "reference library" administration. Even before 1895 the New York State Library, under Melvil Dewey, had made a firm start toward subject specialization in reference service with the inception of special departments for law, manuscripts, medicine, sociology and education. All these, plus the history division added in 1898, now had librarians devoting their entire time to the particular subject field. The goal, Dewey made clear, was to provide desired information with speed and accuracy.[32] The results, if Herbert Baxter Adams' experience was typical, were singularly successful, for Adams maintained that he nowhere enjoyed better facilities and service.[33]

Dewey had foretold the adoption of a similar policy of subject specialization in reference service for the Library of Congress at the hearings of 1896, and the march of events in the national library proved him a successful prophet. Under the administration of Herbert Putnam, the organization evolved at the Library of Congress was a loose arrangement which dispersed reference duties among a number of library departments on a basis roughly corresponding to the level of difficulty and subject of the inquiries.

---

[28] John Crerar Library, *Second Annual Report, for the Year 1896,* p. 4.

[29] John Crerar Library, *Sixth Annual Report, for the Year 1900,* p. 22.

[30] Later members of the reference department of the John Crerar Library included such distinguished librarians as Charles Barr, Charles Harvey Brown, Robert Usher, Harold Leupp, Edward Tweedell and J. Christian Bay.

[31] John Crerar Library, *Twelfth Annual Report, for the Year 1906,* p. 30.

[32] New York State Library, *Eighty-seventh Annual Report...1904,* p. 11.

[33] Herbert Baxter Adams, *Public Libraries and Popular Education* (University of the State of New York "Home Education Bulletin," Number 31 [Albany: 1900]), p. 107.

Most of the simpler work of assistance devolved on the attendants in the Reading Room. In inquiries beyond the time or capacity of the Reading Room force, readers were referred to the more expert service available from the Division of Bibliography and a number of specialized divisions.[34]

The chief effort of the Division of Bibliography went into the compilation of bibliographies rather than into direct aid to individuals, this policy being in line with Putnam's reasoning that the Library of Congress, as the national library, had an obligation to extend its assistance to as wide a circle of readers as possible. However, for important inquirers (i.e., Congressmen or responsible investigators), the Division made extended searches, usually supplying discriminated lists of sources, and occasionally even going so far as to make abstracts of the data required as well.[35] The report for 1902 listed several hundred subjects of inquiry for which the Division had furnished extensive assistance of this kind.[36]

The staff of the Division of Bibliography, though highly qualified, was only prepared to deal with "general" reference questions. For the more abstruse inquiries, readers were referred to the librarians manning the specialized divisions. The manual of 1901 listed the following specialized divisions: the Division of Documents, the Division of Manuscripts, the Division of Periodicals, the Division of Maps and Charts, the Division of Prints, the Division of Music, and the Law Library.[37] Though not set up specifically for informational service, the description of duties furnished by the manual indicated that these divisions were also expected to do reference work in connection with the use of their materials.

> The duty of the division [of manuscripts] with reference to this material, as of the documents, maps, music and prints divisions with reference to the material in the custody, respectively, of each, is not merely to safe-guard it, but to aid in the acquisition, to classify and catalogue, to make it useful to readers, and to answer inquiries which relate to it or which may be answered effectively out of the special knowledge which its custody and administration involve.[38]

With the addition of another special division (for Semitica and Oriental Literature, in 1914), the scheme of organization described in the manual of 1901 remained more or less unaltered for the rest of the pre-war period, but Putnam's reports showed that the work of "interpretation" (his favorite term) was a "sphere of usefulness which [was] constantly increasing."[39] As the revitalized Library of Congress became more truly the national library, it fell heir to inquiries from all over the country asking for information involving the use of materials not available in the local libraries. About 10,000 letters of inquiry a year were being received by 1906.[40]

In 1914 Putnam reviewed his library's progress during his administration, and found cause for satisfaction in its accomplishment. The two million volumes and the well-equipped building provided ample facilities for research. More than that, "the facilities for access to it, for the prompt and convenient use of it, and for the *interpretation of it...* are, as a whole, for the investigator, superior to those of any other American library."[41]

Putnam's pride was probably warranted. The Library of Congress' only real rival among the general research libraries was the New York Public Library, and there the pattern of development

---

[34] U. S. Library of Congress, *Report of the Librarian of Congress for the Fiscal Year Ending June 30, 1901*, p. 244.

[35] *Ibid.*, pp. 241-42.

[36] U. S. Library of Congress, *Report of the Librarian of Congress for the Fiscal Year Ending June 30, 1902*, pp. 39-41.

[37] U. S. Library of Congress, *Report of the Librarian...1901*, pp. 248-278. Part II of the *Report* is a manual describing the constitution, organization and methods of the Library.

[38] *Ibid.*, p. 261.

[39] U. S. Library of Congress, *Report of the Librarian of Congress...for the Fiscal Year Ending June 30, 1903*, p. 47.

[40] U. S. Library of Congress, *Report of the Librarian of Congress for the Fiscal Year Ending June 30, 1907*, p. 77.

[41] U. S. Library of Congress, *Report of the Librarian of Congress...for the Fiscal Year Ending June 30, 1914*, p. 10. (Emphasis by the present author).

and organization was so similar as to reinforce Putnam's belief in the excellence of his arrangements. As in the Library of Congress, reference service was at first limited to the part-time assistance available from the reading room attendants. The Readers' Department organized by Billings combined circulation and reference duties. The scope of the latter was restricted and conventional, stressing instruction in the use of the catalog. According to a description of 1897, "officials are stationed in the reading rooms in each building, whose duty it is to assist readers, to advise in the use of the catalogues, and to aid in finding books on the open reference shelves."[42]

However, the scope of the reference services was soon broadened by the establishment of specialized divisions — the Oriental Department, the Slavonic Department, and the Public Documents Department in 1898-99, and the Prints and Manuscripts Departments in 1899-1900. The process of specialization did not reach full fruition until after the opening of the new building in 1911. Billings himself was responsible for the design of the building, which represented in concrete form the embodiment of his ideas for research library service.[43] In its broad outlines it paralleled rather closely the arrangement of the Library of Congress. The large main reading room, with its 30,000 reference books accessible on open shelves, was primarily for the use of the general readers, with the familiar "information desk," manned by trained librarians, available for their assistance.[44] For the serious investigator and specialist, the library building provided no less than fifteen special reading rooms, each under the supervision of an expert in the particular field, prepared to aid readers.[45]

Most of these divisions had the status of separate departments, but strangely enough, the general reference service for some time further did not gain such recognition, the task of assistance continuing to be only one of the functions of the Readers' Department. A year's experience with the operation of the new building apparently demonstrated the value of establishing the work of assistance to the general public as a distinct department, and led to the creation of the Information Division.[46] Similarly, the reference work devolving on the Documents Division was assigned to a distinct reference section in 1913.[47]

Though no formal evaluation of these amplified provisions for reference service was actually made, their success was in part implied by the large increase in the volume of reference work noted in the reports for 1914 and 1915.[48] Much of the increase was admittedly "occasional" in that it stemmed out of the growing demand for information relating to the European War, but the librarians were not loath to point out that a large share of the credit belonged to the Library itself. Improved facilities and expanded service were drawing a vastly larger clientele, especially of scholarly readers.[49]

The phenomenon was not unique with the New York Public Library. Many other research libraries reported a similar increase in the volume of service, and might well have adduced similar reasons for its occurrence. By 1915, it has been seen, most research libraries could offer their users the service of staff members whose full time was available for the work of assistance, and usually the latter were specially equipped by training and experience for that specific task. Reference work had become a well-defined library function, coordinate in organizational status with the

---

[42] "Introductory Statement," *Bulletin of the New York Public Library*, I (January, 1897), 15.

[43] F. H. Garrison, "Billings, a Maker of American Medicine," in his *Lectures on the History of Medicine* (Philadelphia: Saunders, 1933), p. 187.

[44] John Shaw Billings, "The New York Public Library," *Century*, LXXXI (April, 1911), 844.

[45] "Report for the Year Ending December 31, 1911," *Bulletin of the New York Public Library*, XVI (February, 1912), 80-81.

[46] "Report for the Year Ending December 31, 1912," *Bulletin of the New York Public Library*, XVII (February, 1913), 122.

[47] "Annual Report for the Year Ending December 31, 1913," *Bulletin of the New York Public Library*, XVIII (March, 1914), 231.

[48] "Annual Report for the Year Ending December 31, 1914," *Bulletin of the New York Public Library*, XIX (March, 1915), 214-20, 223; "Report of the New York Public Library for 1915," *Bulletin of the New York Public Library*, XX (March, 1916), 215, 217.

[49] "Annual Report for ... 1913," *op. cit.*, pp. 209-10.

older-established functions of cataloging, circulation and acquisitions, and sometimes even exceeding these in prestige. In addition, a number of research libraries — notably the Library of Congress, the New York Public Library, the Columbia University Library, and a handful of public libraries — had gone well beyond the stage of specialization by function to the more fruitful assistance implicit in sub-specialization by subject. Even for those research libraries, mainly in the university group, which had not yet been able to achieve any great degree of specialist assistance, the path clearly pointed in that direction. After two generations of development, reference service in the general research library was a function in *esse,* and its amplification via subject specialization definitely *in posse*.

Chapter IV

THE NATURE OF REFERENCE WORK IN THE
GENERAL RESEARCH LIBRARIES, 1896-1916:
POLICIES AND PRACTICES

The first great issue in the development of reference services was the value and necessity of personal assistance as a library function. It was settled when the reference department became an integral part of the organization of most American research libraries. Having assumed responsibility for giving reference service, the general research libraries found themselves confronted with a second major issue — the nature and extent of the assistance to be offered. The problem was continuing and multiple. How much assistance, to what classes of readers, and through what means — each of these related questions furnished the subject for debate in the theoretical discussions of reference work, and the answers, explicit or tacit, served as the mainsprings of operational policy.

The "Conservative" Theory of Reference Work

By and large, the policy projected in the literature of reference work was one of cautious and limited assistance. An early statement by A. R. Spofford exemplified the characteristic tone and reasoning. Though by now convinced that no other "aid to the reader" was so effective as "an intelligent and obliging assistant," he thought that the librarian should do no more than to lay before the reader the books likely to supply the requisite information, leaving the reader to extract the data for himself. He concluded succinctly: "It is enough for the librarian to act as an intelligent guidepost, to point the way; to travel the road is the business of the reader himself."[1]

Spofford justified his position by two arguments. The first, severely practical, pointed out that the time of the librarian was limited and the demands on it numerous; extended service to any single patron therefore involved a disservice, actual or potential, to other readers. The second argument suggested that extensive assistance involved a disservice to the inquirer himself![2] According to Spofford, the basic function of the library, whatever the type, was to aid readers in self-development. The job of the reference librarian was to indicate the *means* of gathering information. To do more — to supply direct answers instead of guidance — would thus be to deprive patrons of the invaluable benefits derived from the experience of personal investigation.[3]

These two arguments, repeated with varying form and emphasis, dominated the theoretical discussion of the nature and extent of reference work in the period under review. The university librarians, keenly cognizant of their educational obligations, consistently stressed the role of reference service as a form of instruction and equated assistance with guidance. The policy of the University of Illinois Reference Department, stated its report of 1901-02, was "to help students to help themselves."[4] In an article significantly titled "The Educational Value of Reference Room Training for Students," Willard Austen of Cornell University maintained that reference work was only another means of bibliographic instruction, complementing lectures, courses and tours.[5] At the close of the period, Frederick Hicks of Columbia found the familiar reasoning still acceptable.

---

[1] Ainsworth Rand Spofford, *A Book for All Readers* (New York: G. P. Putnam's Sons, 1900), pp. 204, 213.

[2] *Ibid.*, pp. 203-04.

[3] *Ibid.*, p. 200.

[4] Quoted in Madeline Cord Thompson, "History of the Reference Department of the University of Illinois Library," (Unpublished M.S. thesis, University of Illinois, 1942), p. 107.

[5] *Public Libraries*, XII (July, 1907), 273.

Admitting that the natural zeal of the reference librarian and the tendency of officers and students to ask questions which they might easily answer for themselves made it hard to limit assistance, he still concluded "that a reference librarian is within the proper limits when he confines himself to putting a reader in the way of serving himself, namely, when he assists him in the use of books."[6]

The formula was also popular with public librarians. Public libraries were often called "popular universities," and the analogy led many public librarians to construe themselves as instructors. Thus John Cotton Dana stated flatly that the prime duty of the reference worker in the public library was not to answer the questions, but to instruct the inquirer in the use of the material, so that he might be led to find his own answers.[7]

Not all public librarians were prepared to accept the analogy with the university situation and the limitations it implied for public library reference service. When Dana delivered his paper, he found some dissent from his position, an attempt being made on the part of his critics at a distinction between the academic library engaged in more or less formal instruction, and the public library serving a community which expected of it the more direct services of a bureau of information.[8] Another objection came from Agnes Van Valkenburg, who felt that questions of genuine import deserved more generous aid.[9]

However, even public librarians who doubted the intrinsic logic of rigorously limiting assistance were disposed to accept the practical argument of lack of time. As Van Valkenburg herself noted ruefully, reference librarians in public libraries were invariably so few and their work load so large that they could seldom err on the side of too much assistance.[10] The tone of her comment indicated that she viewed this situation as permanent and inevitable.

The policy of limited assistance received its most extensive and carefully reasoned exposition in an article by William Warner Bishop. For Bishop the issue was clear: reference work was the service given by a librarian *in aid* of a study, the study itself (i.e. the actual extraction of information) was the exclusive responsibility of the reader.[11] Realistically, he based his position, not only on the value of training for "self-help," but on the hard fact that the general reference librarian simply could not be sufficiently expert in the many and varied fields of inquiry to render more than the minimum assistance.[12] The reference librarian could, however, be an expert in *library methods*. In the explanation of the use of the library machinery the reference librarian could thus find a profitable outlet for his desire to be of service to the reader, yet retain a manageable scope for his activity.[13]

In the form given it by Bishop, this theory of reference work was logical and sound within the limits of its assumptions. It struck a neat balance between the claims of service to clientele, economy of library operation, the pedagogical value of "self-help," and the limited abilities of the available library personnel. Wyer has called it "the conservative theory of reference work,"[14] a convenient and accurate term which will be employed henceforth in the present study.

Actually, the assumptions on which the conservative theory rested were numerous and

---

[6]Columbia University Library, *Report of the Assistant Librarian, June 30, 1914*, p. 18.

[7]John Cotton Dana, "Misdirection of Effort in Reference Work," *Public Libraries*, XVI (March, 1911), 109. Cf. also Ida L. Rosenberg, "Problems of a Reference Librarian," *Library Journal*, XXIX (March, 1904), 121.

[8]Dana, *op. cit.*, p. 109.

[9]Agnes Van Valkenburg, "How Far Should We Help the Public in Reference Work?," *Massachusetts Library Club Bulletin*, V (July-October, 1915), 107.

[10]*Ibid.*

[11]William Warner Bishop, "The Theory of Reference Work," *Bulletin of the American Library Association*, IX (July, 1915), 134.

[12]*Ibid.*, p. 135.

[13]*Ibid.*

[14]James Ingersoll Wyer, *Reference Work: a Textbook for Students of Library Work and Librarians* (Chicago: American Library Association, 1930), pp. 6-7.

questionable, though seldom explicitly stated. The argument that the library could not hope to provide sufficient manpower to render more than the minimum assistance assumed, in the first place, that the library would never obtain the financial means to carry out its ideal program, and, in the second place, that reference service would always occupy the same position in the hierarchy of library services that it then had. Conceivably, however, the library could obtain enough support to do all that it wished, and certainly it was quite possible to minimize other library activities in favor of more reference service. In other words, the argument rested on a pessimistic view of the possibilities of financial support for library service and on a value judgment that placed reference work well down in the scale of library responsibilities, rather than on its own intrinsic logic.

The second argument in favor of the conservative theory of reference work derived its support from the supposed pedagogical superiority of guidance over direct provision of information. This argument involved the a priori assumption that the library was an educational institution the objective of whose reference service should be more or less formal instruction — not to mention the more immediate question of whether a hint as to method actually was educationally more effective than direct supply of desired information. Neither of these assumptions rested on very sure foundations, the propriety of the public library as an agency of *instruction* being particularly questionable.

In the same way, Bishop's reasoning that the reference librarian could not hope to be competent in the many possible subjects of inquiry (and hence should restrict himself to assistance with the library apparatus) held good only for the individual reference librarian, not for a whole reference staff. There was no reason, in theory, why the reference staff of a library should not be large enough to provide representatives for the major branches of knowledge, with each librarian learned enough in his own field to be able to offer substantial aid.

Finally, the conservative theory of reference work rested on the assumption that the patrons of the library would be content with the minimal assistance offered. For instance, one statement implied that the truly deserving university student or public library patron would really want no more than hints and guidance.[15] Presumably readers more egregious in their demands were to be rejected out of hand, or to be brought to realize that less aid really did them more good than more aid! Of dubious logic in itself, this assumption also ran counter to the traditions of reference service history. The statements of Green and other pioneers made it clear that reference service was first inaugurated with the idea that more service would increase the popularity of the library with the patrons who supported it. To draw the line of assistance at a point short of real satisfaction to the clientele would therefore be inconsistent with its original *raison d'être*.

Though the assumptions underlying the conservative theory of reference work are thus seen to have been questionable, if not indeed quite ill-founded, the evidence of the library literature shows that they were in actuality *not* questioned. In part, this fact bespeaks the general lack of sophistication and self-consciousness in the American library world of the pre-war era. In greater part, however, the acceptance of the conservative theory may be attributed to the fact that, while shaky in terms of intrinsic logic, it did on the whole fit in rather well with the pattern of contemporary reference work practice. Indeed, it may well be suspected that the theory was mainly a case of ex post facto reasoning — an attempt to provide a rationale for the situation that actually existed. The theory illustrated the practice as much as it anticipated and guided it.

The Practice of Reference Work

The best single indication of the nature of reference work as actually practiced before World War I comes from the references to the type of patrons served. Nearly all the public librarians reported that their major activity was helping the inexperienced library user.[16] The university

---

[15] Cf. the discussion following the paper by Eleanor B. Woodruff, "Reference Work," *Library Journal*, XXII (Philadelphia Conference Number, 1897), 129.

[16] Cf. the statement by George Clark, in the symposium reported by Mary Eileen Ahern, "Reference Work with the General Public," *Public Libraries*, IX (February, 1904), 58.

librarians followed a similar line, focusing their attention on the undergraduate students.[17] As a result of this preoccupation with the inexperienced library user, a principal function of reference librarians in all types of libraries was explaining the use of the bibliographic apparatus. In the university libraries this activity meant that reference librarians often engaged in more or less formal bibliographic instruction, with lectures,[18] courses,[19] and guided tours[20] being some of the methods variously tried.

Nevertheless, the emphasis on instruction and guidance in the use of library materials did not prevent reference departments from also functioning as information bureaus. Most libraries were willing to supply information directly (rather than suggest sources) when the inquiries were limited to straight-forward questions of fact. Such questions, known within the profession as "ready reference questions" or "quick reference questions," came to the reference desk in great numbers. The University of California Library recorded a total of 15,526 such questions during the academic year 1914-15,[21] and a busy public library might well have received as many in a month.

In answering such factual questions, reference librarians tended to lean heavily on the compendia of information known as "reference books." Though it was recognized that optimum performance of reference work involved knowledge of the entire resources of the library, the library literature of the period indicated that the focal point of attention for reference librarians was the subject of "reference books" — their selection, the peculiarities of their use, their relevance for this and that type of library.

This narrow preoccupation with "reference books" may have been heightened by the character of contemporary library education. Singleton's study of the history of the teaching of reference work has shown that the usual method placed heavy emphasis on the knowledge of a selected number of "reference books," most commonly those found in the Kroeger *Guide.*[22] In other words, reference work, as a professional accomplishment, was largely equated with skill in the use of a limited number of "reference books."

While much of the reference work involved no greater effort than the ascertainment of simple facts from the immediate collection of "ready reference books," the service often went beyond such elementary assistance. However much the conservative theory of reference work might counsel a policy of minimum assistance, the demands of the readers and the zeal of the librarians themselves often led the latter into much more elaborate procedures. For many reference librarians it was a point of professional pride — Frances Staton grandiloquently called it "the creed of our Reference Library"[23] — not to give up the chase until all likely sources of information had been exhausted. Indeed, Dana's strictures on the "misdirection of effort in reference work" was explicitly designed to forestall what he considered the reference worker's tendency to over-tenacious grappling with problems.[24]

The preparation of bibliographies and indexes was considered to be a more justifiable outlet for the professional zeal of the reference librarian. Thompson finds another plausible reason for the proliferation of bibliographies in the fact that relatively few printed bibliographies were as yet

---

[17]For example, the "Report of the Reference Department of the University of Illinois Library...1915-16" (unpublished) stated that the work was "almost entirely with students in the University." (p. 1); quoted in Thompson, *op. cit.*, p. 108.

[18]Cf. the annual series of lectures on bibliographic topics given at Cornell by Harris and Austen *(Supra, p. 34).*

[19]For example, the reference librarians at the University of Illinois conducted a regular course (Library Science 12) in the use of the library. (Thompson, *op. cit.*, pp. 146-54).

[20]University of Michigan Library, *Library Staff Manual* (3d ed., Ann Arbor: [Ann Arbor Press], 1912), pp. 23-24.

[21]University of California Library, *University Library,* reprint from the *Annual Report of the President of the University, 1914-15;* p. 13.

[22]M. E. Singleton, "Reference Teaching in the Pioneer Library Schools, 1883-1903" (Unpublished M.S. thesis, Columbia University, 1942), pp. 16, 179.

[23]Frances M. Staton, "Reference Libraries and Reference Work," *Proceedings of the Ontario Library Association,* (Eleventh Annual Meeting, 1911), p. 67.

[24]Dana, *op. cit.,* p. 108.

available, constraining reference librarians to construct their own equipment, so to speak.[25] Whatever the exact reason, the number and length of the bibliographies compiled were such as to leave no doubt that they accounted for much of the reference staff's time. The University of Illinois Reference Department averaged over 100 bibliographies a year before 1915.[26] Stanford University's chief reference librarian reported that her department prepared an average of one long typed bibliography each month on topics of general interest, besides many shorter lists compiled in response to individual requests.[27] The numerous lists regularly prepared by the public libraries of Cleveland and Detroit on behalf of clubs and debating societies are other cases in point.

A surprisingly large proportion of this bibliographic output was extensive and scholarly enough to warrant publication. The *Bulletin of the New York Public Library* and *Special Libraries* contained regular bibliographic contributions by reference librarians of the New York Public Library and Library of Congress, respectively. Even the smaller research libraries often issued printed bibliographies of some extent and consequence.[28]

Most of the printed bibliographies were prepared with the object of exhibiting the resources of the library in an entire department of knowledge, and in that sense were designed to supplement the catalog rather than aid a particular reader. More nearly reference work proper (in the strict sense of personal assistance to the individual inquirer) were the bibliographies prepared in response to requests by correspondence. Nearly all the general research libraries professed surprising willingness to go to considerable lengths in answering mail inquiries; W. N. Carlton of the Newberry Library mentioned answers running up to "three or four quarto sheets of letter paper."[29] It is hard to reconcile this activity with the more or less official policies of minimum assistance, but professional pride and the futility of trying to maintain the objective of instruction with patrons at a distance probably overcame any theoretical objections.

Close knowledge of "reference books" and special competence in the preparation of bibliographies thus came to be seen as the distinctive professional accomplishments of the reference librarian. This points up the larger overall conclusion that reference work had become a specialized technique, with its own lore and methodology. The literature of reference work for this period shows the librarians largely preoccupied with the problems of working out the "rules and routines" of the new technique — how to do reference work with this or that type of material (documents, reference books, clippings, etc.), how to deal with this or that type of reader (the student, the faculty member, the general public, etc.), and how to solve the problems of reference department administration (recording questions, the proper relationships with other library departments, the arrangement of the reference room, etc.).

Like other library techniques, reference work soon established secondary specializations on the basis of process or type of material. The New York Public Library had a reference section operating as part of its Documents Division to answer questions involving the use of government publications.[30] Inquiries received by telephone and mail were thought to demand their own distinctive methods of operation; the Library of Congress' Division of Bibliography functioned largely as a special correspondence reference section.[31] In the large public libraries, such as those in

---

[25]Thompson, *op. cit.*, pp. 127-28.

[26]*Ibid.*, p. 137.

[27]Stanford University Library, "Report of the Librarian," in *Annual Report of the President of the University for the Twenty-Sixth Academic Year Ending July 31, 1917...*, p. 147.

[28]E.g. William Zebina Ripley, *A Selected Bibliography of the Anthropology and Ethnology of Europe* (Boston: Published by the Trustees of the Public Library, 1899); John Crerar Library, *A List of Bibliographies of Special Subjects, July, 1902* (Chicago: Printed by Order of the Board of Directors, 1902); Newberry Library, *Materials for the Study of the English Drama (Excluding Shakespeare); a Selected List of Books in the Newberry Library* (Chicago: The Newberry Library, 1912).

[29]Newberry Library, *Report of the Trustees...for the Year 1910*, p. 16.

[30]"Annual Report for the Year Ending December 31, 1913," *Bulletin of the New York Public Library*, XVIII (March, 1914), 231.

[31] U. S. Library of Congress, *Report of the Librarian of Congress for the Fiscal Year Ending June 30, 1901*, pp. 241-42.

Cleveland, Detroit and Cincinnati, the reference work for women's clubs and debating societies came to be considered a subspecialty requiring its own peculiar technique.[32]

Perhaps the best example of the lengths to which some reference departments went in the refinement of reference work techniques is furnished by the Columbia University Library. Under the direction of Isadore Gilbert Mudge, the Columbia department developed intricate special procedures for particular types of problems such as identification of quotations, location of manuscript letters, bibliographic verification of titles, and location of books.[33]

The Demand for Subject Specialization

Such refinement of techniques, while of undeniable utility, was subject to the valid criticism that it was usually applied to problems of relatively little significance.[34] It was soon recognized that for substantial service to scholarship, specialization in research library reference service had to take the more fruitful form of *subject* specialization.

Melvil Dewey, ever in the forefront of library thought, called for this new approach in reference service as early as 1901. In a prophetic article, Dewey foresaw that the research library's already apparent tendency toward subject specialization in collection carried with it the logical corollary of subject specialization in service.

> In this limited number of great libraries the comparatively modern notion of the reference librarian is bound to develop into what I think we may wisely call the "library faculty." One man cannot possibly do the reference work for a large library from lack of time, and no man since Humboldt presumes to be a specialist on all subjects. A process of evolution is inevitable. As demand and income warrant we shall have reference librarians each limited to history, science, art, sociology, law, medicine, education, or some other topic till we shall have in the library, as in the university, a company of men each an authority in his own field. Such a corps is obviously best named a Faculty, and for a library, equipped with such a staff of specialists I propose the name of "faculty library"...It is certain that reference work must be closely divided if it is to be of high value. [35]

Dewey's was no lone voice. Speaking for the large "reference library," John Shaw Billings noted that "the bibliographies which would be most useful for...those engaged in research work can only be prepared by experts in the different arts and sciences...Every great reference library needs a dozen such experts in different departments."[36] Olive Jones of the Ohio State University Library affirmed the applicability of subject specialization to the university library,[37] and N. D. C. Hodges held that some such plan was equally necessary for the large public library.[38] J. F. Daniels warned the profession bluntly that reference service would run the risk of drifting out of the hands of librarians into those of outside specialists unless libraries could offer research men the intensive service possible only with staff members able to speak the scholars' own language.[39]

---

[32] Cleveland Public Library, *Thirty-ninth Annual Report, for the Year 1907*, p. 35; Cincinnati Public Library, *Annual Report of the Board of Trustees...for the Year Ending June 30, 1905*, p. 29; Detroit Public Library, *Forty-ninth Annual Report... for the Fiscal Year 1913-1914*, p. 15.

[33] Isadore Gilbert Mudge, "History of the Columbia University Reference Department" (Unpublished manuscript, 1941; in Columbia University Library), pp. 89, 102, 116-19, 129-35.

[34] Cf. J. F. Daniels, "The Indeterminate Functions of a College Library," *Library Journal*, XXXII (November, 1907), 489.

[35] Melvil Dewey, "The Faculty Library," *The Library*, n.s., II (July 1, 1901), 239-40.

[36] John Shaw Billings, "Library Problems of Tomorrow," *Library Journal*, XXVII (Boston and Magnolia Conference Number, 1902), 8.

[37] Ahern, *op. cit.*, p. 63.

[38] Cincinnati Public Library, *Annual Report of the Board of Trustees...for the Year Ending June 30, 1904*, p. 23.

[39] Daniels, *op. cit.*, p. 489.

But there were also formidable objections to subject specialization. In the first place, it was questioned if the scholars really wanted or needed such service. A report of the Science Division of the New York Public Library maintained: "Scientists making extended investigations usually know the literature of their subject and are able, once they are familiar with the shelves, to pursue their work with little or no attention from the staff."[40] This attitude was common; in fact, the widespread emphasis on service to the inexperienced reader seems to have been founded in part on the notion that the scholar could very well be left to his own resources.

Some librarians, while admitting the need for specialized assistance, thought that the library staff itself need not necessarily provide it. Walter Briggs claimed that university libraries could simply refer abstruse inquiries to the subject specialists on the faculty.[41] Similarly, Clement Andrews of the John Crerar Library advocated that the independent reference libraries establish working relationships with a group of outside scholars to whom difficult questions might be referred at need.[42]

In any case, as even the proponents of subject specialization ruefully admitted, where was the library to obtain the highly qualified staff required?[43] The distance which libraries had yet to travel in this regard was made clear by the analysis of staff qualifications submitted in the Newberry Library's report for 1914. Of the thirty full time staff members, nine were college graduates, three had had some college education, and eight held high school diplomas. Only ten staff members had had library training or experience before coming to the Newberry Library. Yet the tone of the report was such as to indicate that at the time this record of qualifications was considered as good![44]

Approaches to Subject Specialization

Given the difficulties, both theoretical and practical, in the path of subject specialization in reference service, it is not surprising to find that the achievement of this goal was no overnight occurrence, but the product of a long evolutionary process. As a matter of fact, few libraries even attempted anything like a deliberate, head-on confrontation of the task — perhaps the Columbia University Library under Johnston came closest to doing so — but instead were led into it almost imperceptibly by the concurrent development of their collections, and by the demands of administrative efficiency.

In the very largest research libraries the first impetus toward subject departmentation came from the acquisition of groups of materials whose form or language required special handling. Keyes Metcalf has pointed out that of the fifteen special reading rooms in the New York Public Library's new building, only three were originally organized on the basis of subject.[45] Thus the departments for manuscripts, rare books, prints, music, and maps came into being because in each case the preservation and arrangement of the materials presented unusual problems. Similarly, the Jewish, Slavonic and Oriental Divisions owed their reason for existence to the special problem posed by material in non-Roman alphabets rather than because they represented specific areas of knowledge.[46]

The initial subject departmentation of the Library of Congress might have furnished Metcalf with an equally good example, for, of the "subject" departments described in the manual of 1901, all

[40] "Annual Report [of the New York Public Library] for ... 1913," op. cit., p. 233.

[41] Walter B. Briggs, "Reference Work in Public and College Libraries: a Comparison and a Contrast," Library Journal, XXXII (November, 1907), 493.

[42] Clement W. Andrews, "The Use of Books," Library Journal, XXXII (June, 1907), 252.

[43] Billings, op. cit., p. 8.

[44] Newberry Library, Report of the Trustees ...for the Year 1914; p. 31.

[45] Keyes D. Metcalf, "Departmental Organization in Libraries," in Current Issues in Library Administration, edited by Carleton B. Joeckel (Chicago: University of Chicago Press, 1938), p. 106.

[46]Ibid., p. 107.

except the Law Library pretty obviously had their basis in the special requirements of form or language.[47]

These facts seem to justify Metcalf in his general conclusion that the original division of research libraries was functional in origin rather than by subject.[48] However, once established as separate departments under the direction of specialists, the "form and language" divisions inevitably, and indeed rather rapidly, came to assume responsibility for informational duties in connection with their materials. A. S. Freidus of the New York Public Library's Hebrew Department claimed that "since the organization of this department in 1897, reference work has been a feature receiving our special attention."[49] A report of the Art and Prints Division in the same library noted that its chief was engaged in inquiries that "meant extended and comprehensive investigations."[50]

In the Library of Congress this process may have started even earlier for, as previously noted, the "manual" of 1901 made information duties a definite part of the responsibilities of the specialized divisions.[51] Subsequent reports indicated that this statement represented more than good intentions. The Division of Maps, for example, was called upon for assistance in the settlement of boundary disputes, and in much other litigation as well. Such requests, it was made clear, involved much more than the supply of materials; many were for "information which can be given only by an elaborate search and much comparison."[52]

The approaches to specialization were not always so oblique. Few public libraries other than those of Boston and New York had large collections of material whose form or language problems required special handling, yet they too travelled down the road of subject departmentation. Here the impetus to subject specialization plainly derived from the ideal of service that formed one of the strongest traditions of American librarianship. The general reference department had been established to serve the general reader, but public librarians also recognized the existence in their constituency of large groups with special subject interests. To attract and serve these groups something more than "general service" was necessary. William E. Foster gave the following explicit statement of this common motivation for subject specialization: "While the underlying principle in the development of the Library's service has been that it must in any case, reach and benefit 'the average reader,' or, to put it in another form, the more superficial reader, yet it has always stood equally ready to help the reader who desires to go more thoroughly into a subject."[53]

Probably the most easily identifiable — and influential — of these special interest groups in any metropolitan community is the business and industry group, and so the service to industry was usually the first to be established on a specialized basis. Thus the Providence Public Library, as early as 1900, began to bring together a special collection of books to serve as an "Industrial Library," and, shortly after hired Joseph Wheeler to provide the "aggressive service" by which the materials might be made more effective.[54] The same reasoning accounted for the early establishment of "useful arts" departments at the Cincinnati, Detroit, and Cleveland public libraries.[55]

Another easily identified special interest group was that concerned with music and fine arts. The same process of first segregating the appropriate materials and then setting up a specialized information service in connection with the materials took place in this field almost as early as it

[47]*Supra*, p. 39.

[48] Metcalf, *op. cit.*, p. 107.

[49] "Report of the Director for the Year Ending December 31, 1910," *Bulletin of the New York Public Library*, XV (February, 1911), 69.

[50] "Report for the Year Ending December 31, 1912," *Bulletin of the New York Public Library*, XVII (February, 1913), 106.

[51]*Supra*, p. 39.

[52] U. S. Library of Congress, *Report of the Librarian of Congress for the Fiscal Year Ending June 30, 1903*, p. 31.

[53] William E. Foster, *The First Fifty Years of the Providence Public Library, 1878-1928* (Providence: Published by the Providence Public Library, 1928), p. 32.

[54] *Ibid.*, pp. 33-34.

[55] E.g. Cincinnati Public Library, *Annual Report of the Board of Trustees...for the Year Ending June 30, 1902*, pp. 31-32.

did in the field of "useful arts."[56] Althea Warren has suggested that there were also administrative reasons behind the selection of these two subject areas for special treatment. By segregating the books of most immediate interest to the library's community (science and technology for the men, arts and music for the women), the library was able to make useful savings in space and time.[57]

In most public libraries this process of subject departmentation proceeded by the slow method of accretion, adding new departments (most commonly technology, genealogy, municipal reference) but leaving undisturbed the main lines of the library organization for public services, which was by function. In the Cleveland Public Library, however, the process took the more radical form of almost complete realignment of the library organization along subject lines.

The reorganization effected in 1913 provided a Reference and Information Division, a Popular Library (fiction and popular "classed books,"), and subject departments for Sociology; Religion and Philosophy; Science and Technology; General Literature; History and Archaeology, Biography, Genealogy and Heraldry, Travel and Geography; and Fine Arts. Each of the subject departments had its own staff and was to offer both reference and circulation service.[58]

The new alignment arose out of a variety of motives. On the one hand, it represented no more than an effort to increase administrative efficiency by doing away with a meaningless separation of books on the same subject. Over the years the Cleveland Reference Department had come to include a large store of material going well beyond the usual bounds of "reference books," including such items as bound sets of indexed periodicals, illustrated books, and all volumes considered rare or expensive. The library thus came to consist of two parallel collections, almost equal in size, shelved and cataloged separately, but whose only real difference was in the regulations pertaining to their use. Readers could not appreciate the reasons for the distinction and found the dispersion of materials inconvenient. In this sense the subject departmentation meant only an administrative measure designed for simplification of arrangements and consolidation of like materials.[59]

On the other hand, the Library's administrators also saw in the new arrangement an opportunity for the realization of their desire for a specialized reference service extending to nearly all fields of inquiry, and they planned quite deliberately towards that end. Both motives showed clearly in the following statement: " . . . it is hoped ultimately to have each division in the care of a special librarian. Formerly, the resources on each subject were divided. Now they are brought together in one place, which is more convenient for readers, and also makes possible more specialized service on the part of the library staff."[60]

The reorganization, as already noted, did not do away with the general reference department, but it did bring about a modification of its duties. Under the new system the General Reference and Information Division served primarily as a "ready reference bureau," answering telephone queries and the simpler questions of fact. In addition it functioned as a liaison agency, referring inquiries to the appropriate subject department.[61] In so doing, it filled a place similar to that maintained by the New York Public Library's Information Division and the Library of Congress' Reading Room service.

Cleveland's more or less complete subject departmentation, according to the experience related by Carl Vitz, then in charge of the main library, was not without its liabilities for reference service. It forced a separation of the general reference materials from the material of special fields, tending to make the subject librarians rely on the resources of their own departments even when the general

[56] E. g. Minneapolis Public Library, *Fifteenth Annual Report . . . for the Year Ending December 31, 1904*, p. 22.

[57] Althea Warren, "Departmental Organization by Subject," in *Current Issues in Library Administration*, edited by Carleton B. Joeckel (Chicago: University of Chicago Press, 1938), p. 113.

[58] Cleveland Public Library, *Forty-fifth Annual Report, for the Year 1913*, pp. 35-36.

[59] *Ibid.*, pp. 34-35.

[60] *Ibid.*, p. 39.

[61] Carl P. P. Vitz, "Cleveland Experience with Departmentalized Reference Work," *Bulletin of the American Library Association*, IX (Berkeley Conference Number, 1915), 170.

reference books might have provided easier access to the desired information. The inconvenience to readers whose inquiries cut across departmental lines was also apparent. And of course the employment of specialists inescapably meant increased costs of service. [62]

The difficulties, while real enough, did not induce any change of heart in the Cleveland Public Library's administrators. After two years' experience with the new arrangement, Vitz was satisfied that the Library had made a significant gain in the range and depth of its reference service, for against the inconveniences of decentralization it could offer to its readers a benefit that outweighed them: "...the special guidance so often essential; the opportunity for cooperation with outside interests, and *help in research to the continuous worker in some special field.*"[63]

The arguments in favor of reference service on a subject department basis received confirmation of a practical sort in 1914, when the Los Angeles Public Library adopted a very similar arrangement. The results, again, proved encouraging, for the Library found that the emphasis on reference work inherent in the new arrangement was helping to make it "an ever increasing force in the dissemination of knowledge." [64]

Subject specialization in university libraries. — It has already been pointed out that the university libraries generally lagged behind in the development of reference service. Most university libraries were only beginning upon the primary specialization by function when other types of research libraries were already well on their way toward secondary specialization by subject. Since subject specialization was basically only an extension and intensification of general reference service, it is not surprising that few university libraries could show developments in this direction to rival those in the Library of Congress or the Cleveland Public Library.

Against these considerations stood the fact that the whole university situation seemed to impel the academic library towards subject departmentation. The universities themselves, having discarded the shackles of the prescribed curriculum, had long since adopted a thorough and even minute subject departmentation as the basic principle of their organization, and in some respects the library services had already followed suit. By 1905 nearly all but the smallest and most recently established universities could show a network of departmental libraries.

The departmental libraries, by segregating the materials of a particular field of knowledge, thus already represented an important step toward subject specialization. It was natural and easy for university librarians to see in the existence of the departmental library system an opportunity for subject specialization in reference services as well.[65]

Practically, however, the plan proved difficult of realization. As already noted, many departmental libraries were operated quite blithely as private departmental enclaves, with staff members independent of main library supervision and oblivious of even the most rudimentary notions of library economy. And even for those libraries coming under the central library administration, the problem of finding personnel both expert in library science and competent in the particular subject fields proved to be all but insuperable.

To be sure, scattered examples of departmental libraries providing specialist reference services of a high order were to be found. The librarian for landscape architecture at Harvard prepared extensive bibliographies and had a well-organized plan for keeping faculty members in touch with the current materials pertaining to their special fields of interest.[66] The services of Edward R. Smith as Avery Librarian (architecture) at Columbia University drew high commendation from

---

[62] *Ibid.*, p. 172.

[63] *Ibid.*, p. 173. (Emphasis by the present author).

[64] Los Angeles Public Library, *Twenty-sixth Annual Report, 1913-1914*, pp. 10-11.

[65] Frederick C. Hicks, "Department Libraries," *Columbia University Quarterly*, XIII (March, 1911), 187.

[66] Harvard College Library, *Report of Archibald Cary Coolidge ... Including the Seventeenth Report of William Coolidge Lane, Librarian, ... 1914,* reprinted with additions, from the *Report of the President of Harvard University for 1913-14;* p. 23.

Canfield.[67] A Yale University Library report gave clear indication that its Day Missions Research Library was offering intensive service to scholars both on and off the campus.[68]

However, service of this quality was exceptional. For the most part, the departmental libraries must have presented themselves to the hard-pressed university librarians more nearly in the guise of threats than of opportunities. Quite aside from any theoretical arguments in favor of the principle of unity of knowledge, the physical dispersal of collections and the decentralization of control characteristic of the departmental library system still presented too many problems in library administration to be a wholly acceptable solution for the problem of achieving subject specialization in reference services.

In any case the problem, in 1915, at least, was still remote for most university libraries. The Columbia University Library had undoubtedly gone as far as any university library in achieving a strong general reference service, yet even there the day-to-day tasks of the reference departments still included many duties that could hardly be called professional, let alone reference work proper. Before 1911, according to Mudge, the reference staff was responsible for the filing of all the catalog cards, and for some years later the department continued to be saddled with the task of handling "class reserves."[69]

When so much remained to do in the matter of primary organization of reference services, the university library might well have found substantial justification for the theory of minimum assistance. In the public and reference libraries, whatever the conservatism of official policy statements, the practice of reference work had already gone some considerable distance toward the more liberal assistance implied in the employment of subject specialists. For the university libraries the pedagogical objections to intensive specialization (via the departmental library) presented unusual administrative difficulties. Above all, they had a longer way to go.

---

[67] Columbia University Library, "Report of the Librarian...," in *Annual Reports of the President and Treasurer...for the Year Ending June 30, 1907,* p. 189.

[68] Yale University Library, *Report of the Librarian...July 1, 1916--June 30, 1917,* reprinted from the *Report of the President of Yale University, 1917;* p. 21.

[69] Mudge, *op. cit.,* p. 7.

Chapter V

SPECIAL LIBRARIANSHIP AND THE CONCEPT OF AMPLIFIED SERVICE:
LEGISLATIVE AND MUNICIPAL REFERENCE WORK,
1900-1916

In the nineteenth century the research library meant the *general* research library; the history of American research libraries after 1900 must accord a prominent place as well to the *special* library. The importance of the special library in the twentieth century development of library facilities for scholarship was succinctly stated by Frederick Austin Ogg in 1928: "The growth of special libraries is the outstanding feature of library history in the past twenty years."[1]

Ogg properly emphasized the comparative recency with which the special library had come into prominence, for the real impetus in special library development came only at the beginning of the twentieth century and then with such emphasis and vitality as to have the status of a new movement. To be sure, many medical, legal, and historical society libraries by then already had a history of a century or more,[2] but the special library movement had little connection with these professional libraries. When R. H. Johnston drew up a list of fifty representative institutions to illustrate his more or less official report on special libraries, he included no medical, legal, or historical society libraries.[3]

The omission was deliberate and thus indicated that the term "special library" was being used in a new sense. The old-established professional libraries were "special" only in that they represented collections on limited fields, their purposes and methods being similar to those of the general libraries. The special library, as represented in the Johnston list, was also limited in scope of subject, but it meant something more and different as well.

The Concept of Amplified Service
as the Criterion of Special Librarianship

If the "new" special library was neither a general library nor merely a special collection, what was it? The special librarians felt that they formed a distinct professional group and gave institutional expression to this sentiment by the establishment of the Special Libraries Association in 1909. The distinction was, however, more easily sensed than characterized. The early literature of special librarianship was very largely the record of an emergent professional group's essays at self-knowledge, an agreement on the essential criterion of special librarianship being reached only after a decade of discussion and definition.

Though a number of features were variously suggested as characteristic of special librarianship,[4] eventually the focal point of distinction was seen to rest on the nature of reference service

---

[1] Frederic Austin Ogg, *Research in the Humanistic and Social Sciences; Report of a Survey Conducted for the American Council of Learned Societies* (New York: The Century Company, 1928), p. 381.

[2] Albert Predeek, *A History of Libraries in Great Britain and North America*, translated by Lawrence S. Thompson (Chicago: American Library Association, 1947), p. 97.

[3] Richard H. Johnston, "Special Libraries — a Report on Fifty Representative Libraries...," *Library Journal*, XXXIX (April, 1914), 280-84.

[4] For John Cotton Dana, the distinctive feature of special librarianship was its utilitarianism; he defined the special library as "the library of a modern man of affairs." ("The President's Opening Remarks," *Special Libraries*, I [January, 1910], 4). John Lapp highlighted the special librarian's use of materials outside the usual scope of general library collecting — clippings, bills, photographs, and pamphlets. ("What Is a Special Library?," *Special Libraries*, III [September, 1912], 147). A number of other papers discussing the nature of special librarianship are summarized in an article by Ethel Johnson. ("The Special Library and Some of Its Problems," *Special Libraries*, VI [December, 1915], 157-61).

in the special library. Here special librarians found it easiest to characterize their own methods and aims in terms of their difference from those of the general library. (The comparison, perhaps needless to say, was usually favorable to the special library). As against the limited assistance available in the general library, R. H. Johnston described the special library as being ready to devote "the entire time of its force for days or weeks to an individual reader."[5] The general reference librarian, according to Matthew Dudgeon, was essentially a technician whose only special qualification lay in his ability to construct and use a complex library apparatus; the special librarian, he claimed, "must have special knowledge as well as library technique."[6] The general reference librarian, said Guy Marion, emphasized guidance; ordinarily only in the case of simple questions answerable from "ready reference books" was he likely to supply information directly. The special librarian, in his view, was a much more active participant in the whole process of investigation; not only did his subject knowledge enable him to deal with inquiries beyond the depth of his general library counterpart, but he undertook to interpret and analyze the material as well as locate it.[7]

A final important distinction raised by the special librarians related to the form in which the information was presented to the consumer. The special library served adults who knew what they wanted and were paying to have it furnished quickly and in good order. Since his whole justification for existence consisted in the savings of time he effected for his employer, the special librarian thus had to go much further than the general reference librarian in *adapting* data to suit the client's convenience. As Dudgeon put it, "the special librarian must select the material so that only the parts wanted are delivered. It must be cut down in bulk by extracting, summarizing, generalizing, and even tabulating. It must be portable, readily transferable, negotiable."[8]

On all these points there was substantial agreement among the special librarians, and they added up to the consensus opinion that the essential criterion of special librarianship was an amplified reference service. In 1915 Ethel Johnson undertook to pick out from a decade's essays at self-definition the common feature that would most clearly identify the distinctive nature of the emergent profession. She concluded:

> From the foregoing discussion it is evident that the most distinctive feature of the special library is not so much its subject matter as its service. Before everything else, it is an information bureau. The main function of the general library is to make books available. The function of the special library is to make information available.[9]

In this sense, and only in this sense, the special library really was new. Reference service was only one of the general library's functions, but to the special library it was its principal reason for being. When John Lapp, onetime editor of *Special Libraries*, sought to fix the essential nature of special librarianship in a single phrase, he called it the "growth of a big idea."[10] The "big idea" was the functioning of a library as an intelligence bureau rather than as a repository of materials, and its product was the emergence of a new kind of reference librarian: "the librarian-specialist, whose function it is to gather information, condense and combine it, and interpret the results to the man on the job."[11]

Special Librarianship in Practice: The Legislative Reference Library

The first well-known application of special librarianship was in the field of legislative reference work. There is little doubt that the legislative reference librarians were the most influential in the

[5]Richard H. Johnston, "The Man and the Book," *Special Libraries*, VI (December, 1915), 162.

[6]Matthew S. Dudgeon, "The Scope and Purposes of Special Libraries," *Special Libraries*, III (June, 1912), 131.

[7]Guy Marion, "Résumé of the Association's Activities, 1910-1915," *Special Libraries*, VI (November, 1915), 143.

[8]Dudgeon, *op. cit.*, p. 132.

[9]Johnson, *op. cit.*, pp. 158-59.

[10]John A. Lapp, "The Growth of a Big Idea," *Special Libraries*, IX (June, 1918), 157.

[11]*Ibid*.

launching of the special library movement and did the most to establish its basic character. A contemporary statement by R. H. Johnston affirmed that "to the general librarian the work of the typical legislative reference library...may best illustrate the work and methods of the special library,"[12] and Louis Bailey's review of the history of the legislative reference library credited it with having "led the way to a library development in many diversified fields which has resulted in the strong Special Libraries Association of today."[13]

A quantitative analysis of the early literature of special librarianship confirms this testimony as to the predominating influence of the legislative reference librarians on the special library movement before World War I. Of the 110 articles which H. H. B. Meyer thought it worthwhile listing for his selected bibliography of special librarianship (1912), some forty dealt with legislative reference work.[14] Similarly, of the some eighty entries given for special library literature in *Library Work Cumulated, 1905-1911,* no less than half related to legislative and municipal reference work.[15]

The basic idea of legislative reference work — library service for legislators as an aid in their work — was implicit in the very founding of state libraries, and thus had a lengthy history.[16] However, the first substantial step toward the development of a specialized information service for legislators was not taken until 1890, when Melvil Dewey established a "legislative reference section" at the New York State Library.

The work of the New York State Library's legislative librarians was high in quality, but essentially of the same order as conventional reference work. Their chief effort went into the compilation of an index of state legislation, which was later supplemented by a review of comparative legislation and by a digest of governors' messages. All three were issued in a competently edited and regularly appearing series of published bulletins, which were highly regarded in the library world but which, at the same time, were recognized as not breaking new ground.[17]

The New York State Library's "legislative reference section" was thus the forerunner rather than the progenitor of legislative reference service. In so far as legislative reference work represented a distinct and radical change in the conception and practice of reference service, its inception did not come until a decade later. It has been identified by an overwhelming majority of the writers on the subject with the work of Charles McCarthy in the Legislative Reference Department of Wisconsin.

Ernest Bruncken, himself the pioneer legislative reference librarian in California, named McCarthy as "the chief exponent of the new policy."[18] Don Mowry, another eye-witness of the beginnings of legislative reference service, acknowledged the contribution of Dewey and his staff, but averred that "we can truthfully say that it was not until the establishment of the Wisconsin legislative reference library in 1900, with Dr. Charles McCarthy as its chief, that the reference idea began to receive more than passing attention."[19] The encomiums of McCarthy's contemporaries have been unchallenged by the passing of time, for a recent detailed examination of McCarthy's career gives no less credit to McCarthy's role in the initiation of legislative reference work.[20]

[12]Johnston, "Special Libraries — a Report on Fifty Representative Libraries," *op. cit.,* pp. 280-81.

[13]Louis J. Bailey, "Legislative Reference Service," *Special Libraries,* XXI (January, 1930), 7.

[14]H. H. B. Meyer, "Select List of References on Special Libraries," *Special Libraries,* III (October, 1912), 172-76.

[15]*Library Work Cumulated, 1905-1911; a Bibliography and Digest of Library Literature,* edited by Anna Lorraine Guthrie (Minneapolis: The H. W. Wilson Company, 1912), *passim.*

[16]John Boynton Kaiser, *Law, Legislative, and Municipal Reference Libraries; an Introductory Manual and Bibliographical Guide* ("Useful Reference Series," No. 9; Boston: Boston Book Company, 1914), p. 72.

[17]Herbert O. Brigham, "The Legislative Reference Movement," *Special Libraries,* XV (December, 1924), 240; "Legislative Reference Bureau," *The Chicago City Club Bulletin,* II (December 9, 1908), 200.

[18]Ernest Bruncken, "The Legislative Reference Bureau," *News Notes of California Libraries,* II, Supplement (February, 1907), 97.

[19]Don E. Mowry, "Municipal Reference Libraries," *City Hall,* X (October, 1908), 131.

[20]Edward A. Fitzpatrick, *McCarthy of Wisconsin* (New York: Columbia University Press, 1944), pp. 48, 65.

McCarthy was, of course, no explorer sailing completely uncharted seas. He was, his friend John Commons pointed out, familiar with the specialized service offered to legislators by the New York State Library.[21] However, the circumstances under which the Wisconsin Legislative Reference Department came into being were such as to leave no doubt that the whole scheme owed more to McCarthy's personal conception and initiative than to any antecedents or outside influences.

The development of legislative reference work in Wisconsin had no formal beginning but was the product of an evolutionary process, arising out of McCarthy's on-the-job exploration of the means for service to legislators. The initial opportunity was supplied by the passage of a law in 1901 authorizing the Wisconsin Free Library Commission to maintain a library in the state capitol for the use of the legislature and executive departments.[22] The law itself hardly contemplated anything more than the maintenance of a stock of reference books and documents at the capitol, and McCarthy was actually hired only as a "document cataloger."[23] Quite on his own initiative, however, McCarthy began offering the members of the legislature extensive assistance in securing information useful to them. As McCarthy's work won the appreciation of the legislature, it made a specific appropriation in 1903 for legislative reference work, and subsequently increased the funds available for it until the point where, for the bienniums of 1907-08 and 1909-10, the then large sums of $15,000 per year were being appropriated for the purpose.[24] McCarthy's own title went through a series of changes that reflected this progression. Beginning as "document cataloger" in 1901, he became "librarian, Document Department" in 1905, "chief, Document Department" in 1907, and only from the 1907-09 biennium on was he actually named as "chief, Legislative Reference Department."[25]

McCarthy had had no formal training in librarianship. He was a student of government, (Ph.D., Wisconsin, 1901) and his promotion of legislative reference work arose out of his desire for the improvement of governmental processes rather than out of any interest in the development of library techniques per se.[26] McCarthy was a reformer who sincerely believed that the successful working of the whole system of representative government hinged in large part on the degree to which legislation was based on sound, full information. In the state capitol he saw legislators quite untrained in research, puzzled by the increasing complexity of the social problems demanding solution, victimized by the partisan propaganda of the lobbyists — all but helpless to get for themselves the accurate, impartial information they needed for the formulation of effective laws. The need was great, and it was apparent that the demands on his library (at least potentially) were such that they could not be met without a radical extension of the ordinary library methods.[27]

Therefore, from the inception of his work, McCarthy adopted a policy of very far-reaching assistance, aggressive in seeking opportunities for service, meticulous in supplying the information wanted in the most readily usable form. "Go to the legislator," he advocated, "make yourself acquainted with him, study him, find anything he wants for him, never mind how trivial, accommodate him in every way."[28]

The information itself was very carefully prepared by the library staff before presentation to the inquirer — boiled down, tabulated, presented often in the form of a digest or précis.[29] As Commons described it, "No member was left to read through a lot of treatises or law books and

---

[21]John R. Commons, "One Way to Get Sane Legislation," *American Monthly Review of Reviews*, XXXII (December, 1905), 722.

[22]Fitzpatrick, *op. cit.*, p. 44.

[23]Wisconsin Free Library Commission, *Fourth Biennial Report...1901-1902*, pp. 18-19.

[24]American Bar Association, *Report of the Special Committee on Legislative Drafting, to be Presented at the Meeting of the American Bar Association at Montreal, Canada, September 1-3, 1913* (The Association? 1913?), p. 27.

[25]Fitzpatrick, *op. cit.*, pp. 52-53.

[26]Charles McCarthy, *The Wisconsin Idea* (New York: The Macmillan Company, 1912), pp. 213-16.

[27]*Ibid.*, p. 214.

[28]Wisconsin Free Library Commission, Legislative Reference Department, *Legislative Reference Department* ("Circular of Information," No. 6 [2d ed., Madison: 1911]), pp. 7-8.

[29]*Ibid.*, p. 9.

laboriously digest a subject, but Dr. McCarthy put in his hands the already digested work of others who were studying or acting on the same line."[30]

If the subject was a larger one, likely to be of interest to the whole legislative group, McCarthy had the data prepared in the form of small printed booklets, which summarized the existing law of Wisconsin, reviewed the pertinent legislation of other states, and gave a résumé of the main arguments for both sides of the question, with references to the chief authorities.[31] Where the subject of inquiry was of more than local interest, the data collected was published in the Legislative Reference Department's *Comparative Legislation Bulletin* series. No less than twenty-two of these bulletins were issued by 1911, with such titles as *Railway Co-employment, Lobbying,* and *Corrupt Practices at Elections* being representative of the subjects covered.[32]

To make good their objective of supplying the fullest and most reliable information, McCarthy and his staff went to unusual lengths in gathering data. Not content to rely on the easily used (but often out of date) standard sources, they found means to exploit such hitherto neglected materials as newspaper clippings, bills and pamphlets. Moreover, McCarthy did not balk at going beyond published materials, making heavy and constant use of telegraph and correspondence to elicit data from outside experts, and, on occasion, personally making field trips to gather first-hand information.[33] Commons recalled how startlingly energetic McCarthy's service seemed in comparison with that of the conventional library.

> But, in 1905, in drafting the civil service bill, I found that here was an entirely new kind of library. It was telegraphic. McCarthy wired to civil service organizations, to state governments, to individuals, for statutes, bills before legislatures, clippings and comments. Within a day or two after La Follette requested help on the bill, McCarthy had me supplied with everything one could need in drafting that bill.... I never before had known such a quick-action library.... McCarthy had, or would get immediately, almost everything one might need on all sides of every debatable issue before the public, or the legislature, or Congress.... Most of all, his stubborn criticism of every detail in my work, his participation in our conferences, and his fertile suggestions forced me to the most careful self-criticism that I had ever known except during my apprenticeship under Easley.[34]

The latter part of Commons' statement is particularly interesting in that it shows that McCarthy held himself responsible, not just for the collection and presentation of data, but also for its *validity*. The usual practice in the New York State Library had been simply to indicate to the legislators the pertinent laws of other states, without comment on their merit. McCarthy thought that such service was inadequate and even misleading, for it tended to make for blind copying of what might well be antiquated or wholly unsuccessful legislation.[35] He himself would evaluate the data, or in other cases, would solicit criticism and advice from outside authorities such as professors at the University of Wisconsin. Thus, for example, Commons and Ely would be asked to aid in questions on labor, and Van Hise on conservation.[36]

Despite occasional politically-motivated outcries against his "undue influence" in the law-making

---

[30] Commons, *op. cit.*, p. 723.

[31] Cf. McCarthy's testimony in: U. S. Congress, Senate, Committee on the Library, *Legislative Drafting Bureau and Reference Division*, Senate Report 1271, to accompany S. 8337, 62d Cong., 2d Sess. (Washington: Government Printing Office, 1913), p. 106. This report includes as Appendix B: "Hearings before the Committee on the Library of the House of Representatives, Feb. 26 and 27, 1912, Relative to a Congressional Reference Bureau."

[32] A full list of the *Comparative Legislation Bulletins* published by 1911 is given in Wisconsin Free Library Commission, Legislative Reference Department, *op. cit.*, p. 29.

[33] U. S. Congress, Senate, Committee on the Library, *op. cit.*, p. 101.

[34] John R. Commons, *Myself* (New York: The Macmillan Company, 1934), p. 109.

[35] Fitzpatrick, *op. cit.*, p. 61.

[36] S. Gale Lowrie, "The Function of the Legislative Reference Bureau," *Library Journal,* XXXIX (April, 1914), 275.

process, McCarthy's work on the whole enjoyed exceptional esteem and support from his own state's legislators.[37] Elsewhere in the country his library's success became a chief argument for the inception of legislative reference work, and his methods the model for similar enterprises. John Brindley's scholarly analysis of the development of the legislative reference movement attributed the rapidity with which the movement grew as in no small degree due to the influence of Dr. McCarthy.[38] Ernest Bruncken, the first legislative reference librarian in California, was a former assistant of McCarthy's, as were C. B. Lester and John Lapp, who pioneered in legislative reference work in Indiana. When Nebraska organized its department, it sent Addison Sheldon to Madison to learn McCarthy's methods.[39]

If McCarthy's influence proved germinal, it was largely because the times were propitious for the inception of legislative reference work. Bruncken pointed out the fact that the period from 1900 to 1915 was notable for the wide public interest in and support for measures of governmental reform.[40] In a more immediate sense, the growth of legislative reference libraries was associated with the pronounced contemporary movement toward the enlistment of *expertise* in the governmental process, manifested in the organization of boards, bureaus, and commissions for the collection of facts and recommendation of appropriate legislation.[41]

Under these favoring circumstances, the decade from 1905 to 1915 saw a remarkable increase in the incidence of legislative reference work. The California State Library began such service in 1905 without any formal action on the part of the legislature. The Indiana State Library did likewise in 1906; departments were organized in Michigan and North Dakota in 1907. By 1915 thirty-two states had made arrangements of some sort for the provision of reference service to legislators.[42]

The desire for better legislation plus the visible success of the state legislative libraries also prompted a lively agitation for the establishment of a similar service for Congressmen. Commercial and professional associations recommended the creation of a federal bureau of legislative reference,[43] and in Congress itself a number of members (mainly from Wisconsin) introduced bills designed for that purpose.[44] Though these bills received favorable reports in committee, no positive action was taken until 1914, when an amendment to the legislative, executive and judicial appropriation included the following item: "Legislative Reference: to enable the Librarian of Congress to employ competent persons to prepare such indexes, digests and compilations of law as may be required for Congress and other official use pursuant to the act approved June 30, 1906 . . . $25,000."[45] Technically, the amendment merely revived an appropriation made from 1906 to 1911 for the indexing of the federal statutes, but the debates made it clear that Congress intended it to provide for the establishment of a full-fledged legislative reference service (excluding bill-drafting).[46] The appropriation was renewed annually, though varying slightly in wording and amount, and stood as the

---

[37] Fitzpatrick, *op. cit.*, pp. 278-80.

[38] John E. Brindley, "The Legislative Reference Movement," *Iowa Journal of History and Politics,* VII (January, 1909), 135.

[39] Fitzpatrick, *op. cit.*, pp. 65-66.

[40] Bruncken, *op. cit.*, p. 101.

[41] Brindley, *op. cit.*, p. 133.

[42] Nebraska Legislative Reference Bureau, *Legislative Reference Service for a State* ("Bulletin," No. 1 [rev. ed.; Lincoln: 1926]), p. 1.

[43] Cf. American Bar Association, *op. cit.*, p. 14; Chamber of Commerce of the United States of America, *Referendum No. 6: On the Question of the Establishment by Congress of a Bureau of Legislative Reference and Bill-drafting* (Washington: 1913), p. 171. The results of the poll taken of the members of the Chamber of Commerce of the United States on the above question showed an overwhelming sentiment in favor of the proposal — 625 affirmative votes as against only sixteen in the negative.

[44] An account of these abortive attempts to establish a federal legislative reference service is given in J. H. Leek, *Legislative Reference Work: a Comparative Study* (Ph.D. dissertation, University of Pennsylvania; Philadelphia: n.p., 1925), pp. 59-63.

[45] Quoted in U. S. Library of Congress, *Report of the Librarian of Congress . . . for the Fiscal Year Ending June 30, 1914,* p. 14.

[46] *Congressional Record* (Daily Edition), June 26, 1914, pp. 12219-20; cited, *ibid.*

legal basis for legislative reference service at the Library of Congress until the Legislative Reorganization Act of 1946.[47]

On the whole, the practice of legislative reference work in the Library of Congress and in the state legislative libraries followed, not surprisingly, rather closely on the lines originally laid down by McCarthy. The main feature of the service was the provision of an extensive and expert assistance that furnished information rapidly and in condensed, readily usable form. The Nebraska Legislative Reference Bureau advertised the following service as available on demand:

> Correct, condensed information upon civic subjects on short notice. Briefs prepared showing the facts, opinions, and arguments upon any public questions. Documents and authorities cited and furnished. Bills, reports, resolutions, and other papers drafted. Research carried on and results published, in matters of public importance.[48]

The tone of the Nebraska bureau's announcement suggested a readiness to assume almost any kind of informational duty for its clients, and in fact many legislative reference departments often did take on tasks rather far afield from ordinary library research. Not infrequently a bureau was used as an agency for the consolidation and revision of the law. Thus the North Carolina department was made responsible for the preparation, publication and distribution of the *Amendments* to the 1905 *Revisal* of North Carolina law — which eventuated in a legal publication of 170 pages.[49] Similarly, the Massachusetts bureau was engaged in a scheme for the continuous consolidation of the state law.[50] The Indiana department was given the task of collecting and compiling the preliminary data for a constitutional convention.[51]

In the process of gathering information, most of the legislative libraries, like the Wisconsin model, were accustomed to go well beyond the confines of published materials into direct collection of data by means of questionnaires, interviews and correspondence. Leek cites the example of one library's sending out questionnaires to more than 200 cities for an inquiry on certain municipal regulations.[52] The Nebraska Legislative Reference Bureau held such service to be its regular responsibility: "Officials and citizens frequently desire information that is not in print, or has not been compiled. *Within its field,* the Bureau serves as the agency for securing the desired information."[53]

Another feature common to the operation of most legislative libraries was the maintenance of a close working relationship with outside specialists, most often the faculty of the state university. The bureau in Ohio was thus reported as having professors in the state university regularly engaged in gathering data, and lawyers from the state law college helping with the bill-drafting.[54] In the state of Washington, the Bureau of Municipal and Legislative Research, which was the state agency for legislative reference work, was actually organized as part of the state university's extension division, and evidently depended heavily on the assistance of the University faculty members.[55]

The only real point of disagreement among legislative reference librarians related to the question of the librarian's responsibility for the validity of the information he rendered. The division of opinion roughly corresponded to the organizational status of the libraries. Legislative reference

[47] Roy W. Schlinkert, "Research for Congress," *Library Journal,* LXXVIII (January 1, 1953), 9.

[48] Nebraska Legislative Reference Bureau, *op. cit.,* p. 1.

[49] North Carolina Legislative Reference Library, *First Biennial Report of the Legislative Reference Librarian, 1916,* pp. 4-5.

[50] Leek, *op. cit.,* p. 88.

[51] *Ibid.,* p. 89.

[52] *Ibid.,* p. 77.

[53] Nebraska Legislative Reference Bureau, *op. cit.,* p. 5.

[54] Lowrie, *op. cit.,* pp. 277-78.

[55] University of Washington Bureau of Municipal and Legislative Research, *Bureau of Municipal and Legislative Research* (Seattle? 1913?), p. 1.

libraries established as adjuncts of general libraries, such as the Legislative Reference Department of the Library of Congress and the Legislative Reference Section of the New York State Library, reflected the conservatism of general library reference theory, and consistently refused to undertake the "critical function." Herbert Putnam maintained that "a statement of the *merits* of the information furnished beyond a quotation of the authorities in argument, is not a safe function even for a legislative reference bureau; it is rather the province of an investigating commission."[56] On the other hand, legislative reference librarians such as John Lapp and C. Rogers Woodruff, working directly in the McCarthy tradition and prominent in the special library movement, considered the interpretation of data a proper and even necessary part of their responsibilities.[57]

Municipal Reference Work

Nearly all details of the foregoing description of legislative reference service would apply equally well to the practice of municipal reference work. In scope, purpose, and methods the municipal reference library was the local government counterpart of the state legislative reference bureau — and was deliberately fashioned after it. Don Mowry described the municipal reference library as "a direct outgrowth of the legislative reference library movement,"[58] and like the latter, it derived its basic methods of operation from the Wisconsin Legislative Reference Department.[59]

Although there were a number of prototype institutions,[60] the first municipal reference library, according to contemporary writers, did not come into existence until 1907, the honor going to the Department of Legislative Reference in Baltimore.[61] From Baltimore the movement spread rapidly, with municipal reference libraries being established under a variety of controls and in a number of organizational forms.[62] Kansas City's municipal reference library was a separate agency, as were Baltimore's and Chicago's. In St. Louis, Cleveland, Portland, Oakland and New York, the municipal reference library operated as a city hall branch of the local public library. The municipal reference work in Milwaukee was carried on as part of the regular public library service but had its own specially earmarked funds. No special administrative provisions for municipal reference work were made by the city of Grand Rapids, but the local public library made a specialty of service to city officials.

The patterns of service showed less variety, in general conforming rather closely to the model furnished by the state legislative reference library. Frederick Rex, the municipal reference librarian of Chicago, supplied a definition of the purpose and scope of municipal reference service which showed how much the latter owed to its predecessor.

> The purpose of the municipal reference library is to collect, arrange and make available for use information and material on matters relating to and touching upon municipal administration and legislation. It is a central depository, serving as a haven to the perplexed alderman, department, bureau and division head as well as the citizen.... It is not sufficient that the library collect material and information but equally, if not more, important, is the fact that it should be put in ready, convenient form so that it may be consulted and used without difficulty and unnecessary trouble.[63]

---

[56] U. S. Library of Congress, *op. cit.,* p. 11.

[57] Leek, *op. cit.,* pp. 77-78.

[58] Mowry, *op. cit.,* p. 131.

[59]*Ibid.*

[60] For a brief account of these, see Don E. Mowry, "Reference Libraries in Cities — Baltimore as a Type," *Public Libraries,* XII (December, 1907), 388.

[61] Kaiser, *op. cit.,* p. 240.

[62] This summary account of the organization of municipal reference libraries is taken from *ibid.,* pp. 240-45.

[63] Frederick Rex, "The Municipal Reference Library as a Public Utility," *Special Libraries,* VIII (February, 1917), 24.

Rex's article included a number of examples of the work done by his own bureau. These showed that, though the municipal reference library served a lower level of governmental officialdom, the assistance it furnished could be quite as extensive as that of the legislative reference library. Thus the Chicago municipal bureau was described as having computed the city's geographical center of area and the center of population, as having compiled a statistical report on taxi-cab rates in the large cities of the world, as having conducted a study on speculation and scalping in amusement tickets.[64] Typically, it should be noted, the results of the Bureau's investigations were given as a report, not merely as a bibliography. [65]

The annual reports of the Baltimore Department of Legislative Reference yield a number of examples of similar far-reaching assistance. In 1907 Librarian Flack sent out questionnaires to cities across the country in order to offer up-to-the-minute information on methods of milk inspection.[66] In his report for 1911, Flack reprinted, as a sample of the *reports* which his bureau regularly provided for the city council, the historical study he had made of the construction of "improved paving" in Baltimore. The study (for it well merited the use of this term) covered twenty-five pages of printed text, including no less than fifteen pages of elaborate statistics.[67] It was an impressive performance, and it showed that in municipal reference work, as in its legislative prototype, the dividing line between assistance and original research was sometimes faint, if indeed not non-existent.

Informational service on this scale was not unusual in municipal and legislative reference work. Precisely what effects such service had on the conduct of state and city government, it is not the province of the present study to determine. It is perhaps sufficient here to say that, as *agencies of government,* the legislative and municipal reference libraries probably eventually disappointed the hopes of their proponents. Both types of libraries were originally organized in the expectation that, by making reliable information readily available to government officials, they might counteract the influence of pressure-group propaganda, and thus effect a substantial improvement in state and city legislation. However, the problems of effective legislation proved beyond remedy by library service, and popular enthusiasm for legislative and municipal reference work noticeably diminished after World War I.[68]

But if the legislative and municipal reference libraries failed to play a large part in the major arena of government, they did have an important role on the smaller stage of library development. Municipal reference libraries and legislative reference libraries were only two of the many types of special libraries, but they have been described in some detail because they represented in themselves the essential characteristics of the special library as it evolved in the generation prior to the first World War. McCarthy and his followers were the first to incorporate in practice — and did much to spread — the concept of amplified service that was the distinctive feature of special librarianship. They enlarged the sphere of reference work, showing that the library could function effectively as a direct information bureau supplying the fullest and most reliable data in the form most convenient for the client's use. The slogan of the special library movement was "putting knowledge to work." This meant, among other things, putting the subject knowledge and professional skill of the reference librarian to more and larger work in the pursuit of information than had previously been achieved.

[64]*Ibid.*, pp. 27, 36-37.

[65]*Ibid.*, p. 27.

[66] Baltimore Department of Legislative Reference, *Annual Report...for the Fiscal Year Ending December 31, 1907*, p. 6.

[67] Baltimore Department of Legislative Reference, *Annual Report...for the Fiscal Year Ending December 31, 1911*, pp. 13-37.

[68] Leek, *op. cit.*, p. 3; Eleanore V. Laurent, *Legislative Reference Work in the United States* (Chicago: Council of State Governments, 1939), p. 3.

Chapter VI

THE INDUSTRIAL RESEARCH LIBRARY: REFERENCE SERVICE
FOR PROFESSIONAL RESEARCH WORKERS

Business and Industrial Libraries Before World War I

No definite year can be set for the origin of special libraries in commerce and industry, but in general they may be said to date from about 1900.[1] C. C. Williamson has given a plausible explanation of the basic motivation for their establishment. In his view, business firms had always found it necessary to devote some effort to gathering the information needed in the conduct of their affairs. When the growth in size and complexity of American business enterprises brought the need for increased specialization in procedures, the various activities designed to gather information were integrated into the distinctive division known as the library.[2]

As Williamson's analysis suggests, the establishment of a library service within most firms was usually the result of a gradual process of evolution. Over the years a company would have found it necessary to accumulate a stock of reference books and other informational materials; eventually this collection would have become large enough to warrant its being placed in charge of a full-time employee. In this larval stage of business library development, the librarian was probably more caretaker and filing clerk than intelligence officer.[3]

Though his responsibilities initially may have called for the physical management of the company collection rather than information service, the self-interest of the company librarian naturally led him to enhance his status by stressing the wider service functions potential in his office. Indeed, it was not wholly a matter of choice on his part, for being part of a business enterprise, the librarian had to demonstrate that his department was a "labor-saving, profit-increasing device."[4] In other words, as revealed by the very titles of their articles,[5] company librarians were always in the position of having to justify their cost to the firm, and they could best demonstrate their "earning value" by showing that they could supply needed information directly, expeditiously, and in convenient form. M. E. Murray's attitude was typical: "The more efficiently and oftener the reference library serves the organization, the more time it saves high-priced executives, and helps the rank and file, the more certain it will become a permanent paying department of the business and make itself indispensable. This is in general how the earning value will be determined."[6]

---

[1] Of the engineering libraries surveyed by Alma C. Mitchill, the oldest was founded in 1892 and the vast majority between 1908 and 1918. ("The Special Library Profession and What It Offers; 15: Engineering and Technical Libraries," *Special Libraries*, XXIX [March, 1938], 74). Betty Joy Cole mentions the library of the N. V. Potash Export My. Inc (established in 1890) as among the earliest organized in the chemical industry. ("The Special Library Profession and What It Offers; 4: Chemical Libraries," *Special Libraries*, XXV [December, 1934], 271). Laura E. Babcock stated that "the idea of establishing a commercial library as a department of a business house, and especially of a manufacturing plant, was still comparatively in its infancy...in...1909. The only business library of a purely reference character of which any account could be found at [that] time, either printed or through correspondence, was the library connected with Stone & Webster of Boston." ("A Reference Library in a Manufacturing Plant," *Special Libraries*, II [February, 1911], 13).

[2] C. C. Williamson, "The Public Official and the Special Library," *Special Libraries*, VII (September, 1916), 112.

[3] Cf. Elizabeth Abbott, "The Studebaker Library and Its Work," *Special Libraries*, I (November, 1910), 66.

[4] Williamson, *op. cit.*, p. 112.

[5] E.g., D. N. Handy, "The Earning Power of Special Libraries," *Special Libraries*, II (January, 1911), 5-6; M. E. Murray, "The Earning Power of a Special Reference Library on Retail Distribution," *Special Libraries*, III (October, 1912), 167-69; "The Business Value of a Special Library," *Special Libraries*, III (October, 1912), 161-62.

[6] Murray, *op. cit.*, p. 168.

As suggested by Murray's statement, the industrial library in the period before World War I was oriented chiefly towards serving the company executive who needed information for the everyday conduct of his business, but who himself was unequipped or reluctant to do the library searching necessary to secure it. Like the service offered by the legislative reference and municipal reference libraries, the reference work in the business libraries was designed for the assistance of the inexperienced investigator rather than for the professional research worker.

There were, it is true, occasional suggestions that extensive library assistance was appropriate to the formal researches of the scientists employed in industry as well as the day-to-day inquiries of the company executives. William C. Ferguson, a chemical engineer, thought that the properly organized industrial research department should include "one competent man" to do the translating and literature searching needed by the department.[7] In his presidential address before the American Chemical Society in 1913, Arthur D. Little maintained that industrial research laboratories "should each be developed around a special library, the business of which should be to collect, compile and classify in a way to make instantly available every scrap of information bearing upon the materials, methods, products and requirements of the industry concerned."[8]

Little's position was based on experience as well as logic, for by 1913 there were already a few special libraries operating in conjunction with industrial research laboratories, one of them in his own firm.[9] These pioneer industrial research libraries not only supplied reference service of the conventional general library type (finding answers to specific factual inquiries) but also functioned as informational clearinghouses, routing periodicals for regular reading by the research staff, notifying individual research men of pertinent publications, and acting as liaison agencies between departments working on allied problems.[10]

On the other hand, the lacunae in service were also well evident. The librarians did not do abstracting or translating, took no part in literature surveys, or in the editing of laboratory reports. The questions they cited as typical of their work were of a rather simple kind. It was evident that inquiries of a more recondite nature and extended searches for information still devolved on the research men themselves.[11]

In general, then, before the first World War industrial research libraries were few in number, and reference service in these libraries not yet highly-developed. In part, this situation reflected the influence of the widely-held idea that the professional investigator was so much the master of the literature of his special field as to require only incidental bibliographic assistance from the librarian.[12] The idea may well have had considerable justification in fact, for the extent of the scientific literature in any given field did not yet have the overwhelming dimensions it was later to assume.

---

[7] William C. Ferguson, "A Plan for Organized Research and Analytical Chemistry in Successful Chemical Manufacturing," *Journal of Industrial and Engineering Chemistry*, IV (December, 1912), 905-08.

[8] Arthur D. Little, "Industrial Research in America," *Electrical Review and Western Electrician*, LXIV (February 28, 1914), 441.

[9] Cf. Guy E. Marion, "The Library as an Adjunct to Industrial Laboratories," *Library Journal*, XXXV (September, 1910), 400-04 (the article describes the "Information Department" of Arthur D. Little, Inc., of Boston); Helen R. Hosmer, "Library of the Research Labratory [sic] of the General Electric Company at Schenectady, New York," *Special Libraries*, IV (September-October, 1913), 169-71.

[10] Marion, *op. cit.*, pp. 403-04.

[11] *Ibid.*, p. 404; Hosmer, *op. cit.*, p. 170.

[12] Ernest Bruncken's analysis of the responsibilities of the library to the various types of users may be quoted in this connection. Though his statement was made in reference to state libraries rather than industrial libraries, it illustrates neatly the general tendency at this time to assume that the professional scholar required no service from the library other than the supply of the materials themselves. "At the beginning comes the thinker, the scientific investigator.... His library needs are the greatest of all; he requires books new and old, covering a vast range of learning.... But he knows his books, knows the bibliography of his special field, presumably far better than any librarian could. Here all the state library has to do is to furnish the books." ("The Legislative Reference Bureau," *News Notes of California Libraries*, II, Supplement [February, 1907], 102). Cf. also the report of the Science Division of the New York Public Library. *(Supra,* p. 48).

A much more direct factor in limiting the demand for industrial research libraries was the small dimensions of industrial research itself at this time. As previously noted,[13] the movement for the incorporation of research departments in industrial enterprises did not really get under way until the end of the nineteenth century. Up to the first World War, industrial research was quantitatively an inconsequential activity, with laboratories few in number and small in size. Only a handful of firms as yet had research departments large enough to warrant the establishment of special libraries.[14]

A final limiting factor was psychological in nature. As J. R. Angell explained, during this period scientists held as something of a fetish the belief that productive research was the result of individual inspiration and creativity. They depreciated the value of teamwork in research, regarding its attendant necessity for administrative organization as a hampering influence on the freedom of the individual worker.[15] In effect, this view denied that the process of scientific investigation was amenable to a division of labor. The corollary, of course, was that the research worker himself should undertake as many as possible of the tasks involved in his work. It left relatively little scope for the collaboration of the librarian.

The Impetus of the First World War

With the entry of the United States into the war, industrial research suddenly became an urgent necessity. No longer able to import the chemicals, dyes, glassware, medicines and pharmaceuticals formerly supplied by Germany, the country had to develop its own materials by an intensive and united effort on the part of the nation's scientists and industrialists. The consequence was a rapid multiplication and expansion of industrial research agencies. Frank B. Jewett of the National Research Council gave a vivid description of the overnight burgeoning of industrial research activity under wartime pressures:

> ... research and particularly industrial research, is very actively in people's minds, and before the public at the present time. Newspapers, magazines and periodicals are continually publishing articles on it; vast numbers of people are talking, more or less knowingly about it; and industries and government departments, which up to a few years ago had hardly heard of industrial research, are embarking or endeavoring to embark upon the most elaborate research projects .... I venture to say that there are possibly ten times as many so-called research laboratories and more than ten times as many so-called investigators in the United States today as there were three years ago.[16]

An important by-product of the war-time mobilization of research skills was the recognition of the validity of the principle of organization and cooperation in research. The needs of a country at war could not wait upon individual inspiration. Of necessity tried, organized industrial research was seen to be highly effective, and in the light of this war-time success the case for organization and cooperation in research became compelling.

World War I brought attention and prestige to the industrial research movement and demonstrated its practical value for the conduct of industrial operations. From the springboard provided by the war the industrial research movement jumped into a period of remarkable expansion. The generation between the wars (1920-1940) witnessed a numerical increase of industrial research laboratories on almost an exponential scale. Expenditures by American industry for scientific

---

[13] *Supra*, p. 10.

[14] U. S. National Resources Committee, Science Committee, *Research — a National Resource* (Washington: Government Printing Office, 1938-41), II, 34.

[15] James Rowland Angell, *The Development of Research in the United States* ("Reprint and Circular Series of the National Research Council," Number 6 [Washington: 1919]), p. 8.

[16] Frank B. Jewett, *Industrial Research* ("Reprint and Circular Series of the National Research Council," Number 4 [Washington: 1918]), pp. 2-4.

research increased from $29,468,000 in 1920 to $234,000,000 in 1940.[17] The number of industrial research laboratories in the United States, as listed in the successive editions of *Industrial Research Laboratories of the United States,* grew from 297 in 1920 to 2,224 in 1940.[18] Data on the number of workers employed in industrial research laboratories reveal the same pattern of dramatic growth, showing an increase in laboratory personnel from about 9,300 in 1920 to over 70,000 in 1940.[19]

The vitality of the movement was best seen in the fact that the great business depression of the early thirties caused only a moderate decline in the number of persons employed in industrial research. Nearly 44 per cent of the laboratories kept their staffs as large as before, and some 13 per cent actually increased the number of their personnel; by 1935 the little ground lost was more than made up.[20] A particularly significant aspect of this pattern of growth was the increase in the number of large laboratories; the number of companies maintaining research staffs of more than fifty persons increased from fifteen in 1921 to 120 in 1938.[21]

The growth of industrial research during and after the first World War provoked a parallel expansion of library activity. The sudden multiplication of industrial research operations in the war years in turn required the compilation and accumulation of technical information on a hitherto unprecedented scale. The need was met with characteristic American energy and dispatch. As Charles Reese described it,

> ... investigators and industries became aware that knowledge of conditions, discovery, invention, production — in a word, efficiency of effort was lacking. Intelligence bureaus, informational departments, staffs of abstractors, indexers, compilers and purveyors appeared suddenly all over the country... we were compelled to try to create information bureaus at high speed and with feverish haste.[22]

These *ad hoc* measures for informational services, taken to meet a wartime need, were seen to have such general utility as to commend them for adoption in peacetime operations as well. This realization prompted the establishment of many new industrial research libraries in the years immediately following the end of the war. Such prominent firms as the Aluminum Company of America, Proctor and Gamble, the National Aniline and Chemical Company, and the Standard Oil Development Company all organized research libraries in 1919, and the Eastman Kodak Company did likewise in 1920.[23]

From 1920 on, as in the case of the industrial research movement itself, the history of industrial research libraries was one of steady expansion. Though the vagaries of classification prevent the ascertainment of their exact number, there is no doubt that it became the common practice for libraries to be established in conjunction with research laboratories of any considerable size. However, the relationship of the library to the laboratory varied considerably according to the theories of service held. These are examined in the following section.

[17]U. S. Office of Scientific Research and Development, *Science, the Endless Frontier; a Report to the President,* by Vannevar Bush... (Washington: Government Printing Office, 1945), p. 80.

[18]National Research Council, *Industrial Research Laboratories of the United States* ("Bulletins of the National Research Council," Numbers 2, 16, 60, 81, 91, 102, 104 [Washington: National Research Council, 1920-40]).

[19]U. S. National Resources Committee, Science Committee, *op. cit.,* II, 37.

[20]*Ibid.*

[21]George Perazich and Philip Field, *Industrial Research and Changing Technology,* National Research Project Report, Number M-4 (Philadelphia: Work Projects Administration, 1940), p. 8.

[22]Charles L. Reese, *Informational Needs in Science and Technology* ("Reprint and Circular Series of the National Research Council," Number 33 [Washington: 1922]), p. 3.

[23]Cole, *op. cit.,* p. 272.

The Role of the Librarian in Industrial Research:
Theories of Service, 1920-1940

The post-war increase in the number of industrial research libraries was prima facie evidence of the importance research workers attached to the use of the library. This supposition is supported by a number of direct statements from the research men themselves. Weidlein and Hamor stressed the need for good technical libraries, for "the scientific use of literature . . . is indispensable in laying the foundation for scientific research."[24] The National Resources Committee set a substantial dollars and cents valuation on the use of the library: " . . . a thorough study of a problem in a good library prior to and during the prosecution of research on it will save on the average 10 per cent of the total cost in time and money."[25]

Such statements, while attesting to the increased prestige of the industrial research library, referred primarily to the library as the repository of pertinent information, and not to the work of the library staff. There remained the very large question of by whom and by what means that information was to be brought out for most effective research use.

It was clear that to set a high valuation on the usefulness of a thorough library search was not necessarily to concede to the librarian a much greater part than that of making the materials available. When asked to indicate what qualifications he, as a research worker, expected from the librarian, Dr. J. A. Leighty of the Lilly Research Laboratories mentioned only the pedestrian virtues of accuracy, courtesy and knowledge of general library methods. He did not expect the librarian to prepare translations or abstracts for him, but was obviously satisfied with good "mechanical" service — the circulation of published abstracts, location of literature reviews, the prompt identification and supply of materials requested.[26]

Even more revealing was the attitude of G. M. Dexter, a mechanical engineer. While keenly cognizant of the value of "the library as an engineering tool," he denied that the librarian could make an effective search of the literature. "Much better results," he stated decisively, "could be obtained by an engineer instead of a librarian."[27]

Dexter's principal objection to the librarian's doing literature searches for laboratory staff lay in the librarian's supposed lack of subject knowledge. This view was not uncommon among research men. In its most extreme form it identified the librarian with the old stereotype of "custodian of books." Byron Soule, for instance, made a scathing denunciation of the typical "trained librarian."

> To whom shall he [i.e. the research chemist] turn for library aid? The obvious person is the trained librarian. Unfortunately, as now released from our schools of library science, she is not personally acquainted with laboratory operations. The language of the sciences is unfamiliar to her so the technical association of ideas and subjects is impossible. When asked for a particular volume she can promptly find it, but in general her training is confined to book buying and guardianship. Her responsibility ends at the cover.[28]

Soule, of course, failed to realize that the "typical librarian" he had in mind was by no means representative of the range of abilities to be found within the profession. A more moderate position conceded that there were special librarians with a very fair degree of subject knowledge, yet still

[24] Edward R. Weidlein and William A. Hamor, *Glances at Industrial Research, during Walks and Talks in Mellon Institute* (New York: Reinhold Publishing Corporation, 1936), pp. 135-36.

[25] U. S. National Resources Committee, Science Committee, *op. cit.*, I, 179.

[26] J. A. Leighty, "What the Research Worker Expects of the Librarian," *Special Libraries*, XXI (July-August, 1940), 264-65.

[27] Gregory M. Dexter, "The Library as an Engineering Tool," *Mechanical Engineering*, LIX (November, 1937), 849.

[28] Byron A. Soule, "Finding the Literature," *Journal of Chemical Education*, XXI (July, 1944), 333.

doubted that anyone other than the research worker himself was really competent to cope with the highly technical inquiries into which his minutely specialized investigations led him.[29]

A similar line of reasoning prompted C. K. Mees, the well-known research director of the Eastman Kodak Company, to cast doubts on the feasibility of the company librarian's preparing abstracts for the laboratory workers. It was probably better, he maintained, to arrange for the research workers themselves to prepare abstracts dealing with their own special section of science, with the librarian's part limited to classifying and distributing the abstracts received.[30]

An obvious alternative solution for the problem of abstracting, but again one that tended to minimize the role of the librarian, was simply to utilize the ready-made abstracts available in published form from such "services" as *Chemical Abstracts*. In fact, E. J. Crane, the editor of *Chemical Abstracts*, implied that only some such organization as his own, which could muster to the task of abstracting highly trained scientists possessing unusual knowledge of the subject field and special competence in the use of words, could produce really satisfactory results.[31]

Indeed, the existence of regular "services" such as *Chemical Abstracts* represented the embodiment of an old hope that, implicitly at least, ran counter to the whole idea of library reference work. For in theory such a centralized information service, providing an expertly prepared condensation of the entire literature of the subject, would render the individual researcher all but self-sufficient in so far as his informational needs were concerned. He would have to depend on the librarian only for the physical supply of the materials identified as pertinent by his abstracting and indexing service. It was the same hope that had actuated the preparation of the *Index-Catalogue of the Surgeon-General's Library*, and an analogous belief had once held that the catalog could be the single key that would unlock the entire contents of the library.[32]

In the twenties, the hope must have seemed bright, for the inadequacies of the centralized bibliographic "services" had not been made manifest. Hasse saw in the proliferation of such "services" a very real possibility that they would lead to the atrophy of reference service to research workers. "It would seem then that the apparent trend is that libraries will concentrate upon the care and collecting of books and book materials, but that the analysis of this material will more and more become the work of special groups."[33]

Hasse proved to be a false prophet, for she failed to take into consideration factors that militated against the success of the published "services." However technically proficient, abstracts prepared by a central bureau could not be as timely as those prepared locally. Moreover, as "ready-made" articles, the former would not be so directly relevant to the particular interests and viewpoints of the individual research team as abstracts "tailored-to-fit."[34]

Even more pertinent was the increasingly apparent fact that the coverage of the bibliographical services could not keep pace with the increasing volume and complexity of the literature. *Chemical Abstracts*, it was true, continued to provide a reasonably adequate survey of the literature of chemistry. Even so, a complete search of the literature of any subject in the field of chemistry, especially one involving cross-relationships with other sciences, necessarily required consultation of many other bibliographic sources. For most other areas of industrial research nothing nearly so broad in coverage as *Chemical Abstracts* was available, and the astounding rate of increase in

---

[29] For example, Dana Wood, an engineer, maintained that "only the engineer himself can tell whether he has found what he wants and to do this he must personally review [the material].... No library worker, even if trained along general engineering lines, could expect to become highly specialized along all lines as would be required to meet the diversity of questions likely to be submitted." ("Use of the Library by the Engineer," *Special Libraries*, XVI [April, 1925], 114).

[30] Charles E. K. Mees, *The Organization of Industrial Research* (New York: McGraw-Hill, 1920), pp. 138-39.

[31] E. J. Crane, "The Abstracting and Indexing of Scientific and Technical Literature," *Special Libraries*, XXXI (July-August, 1940), 261.

[32] *Supra*, p. 31.

[33] Adelaide R. Hasse, "Bibliography: Today and Tomorrow," *Special Libraries*, XXI (March, 1930), 78.

[34] See the discussion following Crane's paper; Crane, *op. cit.*, p. 264.

technical literature was steadily widening the gap. As early as 1932 an overall appraisal of the means available for the bibliographic control of technical literature concluded: "Technical literature has become so voluminous and its rate of increase so rapid that need for skillful management of information service has grown up faster than the requisite skill has developed."[35]

It thus became clear that subscription to a "service," — or even a number of them — provided no easy solution for the bibliographical problems of industrial research workers. Information service remained perforce a local responsibility. If, then, the research team could not have the requisite information served up in package form by a central bureau, how was the literature to be tapped?

As already seen, one school of thought among research workers held that the appropriate means was to have the researcher do it for himself. But a necessary preliminary to effective literature searching was an intimate knowledge of the bibliography of the subject and mastery of library techniques — this much was conceded even by those most convinced that the researcher should do his own literature work.[36] Though no reliable data were available to indicate the exact extent of the average research worker's bibliographical competence, the weight of opinion estimated it as being of a very low level. "Most technical schools," Catherine Davies explained, "neither require nor offer courses in library research; hence research men know laboratory techniques much better than library techniques."[37]

Not only was the average research worker ill-prepared for the work of literature searching, but also it was unlikely to elicit his interest. Most scientists, according to Arthur Connolly, had little taste for what appeared to them as a plodding, time-consuming consultation of indexes, bibliographies and abstracts.

> The romance of discovering the secrets of nature in the laboratory still appeals much more to the average research scientist than the drudgery of carefully considering, digesting, and correlating technical treatises, publications and patents .... the average research scientist is temperamentally wedded to the laboratory. He prefers the manipulation of beakers, test tubes, autoclaves, etc., to the dull task of studying the literature.[38]

The most comprehensive argument for extensive reference service held that, even when the research man was competent and willing to undertake his own bibliographical work, it was unprofitable for him to do so. The research worker was a highly paid specialist whose time was most valuable to the employing firm when it was spent on tasks directly connected with his specialty — laboratory investigation. A basic principle of the organization of research was the division of labor. This principle meant that no task involved in the research process should be assigned to the scientist himself if it could be done efficiently by a lesser-paid employee. Illustrating the application of this principle, Mees showed how such activities as electrical measurements, lens optics, photometric measurements, lantern-slide making and instrument-making, all at one time devolving on the research worker himself, had, with the advances made in the organization of research, become "service tasks" delegated to specialists.[39]

To many observers, both librarians and scientists, the same principle seemed to point to the employment of "literature specialists" who would be responsible for the satisfaction of the literature needs of the research organization. As early as 1922, research directors Fleming and Pearce averred that ["literature work] is most effectively carried out by a specially trained staff at a much

[35]Julian F. Smith and Irene F. Smith, "Information Service in Industrial Research Laboratories," *Industrial and Engineering Chemistry,* XXIV (August, 1932), 949.

[36]Dexter, *op. cit.,* p. 849; William A. Hamor and Lawrence W. Bass, "Bibliochresis: the Pilot of Research," *Science,* LXXI (April 11, 1930), 375-78.

[37]A. Catherine Davies, "The Role of the Technical Librarian in the Paper Industry," *Paper Trade Journal,* CXV (October 29, 1942), Technical Section, 32.

[38]Arthur Connolly, "Library Versus Laboratory Research," *Journal of Chemical Education,* XX (November, 1943), 531-32.

[39]Charles E. K. Mees, "The Organization of Industrial Scientific Research," *Science,* XLIII (June 2, 1916), 771.

lower cost than is entailed if it is distributed among research workers."[40] Similarly, Lucy Lewton, in defining the functions of the librarian, thought that such activities as presentation of data in summarized form, abstracting, preparation of bibliographies, translating, even analysis of patent novelty points were "services obviously within the library's scope."[41]

Even Soule, so acrimonious a critic of the ordinary product of the library school, nevertheless felt that, given the optimum training, a librarian could logically take complete responsibility for the laboratory's literature work.

> Without an intimate knowledge of searching aids or the skill to use them efficiently, the task of locating obscure data is too much for anyone who must spend his best hours in the laboratory. He should gladly pass the work on to a specialist exactly as he does when intricate electrical devices and complicated glass apparatus are required. His triumph comes in the use of these adjuncts, not in their construction.... The library technologist is the logical person to assume the responsibility for these special searches.... He can handle the library part of an investigation exactly as the laboratorian deals with the manipulative part.[42]

After a generation of discussion, the literature of special librarianship still showed no agreement on how far the librarian was to go in his assistance to the industrial research worker. Probably, in the final analysis, no single, overall answer could be given, for it depended on the ability and desire of the researcher to do his own literature work and on the competence of the librarian, all three of these factors being variables of wide range.

The end result was, then, a series of answers. The minimum position held that the research worker must himself be primarily responsible for the performance of his literature work, but even then never to the point of completely dispensing with the reference service of the librarian. It was recognized that the sheer complexity and extent of the scientific literature would ordinarily require the assistance of the librarian at least for the choice of index headings, the indication of possible sources in related fields, the verification of obscure references, et cetera.[43]

The maximum position — which assumed that the research worker was willing and the librarian able — held that the reference service might logically encompass the whole range of literature work involved in research, including literature searches, translations, abstracting, and editorial assistance.[44]

Probably the usual position was somewhere in between, but chronologically the literature showed a distinct disposition for opinion to favor increased assistance by the librarian. Unquestionably the post-war theory of industrial research accorded a definite place — under favorable conditions a very large place — to library reference services in the research process. This meant an important enlargement of the role of the reference librarian. He had already shown himself to be an effective aid in the informal investigations of the untrained legislator and businessman. He was now being increasingly recognized, at least in theory, as the potential collaborator of the professional research worker.

---

[40] A. P. M. Fleming and J. G. Pearce, *Research in Industry, the Basis of Economic Progress* (London: Sir Isaac Pitman and Sons, Ltd., 1922), p. 142. The authors were English but they had a wide acquaintance with American industrial research and their reasoning was undoubtedly applicable to the American situation.

[41] Lucy O. Lewton, "Delimiting the Library Field," *Proceedings of the Special Libraries Association,* I (Thirtieth Annual Conference, 1938), P45.

[42] Soule, *op. cit.,* p. 333.

[43] Cf. Smith and Smith, *op. cit.,* p. 952.

[44] Cf. Fleming and Pearce, *op. cit.,* p. 148.

The Industrial Research Library, 1920-1940:
Patterns of Service

It is difficult to find sufficient common denominators in the working methods of industrial re-search libraries to serve as the basis for a reliable general description of their practices.[45] The fact that few industrial research libraries make available their reports adds to the difficulties of classification and appraisal, since the published descriptions in *Special Libraries* and technical journals are almost invariably brief, chatty rather than probing, and often so highly colored by the personal interest of the author as to be mere claims rather than objective observation. The lack of annual reports also makes it difficult to discern chronological development in service.

Nevertheless, one may distinguish several more or less distinct levels or patterns of reference service among industrial research libraries, corresponding fairly closely to the different theories of service. At the lowest level, the only thing "special" about the industrial research library was its collection and classification, with the librarian's assistance being engaged only for the simpler factual inquiries and for the verification of titles. A service of this type was described by the li-brarian of the Mellon Institute of Industrial Research in Pittsburgh. She did little reference work, she explained, because the staff members did all their own literature searching and abstracting. As a general rule, they called upon her for assistance only in locating files of journals in other li-braries and in tracking down obscure references.[46]

However, instances of such limited service were extremely rare.[47] In this case at least, it was obviously the product of the special conditions obtaining at the Mellon Institute. Though the Institute did scientific research on a contractual basis for industrial corporations, its chief *raison d'être* was the training of young scientists in the techniques of research by a system of "industrial fellow-ships." The skillful use of technical literature was considered an important part of that training, hence the "fellows" were deliberately enjoined to seek only the minimum amount of assistance from the librarian. [48]

A purely commercial research laboratory naturally felt no such responsibility for the training of its staff members, and looked upon the librarian's services as a straight labor-saving device, to be given the maximum exploitation consistent with the desires of the researchers and the capa-bilities of the librarian. Where these two limiting factors were still of some weight, the result was an intermediate level of service, which characteristically (though never exactly so in any one in-stance) featured the following types of activity.

In response to specific requests, the librarian would be expected to indicate the physical loca-tion of materials, to identify and verify references, and to supply factual information directly (i.e. without involving the use of the material by the inquirer), when such information was readily as-certainable from standard reference books and did not necessitate special subject knowledge for its interpretation. In inquiries of larger scope, demanding a review of the literature rather than specific facts, the librarian would prepare a bibliography of pertinent references. At this interme-diate level, such bibliographies would be selective but not "critical" or evaluative — that is, the librarian would not be prepared to assess the reliability of the data, but would be expected to know enough about the subject of inquiry to guarantee the relevance of the material listed.[49]

---

[45] Linda Morley has stressed the fact that special libraries vary much more in their policies and operating methods than do public or university libraries. She has estimated the extent of variation among public libraries at 15 per cent, among univer-sity libraries at 25 per cent, and among special libraries as at least as high as 50 per cent. ("The Adaptation of Policies and Methods to Special Libraries of Different Types," *Special Libraries*, XXIII [July-August, 1932], 296.

[46] Lois Heaton, "The Library of Mellon Institute of Industrial Research," *Industrial and Engineering Chemistry, (News Edition)*, VIII, (October 10, 1930), 9.

[47] The special library literature may well be deceptive on this point, since it is likely that only the more imposing records of service would be written up for publication.

[48] William A. Hamor, "Bibliography, the Foundation of Scientific Research," *Special Libraries*, XIV (March-April, 1923), 17.

[49] Cf. Pyrrha S. Cafferata, "The Operation of a Technical Specialized Library," *Special Libraries*, XVI (October, 1925), 327-28.

This left the exhaustive bibliographies and literature summaries to be prepared by the research men themselves, but even in these tasks the librarian would have an important share, utilizing his technical knowledge of bibliography to suggest lines of approach, references from related fields, materials likely to be overlooked by the research worker (such as chapters in general books and articles in obscure journals) and sources of information outside the local library.[50]

In addition to information supplied for specific inquiries, the "intermediate" library customarily sought, by a variety of means, to keep its clientele up-to-date on the current developments in the field. Many industrial research libraries maintained a "routing service," regularly dispatching incoming materials, especially periodicals, to the members of the research staff. Over and above this more or less "mechanical" service, the librarian was expected to have a close enough knowledge of the individual interests of the research workers to be able to call their attention to specific publications of use to them. As Greenman graphically described the operation of such service in the Arthur D. Little Inc. library, "the librarian serves as the eyes of the organization, searching for literature of interest and value to the specialists engaged in relatively different fields of chemical research."[51]

A common alternative (in some cases a supplement) to the circulation of the materials themselves was the preparation and distribution of a list or bulletin identifying the important current literature received. The bulletin might be merely an accessions list, giving only the references in classified form,[52] but more often it also supplied abstracts or annotations of the articles listed. At the "intermediate level" of service, however, the writing of the abstracts did not devolve upon the library staff. Either the abstracts were copied verbatim from the published services such as *Engineering Index* or *Chemical Abstracts*,[53] or, where the desire for promptness precluded waiting for published abstracts, the abstracts were prepared by the research workers themselves, with the library staff merely being responsible for their reproduction and dissemination.[54]

It is thus seen that at the "intermediate level" of reference service the research workers still retained the major responsibility for the literature side of their investigations. In libraries of the third type — giving maximum service — the division of labor between laboratory and library workers was nearly complete, with the library staff taking over almost all the bibliographical tasks involved in the research process. Since conventional reference work represented only a part of such service, some writers on special librarianship have preferred to apply a new, more inclusive term for it, such as "literature service work" or "research information service."[55]

The activities involved in such "literature service work" were roughly of the same general types already described, but required a maximum degree of participation and knowledge from the library staff. In inquiries requesting specific facts, the "literature specialist" might be expected not only to supply the information directly (rather than indicate sources), but often would also be prepared to give an immediate answer from personal knowledge, without recourse to published sources. In either case, the literature specialist assumed responsibility for the validity of the information, supplying where necessary, critical statements indicating the limitations and applicability of the data.[56]

---

[50] Cf. Francis E. Cady, "The Research and Technical Library," *Special Libraries*, XIII (October, 1922), 124.

[51] E. D. Greenman, "The Functions of the Industrial Library — That of Arthur D. Little, Inc., a Type," *Special Libraries*, X (October, 1919), 190.

[52] Cf. Edith Joaness, "A Fifty-Year Old Technical Library," *Special Libraries*, XXX (October, 1939), 256.

[53] E.g. as in the library of the General Motors Research Laboratories Division (Caroline W. Lutz, "Contacts with Our Clientele," *Special Libraries*, XXVIII [December, 1937], 361). Cf. also Thelma Reinberg, "Among Libraries — the Battelle Memorial Institute," *Special Libraries*, XXX (November, 1939), 295.

[54] Gertrude Reissman, "The Kodak Park Library," *Special Libraries*, X (May, 1919), 95; Mary Elizabeth Key, "The Technical Department Library of Aluminum Company of America," *Special Libraries*, XIX (February, 1918), 40.

[55] Lura Shorb and Lewis Beck, "Opportunities for Chemists in Literature Service Work," *Journal of Chemical Education*, XXI (July, 1944), 315-18.

[56] Linda H. Morley, "Report of Professional Standards Committee," *Special Libraries*, XXXI (July-August, 1940), 216.

More often, the request from the researcher necessitated an overall survey of the literature of an area rather than specific items of information. In such cases the "literature specialist" made a thorough and careful review of the pertinent publications, submitting either a critical bibliography (in case the researcher wished to consult the material for himself), or a formal report summarizing the findings of the literature.[57] Such reports, describing "the state of the art," were commonly required by many research laboratories as a necessary preliminary to the inauguration of any new research project.

Though this sort of literature search usually preceded laboratory research, it did not necessarily cease at that point. The literature search often proceeded concurrently with the laboratory work, with the literature specialist participating in the conferences of the research men, providing the ideas suggested by the current literature as his share in a continuous collaboration on plans and methods.[58]

While the *literature survey* probably ranked as the most important single function of the industrial research library, quantitatively it represented only a small part of "literature service work." The established policy of top-level industrial research librarians was to be aggressive in their service, not waiting for inquiries, but as far as possible anticipating the informational needs of their clientele by preparing and disseminating a steady supply of current data. [59]

The favorite medium for the accomplishment of this purpose was the *abstract bulletin*, customarily issued in mimeographed form at weekly or monthly intervals. Like its counterpart in the other types of industrial research library, the abstract bulletin of the top-level library was designed to keep the laboratory staff abreast of the current technical literature, but, being prepared by the local literature specialist rather than reproducing published abstracts, it had the important advantage of being both broader and more selective in its coverage. It was broader in that it commonly covered not only the published literature but also the company's own confidential research reports, more selective in that the literature specialist utilized his intimate knowledge of the firm's special interests and viewpoint to bring out the aspects of the literature that had the most relevance for the company's particular problems.

Almost inevitably, the industrial research libraries commanding the talent and resources to offer such intensive assistance were drawn into, or assumed on their own initiative, many miscellaneous services as well. C. R. Whittemore mentioned that many such libraries were responsible for the maintenance of statistics relating to the economic interest of their firms.[60] The library staff of the International Nickel Company compiled an annual review of the growth of the nickel industry.[61] A translation service, at least for French and German, was commonly expected, and in many firms the librarian had important responsibilities in connection with editorial work and writing — preparing manuals and descriptive bulletins, editing technical reports for publication, sometimes even "ghost writing" papers for company executives.[62]

In the absence of any overall survey of reference services in industrial research libraries, no wholly reliable estimate can be made of the incidence of the various types of service. It seems highly probable, however, that the general trend between 1920 and 1940 was to have the librarian assume an increasingly important role in the research process. By 1934, when Cole made a more or less official description of the work of the special librarian in the chemical industry, the functions

[57] For example, the du Pont Company's "library chemist" was asked to prepare a report describing and evaluating the methods for manufacturing white lead. (A. W. Kenney, "The du Pont Experimental Station Library; a Chemical Special Library." *Special Libraries,* XVII [March, 1926], 101).

[58] D. B. Keyes, "An Informational Service for a Chemical Manufacturing Concern," *Chemical and Metallurgical Engineering* XXVII (July 12, 1922), 58.

[59] Cf. J. A. Dean, "Shell Oil Company of California Information Service," *Special Libraries,* XVII (June, 1926), 229-30.

[60] C. R. Whittemore, "The Function and Organization of the Technical Library in the Service of the Mining, Metallurgical, and Chemical Industries," *Canadian Mining and Metallurgical Bulletin,* Number 213 (1930), 123.

[61] Lucy O. Lewton, "An Engineering Library," *Special Libraries,* XXIX (January, 1938), 14.

[62] Shorb and Beck, *op. cit.,* p. 317.

of the librarian were held to include all of the following tasks: answering of factual inquiries, preparation of bibliographies, scanning and referral of incoming literature, preparation of an abstract bulletin, translations, and making of literature surveys.[63] Similarly, Brown's survey of services in petroleum libraries showed that in 1937 the large majority of these libraries were doing translations, abstracting, and literature searches, as well as the conventional reference work.[64]

In the final analysis, however, it does not much matter whether such extensive reference service actually represented the norm in industrial research library operation, for the existence of even a few instances of such service would have been sufficient to demonstrate its feasibility. Theorists had long maintained, on the basis of intrinsic logic, that given proper training and sufficient responsibility, the reference librarian could provide an efficient and economical substitute for expensive library research by the client himself. In the industrial research library, this division of labor between librarian and client, which had already proven profitable for the legislator and the company executive, was applied to the needs of professional research personnel — and it worked.

---

[63] Cole, *op. cit.*, pp. 273-75.

[64] Delbert F. Brown, "Petroleum Libraries; Their Present Situation and the Outlook for the Future," *Special Libraries,* XXVIII (January, 1937), 3-7.

Chapter VII

REFERENCE SERVICE IN THE
GENERAL RESEARCH LIBRARY, 1917-1940

To general research libraries, as to other social institutions, the First World War brought the need for adaptation to novel conditions; inevitably reference departments suffered their share of dislocations and rearrangements. Shortage of trained personnel was common, and in the case of the Yale University Library it was severe enough to bring about the temporary elimination of the position of reference librarian.[1] Conversely, elsewhere the increased informational demands of war-stimulated research greatly accelerated reference activity; the Columbia University Library provided quarters and assistance for a team of government investigators and went to exceptional lengths in supplying information.[2]

On the whole, however, radical variations from the normal pattern in reference work were as short-lived as the emergency by which they were called forth. As previously shown,[3] by 1916 reference service could look back on nearly two generations of development, and had achieved a stability proof against wholesale dislocation even by the massive stimuli of war. Accordingly, the history of reference service between the wars was marked by no sharp changes in direction, but instead was characterized by the further exploration and intensification of practices and trends already clearly outlined in the pre-war era.

In strictly quantitative terms, the tendency toward an increase in the volume of reference work done and in the number of reference workers employed continued almost unabated throughout the entire post-war period, with only a temporary depression-caused reduction in personnel during the first years of the thirties to interrupt the steady upward progression of the statistics. To cite an example typical of many public libraries, the Minneapolis Public Library estimated that in the period from 1899 to 1939 there was a more than twenty-fold increase in the volume of its reference work.[4]

The university libraries could claim similar gains. Carl White's study of the personnel statistics for eight university libraries showed that twice as many reference librarians were employed in 1937-1938 as in 1918-1919.[5] Many an individual university library could point to an even more impressive record. Yale, which had no full-time reference librarian in 1920 and only one up to July, 1922, had three reference librarians by 1924-1925, and ten by 1938-1939.[6] The University of Minnesota Library had one reference librarian in 1921 and nine in 1941.[7]

---

[1] Yale University Library, *Report of the Librarian...July 1, 1920-June 30, 1921*, reprinted from *the Report of the President of Yale University, 1921*; p. 15.

[2] Isadore Gilbert Mudge, "History of the Columbia University Reference Department" (Unpublished manuscript, 1941; in Columbia University Library); Columbia University Library, "Reference Department Annual Report, July 1st, 1918 to June 30, 1919" (Unpublished report), p. 4.

[3] *Supra*, pp. 40-41.

[4] Minneapolis Public Library, *Minneapolis Public Library; Fifty Years of Service, 1889-1939* (Minneapolis: The Library?, 1939), p. 31.

[5] Carl M. White, "Trends in the Use of University Libraries," in *College and University Library Service; Papers Presented at the 1937 Midwinter Meeting of the American Library Association*, edited by A. F. Kuhlman. (Chicago: American Library Association, 1938), pp. 29-30.

[6] Yale University Library, *Report of the Librarian...July 1, 1924-June 30, 1925*, reprinted from the *Reports Made to the President...by the Deans and Directors...for the Academic Year 1924-1925*, pp. 24, 26; Yale University Library, *Report of the Librarian...for the Academic Year 1938-1939*, p. 12.

[7] University of Minnesota Library, "Report of the University Library and Division of Library Instruction...for the Year Ending June 30, 1941; Including a Twenty Year Summary, 1921-1941" ("Presented as unpublished manuscript"), pp. 88-89.

With the increase in volume of reference work there came an increase in its prestige, at least in the eyes of librarians themselves. A report of the Cleveland Public Library called reference work "perhaps its most valuable service."[8] For J. Christian Bay of the John Crerar Library, reference service was "the Library's most vital function,"[9] and Joeckel and Carnovsky suggested that reference service constituted the chief justification for the public library's claim to be an educational institution.[10]

Policies of Reference Service

Agreement on the importance of reference service did not prevent librarians from differing considerably on policies for the actual conduct of reference work. The central issue of reference service policy—the nature and extent of the assistance to be offered—had not been resolved by the discussions of the pre-war period, and this continued to be the subject of a lively debate in the quarter-century that followed.[11]

The "conservative theory" never ceased to find adherents. It had a particularly strong following among university librarians, many of whom, thinking it educationally advantageous to foster a spirit of self-dependence on the part of library patrons, stressed reference work as a means of instruction, with a corresponding de-emphasis on its function as an information service. A statement in a Princeton University Library report may be taken as typifying this belief: "The function of the Reference Librarians in a university is not to find the material which is needed, but to show the student how to discover it for himself."[12]

The same attitude was often carried over imperceptibly, if not logically, to service for faculty. Thus Wayne Yenawine affirmed that "personal resourcefulness and independence on the part of the student and *of the faculty* are to be desired and encouraged at all times [by reference librarians]."[13] Similarly, Margaret Hutchins observed that reference librarians considered it "part of their objectives to foster self-dependence on the part of students and *faculty*."[14]

Just what educational purposes were being served by denying to faculty more than minimal assistance was seldom made clear. Tacitly, however, the policy was undoubtedly based on the old assumption that the mature scholar did not need help — or at any rate *ought* not need it.

The assumption — and its corollary that reference service was basically "help for the helpless" — was held by a number of public librarians as well. The American Library Association's *Survey of Libraries in the United States* indicated that the policy of the public libraries of New York, Oakland and Toledo, among others, was to supply the actual information only for readers who appeared incapable of finding it for themselves.[15] The statement of the Washington (D.C.) Public Library was a particularly forthright exposition of this point of view:

> Students are encouraged to help themselves and do their own work. Inquirers of sufficient mental calibre can go on to do their searching after direction and help. Helpless

---

[8]Cleveland Public Library, *Fifty-fifth Annual Report, April 1, 1923-March 31, 1924*, p. 30.

[9]John Crerar Library, *Thirty-sixth Annual Report for the Year 1930*, p. 18.

[10]Carleton B. Joeckel and Leon Carnovsky, *A Metropolitan Library in Action; a Survey of the Chicago Public Library* (Chicago: University of Chicago Press, 1940), p. 314.

[11]*Supra*, pp. 43-44.

[12]Princeton University Library, "The University Library," in *Report of the President for the Academic Year 1934-1935*, p. 79.

[13]Wayne S. Yenawine, "Wanted: a Functional Reference Room," *Library Journal*, LXII (March, 1937), 238. (Emphasis by the present author).

[14]Margaret Hutchins, *Introduction to Reference Work* (Chicago: American Library Association, 1944), p. 177.

[15]American Library Association, *A Survey of Libraries in the United States* ... (Chicago: American Library Association, 1926-27), II, 112-14.

inquirers, foreigners, and timid people, are helped to use the material so that the assistant is sure that the desired information is found. [16]

If the "conservative theory" of reference work undeniably persisted, it was not without mounting criticism and challenge. J. Christian Bay felt that mere "guidance" was inadequate. Library patrons, he stated, should secure "critically sifted information... The ideal for anyone connected with reference work is not merely to indicate a mass of literature but to illumine it."[17] Similarly, W. S. Learned made a pointed contrast between the public library's potentialities as a "community intelligence service" and the "trifling service" which, in many institutions, serious inquirers could then actually command. [18]

On the positive side, opposition to the "conservative" view of reference work manifested itself in the support of various counter-theories that looked toward the provision of a more generous, more thorough, more scholarly reference service. While these theories actually represented a fairly wide spectrum of opinion, they shared enough features in common for J. I. Wyer to be able to group them into two major categories: the "moderate" and the "liberal" theories of reference work. [19]

The "moderate" position was best represented by the exposition of reference work written by Charles McCombs for the American Library Association's *Manual of Library Economy*. McCombs defined reference work as

> help given by the librarian to a reader in finding books or facts needed for some sort of study or for some other particular purpose.... The librarian is not concerned with the study itself, when once the books needed are identified or placed at the disposition of the reader, or with the interpretation or utilization of the facts, when once they are found or the source of information pointed out.... The function of the reference department, then, is to aid readers in using books. The aim of the department is to see that the inquirer is supplied with information, if it can be found in books or by means of books. [20]

If McCombs' description was reminiscent of the "conservative" position in its assumption that the librarian had no responsibility for the credibility of the information he supplied, it was free of the implication that the direct supply of information (as distinguished from the indication of sources) was somehow suspect. Moreover, he advocated that the policy of minimum assistance apply only to undergraduate students and to the "aimless habitués" of public libraries, conceding that the social importance of his work entitled the scholar to special help.[21] However, he cautiously warned that the *practical* ability of the library to supply special help to the scholar could not often match its willingness to do so. Extensive assistance such as translating, digesting or tabulating the material found could very seldom be extended even to the bona fide scholar except on a service charge basis.[22]

The "moderate theory" thus represented a compromise between guidance and full information service, between a laudable desire to be of maximum assistance in important investigations and realistic reservations about the ability of the library to do so. It offered a workable mean between demand and capacity, and as such provided a policy for reference service that proved attractive to

---

[16] *Ibid.*, p. 114.

[17] J. Christian Bay, "Sources of Reference Work," *Bulletin of the Medical Library Association,* XIV (July, 1924), 11.

[18] William S. Learned, *The American Public Library and the Diffusion of Knowledge* (New York: Harcourt, Brace and Company, 1924), p. 14.

[19] James Ingersoll Wyer, *Reference Work: a Textbook for Students of Library Work and Libraries* (Chicago: American Library Association, 1930), pp. 7-13.

[20] Charles F. McCombs, *The Reference Department* ("Manual of Library Economy," XXII; Chicago: American Library Association, 1929), pp. 1-2.

[21] *Ibid.*, p. 19.

[22] *Ibid.*, pp. 20-21.

many, perhaps a majority, of the general research libraries. The *Survey of Libraries in the United States* reported that nearly half the larger public libraries commonly found the desired information for a reader in preference to merely referring him to the proper sources.[23] Moreover, most libraries of this class did not set arbitrary limits on the time to be devoted to questions, professing to be governed in this respect "by circumstances," and thus implying that exceptionally important inquiries might be accorded a liberal allotment of the reference department's time.[24]

While most general libraries were inclined to favor the "moderate theory," a few librarians were disposed to adopt a much more advanced position — the "liberal theory" of reference service. The most ardent and convincing exponent of the "liberal theory" was J. I. Wyer. In a definition that transcended the usual caution of the textbook, he enthusiastically described this theory as one that

> will assume that every library desires to give the fullest possible attention to demands made on its reference service: that it will wish to find or create ways and means to satisfy every questioner. This will be especially true of that part of its work which has to do with the more serious study of its book collections. The only tenable, impregnable theory of reference work is that which frankly recognizes the library's obligation to give this unlimited service, and such a theory squares with practice in commercial and other fields. It is service, not suggestion that is at a premium.[25]

The "liberal theory" of reference service, as expounded by Wyer, actually united three different, if complementary, ideas. In the first place, it maintained that the full and direct supply of reliable information was a perfectly valid objective of the library.[26] In line with this reasoning, the reference librarian's duty would only be fulfilled when he had given the fullest possible consideration to the accuracy of the information and, where possible, to the convenience of the reader.[27]

In the second place, so far from denying to research workers extensive personal assistance on the grounds that they needed no more than access to the materials themselves, the "liberal theory" accorded such patrons special consideration.[28] It thus implied that there should be a differentiation of reference services within a given library on the basis of level of inquiry, with the important corollary that the "research service unit" would be prepared to offer more, not less, assistance.

Finally, the "liberal theory" of reference service embodied the concept of a library assistance that would be "expert," a service that could guarantee the authenticity and relevance of the information it supplied because it was founded on the firm and impeccable scholarship of the library staff. It visualized the existence of a reference corps with a thorough knowledge of the general tools and methods of bibliography, and equipped as well with the competence to handle the esoteric materials of specific subject fields.[29]

Taken as a whole, the "liberal" concept of reference service represented an ideal, rather than a program for immediate action. Few librarians of the twenties and even of the thirties, were prepared to accept the ideal *in toto,* or regarded it as anything but visionary. Wyer himself admitted that there was no immediate prospect of its achievement. He regarded the consummation of the

---

[23] American Library Association, *op. cit.,* II, 112.

[24] *Ibid.,* 120. How far the perceptible shift from the "conservative" to the "moderate" position was occasioned by the demands of the library public itself is uncertain, but A. E. Bostwick reported, perhaps a little resentfully, that there was an "increasing feeling on the part of the consulting public that it is the librarian's business to obtain the desired information from the books where it may be found and furnish it to the inquirer in convenient and proper form for whatever use he may desire to make of it." *(The American Public Library* [4th ed. revised and enlarged; New York: D. Appleton and Company, 1929], p. 73).

[25] Wyer, *op. cit.,* p. 9.

[26] *Ibid.,* p. 10.

[27] *Ibid.,* pp. 106-07.

[28] *Ibid.,* p. 9.

[29] *Ibid.,* pp. 135-38.

"liberal" program as a goal to which the library profession should work, in the meantime proposing the "moderate" program as the irreducible minimum.[30]

But if the liberal program was too big to be swallowed whole, some of its individual parts appeared readily palatable to many librarians. Of these, the idea that gained the greatest degree of acceptance was the belief that the reference librarians in research libraries should be subject specialists. The idea already had mustered considerable support before World War I,[31] and with the passage of time it gained considerably more momentum, the trend being particularly strong after 1930. Peyton Hurt, for instance, stated categorically that "the highest type of library service calls for special knowledge...a general library must be so administered that individual staff members may devote some of their time to work in special fields."[32] The English librarian H. A. Sharp carried away from his tour of American libraries (1936) the definite impression of a strong sentiment in favor of subject specialization.[33] At the close of the period, Shores' informal survey showed that public and university reference librarians considered subject specialization the most important means for the improvement of reference work.[34]

Like many another "cause," subject specialization was subject to a variety of interpretations. The majority viewpoint associated subject specialization with "departmentalization," understanding by the latter term the segregation of the book collections on the basis of subject. The reasoning here was that the librarian in charge of such a "subject department" would combine subject-training with an intimate knowledge of the library's resources in that field and hence would be able to offer expert service.[35] On the other hand, a few librarians, Hurt for one, felt that reference workers in a general library could specialize in the literature and bibliography of particular subject fields without having the unity of the book collection destroyed by the establishment of separate subject departments.[36]

Neither plan of subject specialization necessarily bespoke a policy of extensive assistance to research comparable to that offered in many industrial libraries. Yet, though not synonomous with such a policy, subject specialization was an indispensable preliminary to it. Any thorough-going program of reference service to research workers was necessarily predicated on the ability of the librarian to know the terminology, methods and bibliography of the special field in which the individual research worker was conducting his line of investigation. Indeed, the focal point of the criticism of the reference service usual in the twenties was that no more than superficial aid could be rendered by a reference librarian trying to offer assistance in inquiries encompassing the whole range of knowledge. Learned exposed the inherent contradiction between "general" and "extensive" service in a trenchant statement.

> Many reference agencies that now exist defeat their purpose by placing in charge a staff assigned to the entire universe. Only the vaguest and most casual service can be expected of such "experts." Applicants for information are handled on the principle of turn and turn about, a procedure that is comparable to rotating courses alphabetically among the instructors on a college faculty.[37]

Thus, while no large general library seriously contemplated the inauguration of the full-scale

[30] *Ibid.*, pp. 12-13.

[31] *Supra,* pp. 47-48.

[32] Peyton Hurt, "Staff Specialization: a Possible Substitute for Departmentalization," *Bulletin of the American Library Association,* XXIX (July, 1935), 421.

[33] Henry A. Sharp, "An Impression of American Reference Work," *Library World,* XXXVIII (January, 1936), 159.

[34] Louis Shores, "The Practice of Reference," *College and Research Libraries,* III (December, 1941), 13.

[35] Wyer, *op. cit.,* pp. 199-200; Amy Winslow, "Experiences in Departmentalization," *Bulletin of the American Library Association,* XXVII (December, 1933), 686-87.

[36] Hurt, *op. cit.,* pp. 417-19.

[37] Learned, *op. cit.,* p. 14.

program of service visualized in the "liberal theory," those institutions emphasizing subject specialization at least were heading in the direction of an expanded service. In particular, the plan for "subject departmentation" implied in effect the organization of a network of special libraries within the framework of a general library, and in so doing held out the promise of a special library-like type of reference service.

The Practice of Reference Work in University Libraries

Any attempt to correlate the practice of reference work with the theories espoused in the professional literature of the time must be cautious. The annual reports of the university libraries seldom indicated the policies on which they operated, a fact which gives rise to the suspicion that few had explicitly formulated policies at all. Indeed, it is well known that pragmatic considerations have usually loomed much larger in the administration of university libraries than doctrinaire adherence to any given set of theories.

With these reservations in mind, it is still possible to see the practice of reference work in university libraries as falling into certain broad categories, or levels of service, corresponding roughly to the policies previously described. At one end of such a scale may be grouped the university libraries which, either from deliberate intention or from sheer financial malnutrition, stunted the growth of their reference services to the point where these could show little improvement over their status in the pre-war period.

The Harvard University Library, for example, did "not believe in doing reference work" for its readers.[38] Reference service there did not have the status of a separate department, and, to judge from the scant mention it received in the annual reports, hardly competed in prestige and attention with other library functions such as cataloging and acquisitions. Not until 1939 was there substantial attention given to reference service; then an addition in personnel "made it possible *for the first time* to give to the students help that is comparable to that given in other good colleges."[39]

Much the same situation existed at Cornell University, a separate reference department there being established only as late as 1947.[40] When Wilson, Downs and Tauber surveyed the Cornell University Library in 1947-48, they found that the reference services there had been "relatively undeveloped when compared with reference work in institutions of similar rank," with even such routine activities as bibliographical aid to students and faculty members and compilation of bibliographies being not yet firmly-established functions.[41]

Probably most university libraries, by intention and achievement, belonged on the level of service corresponding to the "moderate theory." This is to say they did not subscribe to a policy of deliberately minimizing assistance but at the same time were forced to temper aspiration to the harsh winds of reality. And reality for university libraries meant the presence of a number of factors — both within and without the library — tending to limit the development of reference services.

A major problem for the libraries, as for every other division of the universities, arose out of the characteristically heterogeneous functions of American higher education. Abraham Flexner caustically described the variegated, even disparate purposes which the American university attempted to fulfill. It was, he showed, at the same time a secondary school, a college for liberal arts training, a graduate and professional school, a research center, and a "service station" for

---

[38] Keyes D. Metcalf, "Harvard Faces Its Library Problems," *Harvard Library Bulletin*, III (Spring, 1949), 191. The statement was made in 1949, but Metcalf clearly implied that the policy was one of long standing at Harvard.

[39] Harvard University Library, *Annual Report for the Year 1938-39 ...*, p. 4.

[40] Louis Round Wilson, Robert Bingham Downs, and Maurice F. Tauber, *Report of a Survey of the Libraries of Cornell University for the Library Board of Cornell University, October, 1947-February, 1948* (Ithaca: Cornell University, 1948), p. 89.

[41] *Ibid.*

the general public.[42] As a service agency, the university library was obliged to cater to all the functions assumed by the parent institution, and like it, found it difficult to achieve signal success in any one of them. University libraries operated study halls, undergraduate reading rooms, and "reserve book rooms" in the interest of the undergraduate teaching program. They engaged, through extension departments, radio programs, and lecture series, in the furtherance of the universities' adult education ventures. They also gave serious recognition to their responsibilities to research, but in the welter of activities, research needs and services could seldom be differentiated to the point of making optimum provision for them.

The problem of catering to a number of diverse groups and purposes was immensely complicated by the sheer numbers involved. The sharp increase in student enrollment after World War I brought a heavy service load which strained the capacities of facilities and staff. Under this pressure of numbers, the research aspirations of the university libraries could scarcely be realized. In a complaint which might have been echoed at any one of a dozen state university libraries, William Warner Bishop of the University of Michigan stated:

> The financial drains of this direct and necessary service to the student body is, therefore, a very serious consideration in planning the distribution of our funds. The problem of proper aid in research work and of providing the necessary books for that vitally important part of the Library's services becomes increasingly difficult with this growth in direct services to readers, by far the greater part of them undergraduates. The money which is required to build up and maintain a competent technical staff of professional librarians is likewise difficult to secure in the face of necessary provision for this heavy use within and without the library building.[43]

What this pressure meant in terms of performance in a specific reference department was well illustrated at the University of Minnesota Library, where the chief reference librarian reported in 1933 that it was seldom possible to have more than a single attendant at a time available for service at the desk.[44] Yet at that time the Minnesota department's six full time librarians plus three pages made it comparatively large as reference staffs went; few university libraries exceeded it.

The result was, of course, that the extent of assistance offered in each case had to be made commensurate with the total volume of demand rather than with the needs of the individual inquirer. As Harold Russell regretfully described the situation at Minnesota: "People who need to get help get as much of it as we can give; if not many people are about, they sometimes get a great deal; if there is a line-up at the desk, an increasingly common state of affairs, only the most casual assistance can be given."[45]

The pressure of numbers came from without, but some difficulties were internal. From necessity or bad management, the time of many university reference departments were dispersed over a bewildering number of activities, often of the purely "housekeeping" kind. A few examples may suffice to illustrate this point. Until 1925 the reference department of the Columbia University Library issued "reserve books."[46] At Yale the reference department at one time or another during this period undertook the following "tasks:" listing of auction catalogs, compiling a cataloging code for manuscripts, accessioning manuscripts, maintaining a catalog of microfilms, compiling a list of Yale theses, assembling books for the "Library of 1742," collecting and mounting items for the

[42]Abraham Flexner, *Universities: American, English, German* (New York: Oxford University Press, 1930), p. 45 and *passim.*

[43]University of Michigan Library, *Report of the General Library,* reprinted from the *President's Report for 1936-37,* p. 13.

[44] University of Minnesota Library, "Report of the University Library...July 1, 1932-June 30, 1933" ("Presented as manuscript"), p. 25.

[45]University of Minnesota Library, "Report of the University Library, July 1, 1935-June 30, 1936," ("Presented as manuscript"), p. 45.

[46]Columbia University Library, "Report of the Reference Department for 1925-26" (Unpublished report), pp. 1-2.

university print collection, and compiling an annual faculty bibliography.[47] Supervision of the monumental reading rooms, used by many students as mere study halls, was an onerous task that fell to the lot of nearly every university reference department.[48]

It is not, of course, implied that all such activities represented a profitless consumption of professional time. But these miscellaneous activities, even when worthy in themselves, indisputably represented a diversion from the main function of providing direct assistance to readers. The comment of Wilson and Swank, made in reference to conditions in the Stanford University Library in 1947, is probably appropriate to the situation in university reference departments in general before 1940. "Its time and energies are dissipated to some extent by too large an aggregate of miscellaneous duties, for example, cataloging the Stanfordia Collection, preparing exhibits, and checking in theses, all of which are jobs that need to be done but not at the expense of direct service to the reader."[49]

The conjunction of these factors seemed to some observers to impose the conclusion that the university libraries' *service* to scholarship was not commensurate with their resources in materials and bibliographical apparatus. Sidney B. Mitchell asserted in 1939: "Are we not still noticeably short of scholarly librarians, of staffs which measure up to their materials for scholarship, of men and women to whom the teaching and research scholars are willing often even to concede a real understanding of scholarship and its requirements, let alone acknowledge them as active aids or participants in productive scholarship?"[50]

Against this catalog of liabilities, many of them, indeed, familiar hold-overs from the pre-war period, must be set the very real evidences of progress. The many agreements for cooperation and division of fields in acquisitions bespoke a retreat from the previous policy of wholesale — often indiscriminate — collecting that had emphasized acquisitions over service. Louis Round Wilson noted hopefully in 1933 that

> scholarly libraries are seriously asking themselves the question whether they might not serve scholarship more adequately by adding experts to their interpreting staffs than by unlimited acquisition of materials. Stricter limitation of fields with greater provision of expert service might easily result in a more fruitful procedure than that usually followed.[51]

An important technical advance in reference work was the notable facilitation of inter-library lending. By compiling union lists, union catalogs and descriptions of regional holdings for easier ascertainment of locations, and by liberalizing regulations for lending, librarians made available to scholars a wealth of resources formerly to be seen (when located at all) only at the cost of a personal visit. In the decade between 1927 and 1937, according to the data supplied by White, inter-library lending involving university libraries increased nearly 100 percent.[52]

Commendation is also due for the sustained and patient effort that went into the preparation of tools to make the libraries' own resources more useful. The Yale University reference department, for instance, compiled a card list of newspaper holdings, an index of obscure but useful bibliographies, and an index to the *Yale University Library Gazette*.[53] At Columbia University, a list of

[47]Yale University Library, *Report of the Librarian, July, 1947-June, 1948*, pp. 16-17.

[48]Yenawine, *op. cit.*, p. 237.

[49]Louis Round Wilson and Raynard C. Swank, *Report of a Survey of the Library of Stanford University for Stanford University, November, 1946-March, 1947...on Behalf of the American Library Association* (Chicago: American Library Association, 1947), p. 95.

[50]Sidney B. Mitchell, "Libraries and Scholarship," in *The Library of Tomorrow, a Symposium*, edited by Emily Miller Danton (Chicago: American Library Association, 1939), p. 69.

[51]Louis Round Wilson, "The Service of Libraries in Promoting Scholarship and Research," *Library Quarterly*, III (April, 1933), 140.

[52]White, *op. cit.*, p. 33.

[53]Yale University Library, *Report of the Librarian, July, 1947-June, 1948*, pp. 16-17.

the special indexes compiled and maintained by the reference department comprised no less than eight pages.[54]

Such technical achievements, while of indisputable value, must be recognized as representing work preparatory to assistance rather than assistance itself. Advances in the character and extent of the direct help given to university research workers are less easily pin-pointed, but there is evidence to indicate that university libraries made substantial progress in this direction as well.

The most fruitful approach, as suggested by the theoretical discussions, lay in the development of subject specialization. A number of schemes, all having in common the basic plan of placing at the disposal of scholars the more knowledgeable service of reference workers trained both in subject matter and in library skills, but varying in the administrative means used to effect this purpose, were tried.

One version, while avoiding physical dispersion of materials and staff, involved the assignment of members of the main library reference department to specific fields of learning. The Iowa State College Library experimented with a plan of this nature, one of its reports noting that individual members of the reference corps had familiarized themselves with the literature of chemistry and veterinary science in order to give special assistance to faculty members in the location of pertinent literature.[55]

Another approach to subject specialization, involving a partial dispersal of the collections, grouped all the materials, both "reference" and "circulating," into a number of broad subject divisions, each of these under the direction of a librarian with advanced training in one of the subject fields of the division. The scheme, generally known as the "divisional plan," offered, according to its chief proponent, Ralph Ellsworth, "highly specialized service" and bibliographic consultation for those "probing about on the frontiers of knowledge."[56]

The "divisional plan," a development of the thirties, received only a limited try-out in the period under review and then only in smaller universities such as Brown, Colorado and Nebraska. In any case, by the thirties, the larger university libraries were, by tradition, geography, and size, committed to a plan of "departmental" and "collegiate" libraries, and the development of a subject-specialized reference service proceeded perforce within that framework.

Generalizations about the status of reference work in American university departmental libraries during this period can only be few and hazardous, the range in extent and quality of service being exceptionally broad. In many instances there was quite simply *no* reference service, the administration of the libraries being left in the hands of stenographer-librarians with neither the training nor the time to do more than maintain a nominal supervision over the collection.[57]

By contrast, Walter Hausdorfer's survey of forty-seven university departmental and professional school libraries in 1938 showed that all libraries reporting gave reference service, that they considered it their most important activity, and that most of the new activities initiated between 1933 and 1935 were specifically aimed at increasing the scope and quality of their reference service.[58] Hausdorfer clearly implied, though with no conclusive evidence to back the claim, that the quality of assistance rendered in such departmental libraries, because of the specialized subject knowledge of

---

[54]Columbia University Library, "Annual Report of the Reference Department, 1932-1933" (Unpublished report), pp. 30-38.

[55]Iowa State College, *Twenty Year Development Program; Part I: Proposed for the General Administration* (Ames, Iowa: 1935), p. 91.

[56]Ralph C. Ellsworth, "Colorado University's Divisional Reading Room Plan: Description and Evaluation," *College and Research Libraries*, II (March, 1941), 107, 192.

[57]See, for example, Cornell University Library, *Librarian's Report, 1926-27*, p. 5; Columbia University Library, "Report of the Applied Science Library for 1927-28" (Unpublished report), p. 4.

[58]Walter Hausdorfer, *Professional School and Departmental Libraries* (New York: Special Libraries Association, 1939), p. 16.

the librarians and their intimate acquaintance with the collections in their charge, was higher than was normally obtainable from general reference departments.[59]

Hausdorfer's survey did not report any specific illustrations of actual performance in departmental libraries, but undoubtedly the best examples of really extensive service came from those departmental libraries possessing collections sufficiently notable to warrant the appointment of librarians who were themselves recognized scholars. Thus the Williams L. Clements Library at the University of Michigan, the Missionary Research Library at the Union Theological Seminary, and the Hoover Library at Stanford University were able to place at the disposal of inquirers staffs competent to ferret out answers to the most elusive and esoteric questions in their respective fields.[60]

On the other hand, even in these outstanding departmental libraries, extensive assistance seems to have been usually available only for correspondents, with inquirers using the library in person being expected to shift pretty much for themselves.[61] In general, the assistance available in departmental libraries, if presumably more "expert" than in general reference departments, apparently was not carried any further. Hausdorfer thus reported that the usual procedure followed by departmental librarians in the institutions he surveyed was to give the inquirer "a few books or pamphlets," or to direct him to the subject headings in the catalog that promised the best leads for his investigation.[62] In most cases the departmental librarians did not go so far as to provide abstracts or to prepare reports, for, the survey claimed, there was "neither time nor demand for that sort of service."[63]

These facts bespeak the overall conclusion that the typical development of reference services in university libraries during the 1917-1940 period was one of only moderate progress. The chief positive accomplishment was the definite acceptance of reference work as a primary function of the university library, directed not only toward offering occasional guidance but frankly including the direct supply of information as well. This shift from a "conservative" to a "moderate" position was also accompanied by a considerable qualitative improvement in the work of the reference staff, brought about by the emphasis on subject specialization, and visible at its best in the ability of many departmental librarians to handle questions involving considerable specialized knowledge. On the other hand, the problems of support and organization remained numerous and vexing, notably the means whereby to differentiate service to faculty members from the numerically more pressing demands of undergraduate students. On the whole, the reference service of the typical university library remained general, and because general, limited in scope.

Reference Work in Public Libraries

The existence of numerous factors tending to impede the development of reference service in university libraries gave to that development the appearance of a halting advance by tug-of-war. For public libraries the going was smoother, if not necessarily more rapid. They did not, for instance, have to contend with the problem of divided administrative control, which, for the universities, made the departmental library seem a questionable medium for the achievement of subject specialization. Similarly, in public libraries the claims made by the acquisition function for attention and money offered considerably less competition for reference service than they did in university libraries, where eminence often tended to be equated with size of collections. Finally, the public librarian bore little or no responsibility for instruction in the use of the library, and was

---

[59] *Ibid.*

[60] Hollis W. Hering, "The Research Library and the Research Librarian," *Special Libraries*, XXII (January, 1931), 9-11; University of Michigan, William L. Clements Library, "The William L. Clements Library of American History," in *The President's Report for the Year 1928-1929*, p. 202; Stanford University Library, "Director of University Libraries," in *Annual Report of the President of Stanford University for the Forty-first Academic Year Ending August 31, 1932*, p. 357.

[61] Hering, *op. cit.*, p. 9.

[62] Hausdorfer, *op. cit.*, p. 38.

[63] *Ibid.*, pp. 38-39.

free to develop a direct information service with none of the university librarian's nagging doubts about the threat posed by such service to the self-development of the inquirers. The *Survey of Libraries in the United States* made it clear that relatively few public libraries regarded themselves as teaching agencies, any definite efforts to instruct the adult readers in the use of the catalog or of reference books being made normally only at the specific request of the readers.[64]

On the other hand, public libraries could not escape from certain problems in the organization and provision of reference service that were common to all general research libraries. The problem of numbers — the sheer volume of work to be done for a clientele extending into the thousands — was probably even more acute for the public libraries of metropolitan cities than it was for the university libraries. The sharp increase in public library patronage after the first World War,[65] followed by the further increases of the depression decade, placed the reference departments under a continuous, at times almost intolerable, strain, which inevitably had an adverse effect on the quality of service. When, as in the case of the New York Public Library, the congestion was often so severe as to place the mere possession of a seat in the reading rooms at a premium, the director could legitimately complain that "this crowded condition has seriously impeded the work of several investigators of real importance."[66]

While such congestion affected all phases of public library reference service, it hit hardest at the work of the specialized divisions, which found it difficult to maintain high standards of assistance when operating at a "double-time" tempo. A report of the Economics Division of the New York Public Library made plain the dilemma of a division trying to offer expert service, when confronted by demands of a number calling for mass production methods. "Reference assistants, obliged to help nearly a hundred and fifty thousand visitors during the year, to answer inquiries over three telephone lines in constant use, and to look up the answers to letters from many states and foreign countries, are distressingly unable to give visitors the amount of personal attention they are entitled to expect in a special division where even experienced students can not hope to find all they want without the aid of someone familiar with the collection."[67]

To counteract such difficulties, public libraries took certain administrative measures to ensure better accommodation and attention for serious inquirers. One means was to concentrate the scholarly materials and the subject specialists in the main building, leaving to the branches the main responsibility for home loans of popular books and the simpler sort of reference work. The adoption of this type of arrangement, already evident before 1916, became an all but universal feature of public library operation in the post-war period.[68]

The division of fields between main and branch libraries achieved only a rough separation of "learned" from "popular" in reference service.[69] Within the central buildings, certain additional measures looking toward a further differentiation of types of reference service were employed. As in certain university libraries,[70] the maintenance of an "information desk" was a popular and

---

[64]American Library Association, *op. cit.*, II, 110.

[65]The number of readers served in the Reference Department of the New York Public Library in 1920 was 20 per cent greater than in 1919. ("Report of the New York Public Library for 1920," *Bulletin of the New York Public Library*, XXV [April, 1921], 201.)

[66]"Report of the New York Public Library for 1921," *Bulletin of the New York Public Library*, XXVI (April, 1922), 249.

[67]"Report of the New York Public Library for the Year 1938," *Bulletin of the New York Public Library*, XLIII (March, 1939), 249.

[68]In the Boston Public Library and in the New York Public Library, the distinction formed the basis for the official administrative organization, the "reference department" being synonymous with main library (i.e. scholarly) service, and the "circulation department" with branch (i.e. popular) service. Cf. in this connection, Boston Public Library, *Eighty-second Annual Report...1933*, pp. 28-29.

[69]The main libraries were, of course, always open to "general" as well as "serious" readers, though the New York Public Library did find it necessary to impose certain restrictions on the use of its main building by college students. ("Report of the New York Public Library for 1930," *Bulletin of the New York Public Library*, XXXV [June, 1931], 340).

[70]Cf. Ruth M. Erlandson, "An Analysis of the Work of the Information Desk at the University of Illinois," *College and Research Libraries*, V (December, 1943), 36-43; Iowa State College Library, *Report, 1935-1937*, p. 8.

effective device for relieving reference departments from the burdensome chore of dealing with a multitude of minor requests. As described in the *Survey of Libraries in the United States,* the services available from the "information desk" usually included one or more of the following: giving general information concerning the library's organization, physical arrangement, and regulations; help in the use of the catalog and in the selection of desired books; and a simple reference service confined to questions which could be answered with the help of a few "ready reference books" immediately at hand.[71] Since most requests received by public libraries actually were of the above types, the resultant saving in reference departments' time could be considerable, a saving which might be applied to the more consequential inquiries. Thus the Cleveland Public Library, reviewing the first year's work of its Information Service, found the results highly satisfactory. In handling a mass of questions "irrelevant to reference work," the Service had left the regular reference divisions free for "more purely bibliographical work."[72]

Another administrative arrangement for the differentiation of reference service by type of request was the institution of "readers' advisory services." As distinguished from reference work in the ordinary sense, a "readers' advisory service" aims at assisting readers in the choice of materials for reading or study; the emphasis in the former is on supplying information or sources of information, in the latter on helping to select materials appropriate to the reader's program of self-education and development.[73] So long as no special provisions for the latter service existed, public library reference departments were called upon to serve both types of requests. However, from about 1925 on, separate departments or sub-departments for "readers' advisory services" tended to be established in the large public libraries.[74] These departments had then the effect of drawing off from the reference corps a considerable part of the service load which it had formerly been forced to carry, and thus, like the "information desks," made possible a greater concentration of reference librarians' time and attention for the service of research.

At best, however, such contributions were only negative and potential. The existence of an "information desk" and a "readers' advisory service" meant that the reference librarians did *not* have to take care of certain minor or subsidiary tasks and *could* give closer attention to serious informational inquiries. It did not of itself assure superior service. Positively, the only way to ensure a higher standard of service to scholars was to make the assistance rendered more knowledgeable and more thorough. For public libraries, as for university libraries, this meant subject specialization in reference service.

Since decentralization of collections and personnel posed no threat to the administrative unity of the public library, the usual method taken to achieve subject specialization in reference service was "subject departmentalization." Subject departmentalization was either partial or complete. In the former case only a few subject areas, most commonly technology and science, fine arts, business, genealogy and history,[75] were given separate departmental status. When "complete," all fields of knowledge were encompassed within one or another of the subject divisions, with the general reference department, if existing at all, having only very general functions of liaison, referral and "information desk" service.

Most major public libraries went only so far as partial subject departmentalization, retaining functional (i.e. circulation, reference) divisions, and occasionally form and language divisions (periodicals, prints, et cetera) as well. However, six large public libraries carried the principle of subject departmentalization to its ultimate end by adopting plans of complete subject departmentalization. In the public libraries of Cleveland, Baltimore (Enoch Pratt), Los Angeles, Rochester,

---

[71] American Library Association, *op. cit.,* II, 104-08.

[72] Cleveland Public Library, *Fifty-sixth Annual Report; April 1, 1924-March 31, 1925 and Fifty-seventh Annual Report, April 1, 1925-December 31, 1925,* p. 38.

[73] Hutchins, *op. cit.,* pp. 180-81.

[74] J. M. Flexner, *Circulation Work in Public Libraries* (Chicago: American Library Association, 1927), pp. 189-90.

[75] E. W. McDiarmid and John McDiarmid, *The Administration of the American Public Library* (Urbana: The American Library Association and the University of Illinois Press, 1943), p. 81 (Table 10).

Worcester and Toledo, each subject department combined in the one unit all of the library's resources in that area, and was responsible for both reference and circulation service.[76]

The presumption behind the establishment of subject departments was that the librarian in charge, bringing to the position an already comprehensive knowledge of the field and its methods, could, by continued close contact with the collections and clientele, increase that knowledge to the point where it assured expert service for even highly technical inquiries.[77] Probably the generally admitted difficulty of obtaining personnel of the requisite competence held the usual level of practice somewhat below the level contemplated by the theory, but at their best public library subject departments could offer examples of outstanding service. The Technology Department of the Carnegie Public Library at Pittsburgh was, in Spratt's estimation, one of the finest special libraries in its field.[78] The Business Information Bureau of the Cleveland Public Library was able to undertake questions involving considerable technical knowledge and research, including the critical examination of data.[79]

The subject divisions of the large public libraries also could claim credit for a great deal of high-caliber bibliographical work,[80] but most of the extensive bibliographies were prepared only for publication — that is, for the benefit of scholarship at large rather than for the benefit of an individual inquirer. In general, public libraries continued to adhere rather closely to the traditional policy of not making extensive bibliographies, abstracts, summary reports, or literature searches on the grounds that service could not be furnished to one reader that could not be furnished to all.[81]

Exceptions were commonly made only in the case of inquiries received by correspondence, and for the government officials served by the municipal reference libraries. Presumably in the case of requests by correspondence the fact that the inquirer was in a position of greater dependence on the library's help motivated the libraries to go somewhat further in their assistance than usual. The municipal reference libraries were, of course, organized in the first instance to provide especially comprehensive assistance to a specific clientele.[82]

It is clear then that the public library did not greatly change its practice in reference service in terms of *extent* of assistance, as distinguished from its *quality*. The passage of time had brought an increasing interest in and concern for assistance to research and a perceptible gain in competence attendant upon the growth of subject specialization, but no comparable development in range of service. As public institutions, the public libraries could not favor one group of readers over the rest, and when the clientele numbered many thousands, there was no hope of obtaining the financial resources to provide unlimited service for all. The public library could offer the scholar reliable, sometimes expert assistance, but so long as it received no special funds for service to research, its assistance remained limited in extent.[83]

[76] *Ibid.*, p. 74.

[77] *Supra*, p. 78.

[78] H. Philip Spratt, *Libraries for Scientific Research in Europe and America* (London: Grafton, 1936), pp. 183-86.

[79] Rose Vormelker, "The Business Information Bureau," *Special Libraries*, XXIII (July-August, 1932), 300.

[80] E.g., *Business Information Sources; Bulletin of the Business Information Bureau, Cleveland Public Library* (1930-   ); Newark Public Library, Business Branch, *The Business Bookshelf; a List Based on Use*, compiled by Marian C. Manley and Mary E. Hunt... (Newark: The Public Library, 1935).

[81] Cf. Marian C. Manley, *Public Library Service to Business; a Comparative Study of its Development in Cities of 70,000 and More* (Newark: Newark Public Library, 1942), p. 4; Vormelker, *op. cit.*, p. 301.

[82] *Supra*, p. 60.

[83] Cf. "Report of the New York Public Library for the Year 1936," *Bulletin of the New York Public Library*, XLI (March, 1937), 204.

Chapter VIII

"RESEARCH SERVICE" IN THE GENERAL LIBRARY BEFORE WORLD WAR II

The Pressure for Research Service

The greatest deficiency in the usual practice of reference service in general research libraries was the lack of special provision for scholars. Serving groups of readers whose needs were exceedingly diverse, reference departments naturally tended to subordinate service to the research group in the interest of the far more numerous general readers.

To this "argument of numbers" was added the support of the familiar reasoning which held that the scholar did not want or require special service, and that in any case the librarian was really incapable of supplying effective assistance. Harold Moulton, for example, doubted that librarians were competent to do even "fact-finding" in his own field of the social sciences.[1] Similarly, H. J. Webber, an agricultural scientist, described the librarian's role as only that of the "skilled mechanic charged with the duty of keeping the tools in serviceable condition."[2]

To have accepted this reasoning at its face value would have been tantamount to condemning reference service to a permanent position of mediocrity. Some librarians were unwilling to accept such a limitation upon their role and preferred to see in service to research a challenge and an opportunity for wider usefulness.[3] Probably some of their statements were moved largely by the desire to gain for librarians the extra prestige that would come from closer association with the faculty. Even so, they were not without a certain importance, for whether emanating out of sheer self-interest or from altruistic ideals of service, the aspirations of the librarians themselves to become accepted as collaborators in scholarship did help to produce an environment favorable to experimentation in research service.

More convincing arguments came from those who added logic to ardor. William E. Henry, librarian of the University of Washington, based his advocacy of extensive reference service for scholars on the benefits to be gained by the scholars themselves. He hit especially hard at the old assumption that it was somehow wrong for the scholar to delegate any large part of his work to others, as though the value of a study were to be measured by the personal labor of its author.

> We have expected our professors and our advanced investigators to seek out their own bibliographical references, to list them, and to organize them. Upon the whole, this means doing a great deal of hard labor that is in no sense a test, and shows no triumph in skill, in the work that distinguishes the scholar and investigator.... Men with special scholarly tendencies should be relieved of all the drudgery that is not an essential part of their work in organizing material and concentrating it toward their theses.[4]

Henry evidently did not question the ability of the scholar to do his own bibliographical work. However, some research men themselves pointed out that the bibliographical competence of the scholar was actually questionable, that he had to look to the librarian not merely for relief from

---

[1]Harold G. Moulton, "The Special Library and Research," *Special Libraries,* XIX (September, 1928), 227.

[2]H. J. Webber, "The Relation of a Research Worker to the Librarian," *Bulletin of the American Library Association,* XXIV (September, 1930), 377.

[3]E.g. Edith M. Coulter, "The University Librarian: His Preparation, Position and Relation to the Academic Department of the University," *Bulletin of the American Library Association,* XVI (May, 1922), 272; John Boynton Kaiser, "Newer Functions of University Libraries," *Library Journal,* LI (March 1, 1926), 220.

[4]William E. Henry, *Five Objectives of a University Library* (Seattle: University of Washington, 1927), pp. 14-15.

"drudgery," but also for the added increment that would come from the librarian's superior knowledge of bibliographic procedure. The assistant dean of the Harvard School of Business candidly confessed his own inability to undertake the more difficult literature searches, and expressed his appreciation at being able to delegate the task to his departmental librarian.[5] A. C. Noé stated flatly that few natural scientists had the language ability to conduct a literature search of any real magnitude, especially when the subject involved a cross-divisional approach. He urged the formation of special bibliographic departments in university libraries to assist scholars in ascertaining data, especially in fields outside their own narrow specialties.[6]

A similar combination of logical arguments and research workers' demands had led to the provision of extensive reference services in industrial research libraries.[7] The fact that industry had found it profitable to support such service in turn supplied an additional argument for its being furnished to academic research workers. A survey of land-grant colleges and universities reported:

> Many commercial concerns have found the extensive employment of librarians in their research departments desirable. Much of the searching and abstracting... in these commercial firms is done by librarians. The DuPont Co. is spending for library services for its research departments more than $100,000 per year. Unless these services were commercially valuable, the money would not be so used. Libraries of educational institutions might well render part of the service now offered by libraries of many commercial corporations.[8]

Neither the validity nor the number of such statements should obscure the obvious fact that they never constituted more than a minority opinion. Most scholars and librarians were much more cognizant of the need for books and buildings than they were of the need for additional service.[9] Nevertheless, these statements did indicate the existence of a body of opinion advocating that general research libraries provide expert and extensive assistance designed specifically for the research clientele. As a ferment for change, it paved the way for new departures in reference service in the general research library.

Service to Research Workers in Endowed Reference Libraries

The best argument for the provision of extensive assistance to scholars was, of course, its successful application in actual practice. By 1930 a number of precedents for service of this type (other than in the industrial research libraries) were already available in the work of certain endowed reference libraries, notably the John Crerar and Newberry Libraries of Chicago, and the Huntington Library of San Marino, California.

These endowed reference libraries were all general libraries in that they were available to the general public, but the fact that their collections were highly specialized and limited to use on the

---

[5]John C. Baker, "The Place of the Baker Library in the Harvard Business School," *Special Libraries*, XXVI (September, 1935), 201.

[6]A. C. Noé, "The University Library and Research," *Library Quarterly*, IV (April, 1934), 300-01. Unfortunately, no reliable data were available to indicate the exact extent of scholars' bibliographic competence. However, Hurt's study, showing that advanced graduate students had little knowledge of bibliography or of library search techniques, supported the belief that the testimony cited above had not exaggerated the scholars' need of library assistance. (Peyton Hurt, "The Need of College and University Instruction in Use of the Library," *Library Quarterly*, IV [July, 1934], 436-41).

[7]*Supra*, pp. 67-69.

[8]U. S. Office of Education, *Survey of Land-Grant Colleges and Universities*, directed by Arthur J. Klein ("Bulletin," 1930, No. 9; Washington: Government Printing Office, 1930), I, 642.

[9]*Ibid.*, p. 645.

premises tended to restrict their patronage to the scholarly group.[10] In other words, they could effectively concentrate attention on research service to an extent not ordinarily possible in libraries serving a more heterogeneous clientele.

Serving research as their chief *raison d'être,* the endowed reference libraries gave scholars preferential treatment. The Newberry Library reported: "For some research workers we have spent many hours, even days. As this is essentially a research library of source material, we feel justified on proper occasions in going to great lengths to assist a scholar."[11] At the Huntington Library, the official policy was "to be of assistance wherever possible, ...time and trouble are not to be spared, if the contribution is one that will serve the advancement of learning."[12]

Similarly, J. Christian Bay of the John Crerar Library averred that the regular policy in his reference department was to go to considerable lengths, when necessary, to produce a satisfactory answer to scholarly inquiries. He recalled such instances of extensive assistance as the preparation of a history of submarine boats, a survey of some five hundred papers on the absorption of calcium in animal metabolism, and a critical bibliography on the poisonous fishes of the tropics.[13]

This sense of obligation to scholarship was particularly manifest in those queries which drew upon the parts of the collection in which the libraries might claim to be pre-eminent. In such instances the libraries were disposed to regard themselves as "courts of last resort." On the legitimate assumption that the information requested was not likely to be available elsewhere, they provided assistance of an extra measure of thoroughness. Thus the custodian of the Ayer collection at the Newberry Library, notable for its holdings of Americana, reported himself constantly being pressed into service to answer inquiries (chiefly by correspondence) relating to the identification of editions, appraisal of rarities, and verification of historical data.[14]

In the same way, the Huntington Library came to serve as a sort of national information center for inquiries in the field of British and American civilization, and the John Carter Brown Library for questions in its special field of American history before 1820.[15] Many of these questions required highly specialized and expert knowledge from the library staffs. Among the instances of assistance reported by the Huntington Library were such tasks as collating the text of a published work with the original manuscript,[16] and deciphering illegible manuscripts by means of microscope and ultra-violet rays.[17] The John Carter Brown Library was often called upon to identify issues and make collations of rare books in its collections, and the eminence of its librarian in American historical scholarship brought him many requests for advice on research topics.[18]

[10] The Reference Department of the New York Public Library, though probably the most notable endowed reference library in the United States, does not fit in with this generalization. Its collections are general in scope and its patronage is heterogeneous. In many respects the New York Public Library, like the Library of Congress, is simply *sui generis.*

[11] American Library Association, *A Survey of Libraries in the United States ...* (Chicago: American Library Association, 1926-27), II, 121.

[12] Henry E. Huntington Library and Art Gallery, *First Annual Report, July 1, 1927-June 30, 1928,* p. 19.

[13] John Crerar Library, The *John Crerar Library, 1895-1944; a Historical Report Prepared ...by the Librarian, J. Christian Bay* (Chicago: The John Crerar Library, 1945), p. 172.

[14] Newberry Library, *Report of the Trustees ...for the Year 1923,* pp. 24-25.

[15] Henry E. Huntington Library and Art Gallery, *Seventh Annual Report, July 1, 1933-June 30, 1934,* p. 17; Lawrence Wroth, *The First Century of the John Carter Brown Library; a History with a Guide to the Collections* (Providence: Associates of the John Carter Brown Library, 1946), pp. 82-83.

[16] Henry E. Huntington Library and Art Gallery, *Third Annual Report, July 1, 1929-June 30, 1930,* p. 20.

[17] Anthony Gabler, "The Huntington Library from a Reference Angle," *Bulletin of the American Library Association,* XXVII (December 15, 1933), 689.

[18] John Carter Brown Library, *Report to the Corporation of Brown University, July 1, 1921,* p. 2; *Report to the Corporation of Brown University, July 1, 1925,* pp. 3-4.

The Library of Congress
and "Interpretive Service" for Research

The endowed reference libraries had the advantage of operating under circumstances which tended to limit their patronage to the research group. The problem of providing specialized service for scholars when these were far out-numbered by general readers was more difficult. In the Library of Congress and in the university libraries, such service could be achieved only as the result of special ventures, more or less frankly labeled as experimental.

Up to about 1927 the pattern of reference services in the Library of Congress remained essentially that established in the pre-war period. The lack of progress was pointed out by the Librarian of Congress himself. A great research library, declared Putnam, ought to provide for investigators comprehensive collections, ample physical facilities, an adequate bibliographic apparatus, and finally, "human aid in the interpretation of collections." In the first three respects he professed himself well satisfied with the development of the Library of Congress; in the last, it was still deficient.[19]

Technically, Putnam explained, the work of the reference librarians and bibliographers was proficient enough, but it was a proficiency directed toward and adequate for only the general reader, not the scholar. What was needed for service to scholarship, he claimed, was the extra measure of assistance that could come from library staff members who could add to familiarity with the library apparatus a really strong subject knowledge. "In brief, the aid needed by the investigator is an interpretation of the collections and of the apparatus by someone having also an understanding of the subject matter; and it is clear that this involves a special knowledge of the field quite outside of the technique which attends to the orderly treatment of the material and the construction of the apparatus of use."[20]

The wording of this statement was somewhat deceptive and unfortunate, for it implied that professional librarians as a class were inherently only technicians who could claim no close knowledge of the content of books. Actually, the idea that reference librarians should command a real competence in one or more subject fields was already a commonplace. In fact, as previously seen, by 1927 many public and university libraries were already committed to some form of subject specialization in reference work. Elsewhere, Putnam was more careful not to overemphasize the novelty of his proposal for "interpretive service," describing it more accurately as the perfectly natural extension of the tendency and purpose common to all research libraries.[21]

Putnam's proposal did however envisage two important differences from the usual plan of subject specialization: the specialist assistance was to be directed specifically, even exclusively, in the interest of the scholarly readers, and it was to be provided by personnel who had not merely some familiarity with the subject matter but were themselves recognized experts in the subject field. In other words, it was to be a "super-service" — assistance by scholars on behalf of scholars.

His idea was simple and logical enough, but the mechanics of its implementation were unusually complicated. Putnam had little expectation that the federal government would support a service going beyond the conventional type and turned to non-governmental sources for funds to institute it. Actually, the chance accrual of outside funds preceded and may well have germinated the whole idea of "interpretive service." In 1924, Mrs. Elizabeth Sprague Coolidge had set up an endowment fund for the promotion of musical activities by the Library of Congress. One of the incidental features of the gift was the assignment of an annual honorarium to the chief of the Music Division, this stipend to be over and above his regular salary. The officially-stated purposes of this honorarium were to recognize the additional responsibilities imposed on the chief by the promotional activities due under the endowment, and to "assure in the position an expert of the requisite competence."[22]

---

[19] Herbert Putnam, "Interpretive Service in a Library for Research," in *Overbibliotekar Wilhelm Munthe Pa Femtiarsdagen 20. Oktober 1933 Fra Fagfeller Og Venner* (Oslo: Grøndahl & Søns Boktrykeri, 1933), p. 211.

[20] *Ibid.*, pp. 211-12.

[21] Herbert Putnam, "Consultants at the National Library," *Library Quarterly*, I (January, 1931), 21.

[22] U. S. Library of Congress, *Report of the Librarian of Congress for the Fiscal Year Ending June 30, 1928.*, p. 335.

The Coolidge gift seems to have suggested to Putnam the possibility of the Library's obtaining a whole series of endowments for the support of specialist positions. The parallel with university endowments led him to call these positions "chairs." A "chair," he explained, was not a "teaching chair" or a "research chair," but an "interpretive chair," — "whose incumbent will combine with administrative duties an active aid and counsel to those pursuing research in the Library and general promotion of research in his field."[23]

In 1926-1927, the Library of Congress received grants of $75,000 each from William Evarts Benjamin and the Carnegie Corporation of New York for the maintenance of "chairs" in American history and fine arts respectively, the income going for the payment of extra stipends to the chiefs of the Manuscripts Division and the Prints Division. Subsequently, endowments were secured for the support of chairs in aeronautics (1930), geography (1933), and Hispanica (1939). The incumbents in each case were the chiefs of the appropriate Library divisions, who retained their normal administrative responsibilities. The extra stipends forthcoming from the endowments were in recognition of the presumably additional service of "interpretation," which these subject specialists were expected to contribute over and above their regular service in the division.[24]

The five chairs covered only a small part of the whole field of learning. Putnam's aim was to place on the staff a specialist for each of the major subject areas. To this end he recruited a corps of "consultants," to supplement the work of the "chair" holders. Like the latter, the "consultants" were subject specialists expected to provide "interpretive service," and paid from endowment funds. However, the "consultants" were to bear no administrative responsibilities. They were recruited chiefly from the ranks of retired professors, and received no stipend other than small honoraria.[25] The first consultantship was made possible by Archer Milton Huntington's grant of $50,000 to provide service for the field of Hispanic literature. Subsequent grants provided for the establishment of similar consultantships for European history, church history, archaeology, philosophy, sociology, economics, political science, pure science, and poetry.[26]

The system of consultantships was expanded by the addition of "honorary consultants," these being scholars resident in Washington who were willing to serve the Library of Congress without payment.[27] Among the fields of learning eventually covered by the honorary consultants were bibliography, military history, geography, Chinese history, paleography, and Roman law.[28]

Even with the addition of consultants and honorary consultants, the subject fields for which specialist service was available at the Library of Congress never came close to encompassing the whole range of knowledge. This fact points up the chief weakness of the scheme as it actually operated — its wholly patchwork and "occasional" nature. Despite Putnam's rather grandiose, prospectus-like announcement of a highly expert service for all important fields, the "interpretive service" always remained limited to the relatively few subjects which chanced to draw the support of a subsidy, or of a scholar willing to serve as an honorary consultant.

The fact that the financial support for the scheme of special research service came wholly from funds outside the regular library budget probably accounted for another weakness — its poor articulation with the Library's regular reference service. The consultants were only part-time employees of the Library. Since by the terms of their appointment they had no regular duties, their participation in the work of assistance was almost entirely dependent upon chance contact, or the degree to which a query might arouse their personal interest.

[23] *Ibid.*, p. 336.

[24] *Ibid.*, pp. 337-38.

[25] *Ibid.*, p. 3.

[26] U. S. Library of Congress, *Report of the Librarian of Congress for the Fiscal Year Ending June 30, 1937.*, p. 4.

[27] U. S. Library of Congress, *Report of the Librarian of Congress for the Fiscal Year Ending June 30, 1930*, pp. 17-18.

[28] David C. Mearns, *The Story up to Now; the Library of Congress, 1800-1946,* reprinted from the *Report of the Librarian of Congress for . . . 1946* (Washington: 1947), pp. 203-04.

For that matter, there was nothing in their terms of employment to indicate that the consultants were to direct attention solely, even primarily, on the work of "interpretation." Much of their time went into such tasks as analysis of the Library's holdings, compilation of lists of desirable purchases, even the pursuit of private research. Indeed, the duties involved in the tenure of consultant-ships were so vague as not to preclude absence from Washington itself. Thus, in reference to the consultant in poetry, Putnam stated: "As in the case of other consultants, the service to us will not preclude those other interests, [i.e. private interests] nor in his case necessitate continuous residence in Washington, as his service to the public will be largely by correspondence or in the field."[29]

The incumbents of "chairs" were, of course, members of the regular library staff; in each case they served as chiefs of the appropriate library divisions. But except in the case of the "chairs" for aeronautics and Hispanica, the holders of the "chairs" were already serving in precisely that same capacity before the inauguration of the "chairs." It is impossible in these circumstances not to cast serious doubts on Putnam's claim that the installation of these "chairs" represented an important extension of the Library's reference service to research. It seems highly unlikely that, say, the chief of the Maps Division was willing or able to lend any more extensive or more expert assistance to inquirers than previously simply because the endowment of a chair in geography had brought him an extra stipend. What the endowment funds did do, by providing more funds for the same work, was to enable the Library of Congress to pay its highly qualified division chiefs enough money to retain their services.[30] The "chairs" certainly performed a worthwhile function by preventing the dispersal of some of the Library's most valued personnel. Whether they represented a real step forward in the development of its reference services is much more problematical.

Such criticism does not negate the positive contributions made by the venture in "interpretive service to research." The "chairs" for aeronautics and Hispanica did constitute a definite increment to the Library's facilities for assistance, no special service for these fields having been previously available. Moreover, intermittent and occasional as their help was, the consultants were often able to render useful service. Martin Roberts, the head of the Reading Rooms staff, described some of the ways in which they helped the Library and its patrons:

> The aid rendered by the consultants is of diverse character. They discuss with the investigator his problem, interpret our collections, point out likely sources of information and material, furnish highly specialized information by correspondence, clear up important lacunae in our collection by recommendations for purchase, cooperate in advising as to specialized lists of references, suggest methods of procedure besides advising as to matters of style in the preparation of manuscripts, and in many instances exert a profound influence through constructive criticism.[31]

Perhaps the greatest benefit arising out of the whole venture in "interpretive service for research" was indirect. It seems to have brought as a by-product a noticeably heightened emphasis on reference service in the already existing special divisions. From about 1929 on, nearly every division in the Library included in its annual report a special section on "service," in which there were presented instances of notable assistance furnished to investigators, and often requests for an augmented and better trained reference staff.[32]

One effect of this library-wide expansion of the work of assistance was a substantial increase in

---

[29] U. S. Library of Congress, *Report of the Librarian of Congress for the Fiscal Year Ending June 30, 1937.*, p. 4.

[30] Owing to the low level at which such positions were classified in the federal personnel plan, the usual salary limit for division chiefs in 1928 was only $4,400. The added stipend coming from the "chair" funds made the total salary competitive with the university positions to which these specialists might otherwise have been attracted, and thus held for the Library its top-caliber personnel. (U. S. Library of Congress, *Report of the Librarian of Congress for the Fiscal Year Ending June 30, 1928.*, pp. 336-337).

[31] U. S. Library of Congress, *Report of the Librarian of Congress for the Fiscal Year Ending June 30, 1931.*, p. 379.

[32] Cf. U. S. Library of Congress, *Report of the Librarian of Congress for the Fiscal Year Ending June 30, 1928*, p. 85; *Report...for...1930*, p. 148; *Report...for...1933*, pp. 88, 135; *Report...for...1934*, p. 103; *Report...for...1935*, p. 127; *Report...for...1936*, pp. 125-26.

the number of investigators using the Library. Particularly striking was the fact that many agencies doing group research maintained whole staffs of research workers in more or less continuous residence at the Library of Congress during the course of their research.[33] Martin Roberts was confident that the "unusual increase" in scholarly patronage bore a "close relationship" to the improvement and enlargement in reference service, and mentioned the "appreciative acknowledgments that came from the investigators" for the services rendered by the staff and consultants.[34]

Such appreciation gave considerable validation to the essential principle behind the whole venture in "interpretive service" — the idea that mature scholars would benefit by a program of expert reference service designed specifically for them. Unfortunately, in practice the experiment in research was bogged down by a needlessly complicated apparatus of "chairs" and "consultantships," and hindered by the general lack of coordination characteristic of the Library's operations at that time.[35] The "interpretive service" also suffered from a considerable vagueness in definition, it never being made quite clear just what forms of assistance were comprised in the term. Nevertheless, "interpretive service" at the Library of Congress did represent a real advance in reference service in general research libraries, in so far as at least the professed intention was to carry one stage further and in a new dimension the role of library assistance. If the practice fell considerably short of the full implementation of this ideal, it achieved at least enough to demonstrate its potentialities.

"Research Librarians" in University Libraries

By virtue of its size and its position as the national library, the Library of Congress is unique among American libraries, and therefore its procedures are seldom wholly appropriate to other libraries. Putnam's venture in "interpretive service" did arouse considerable interest but had little direct influence. When the university libraries came in their turn to experiment with research service, their undertakings shared with the Library of Congress' scheme the basic objective of providing fuller, more effective assistance to research workers, but the forms of organization were quite different.

As earlier described, the pressure for research service came from scholars as well as librarians. Accordingly it is not surprising that the prime mover in the most important plan for research service in university libraries was a scholar — significantly, a natural scientist. Dr. Harlow Shapley, the well-known astronomer at Harvard, had come to the conclusion that humanistic and social science research in the universities was badly organized, with the scholars themselves having to do far more work than was necessary or desirable.

In the natural sciences, he pointed out, the principle of division of labor had long been in effect, the research worker having commonly at his disposal a number of laboratory technicians and research assistants to perform the lesser tasks.[36] For research workers working primarily in the library rather than in the laboratory, such assistance was generally not available. Yet the principle, Shapley claimed, was equally applicable to research outside the natural sciences. The process

---

[33] U. S. Library of Congress, *Report of the Librarian of Congress for the Fiscal Year Ending June 30, 1931.*, p. 378.

[34] *Ibid.*, p. 379.

[35] For most of the period under review, the various units of the Library of Congress furnishing reference service had no organizational connection with each other. In 1933 William Adams Slade was appointed Chief Reference Librarian with responsibility for supervision of the reference services as a whole, with the hope that he might be able to bring to bear upon a particular problem the full resources of the Library's manpower for personal assistance. (U. S. Library of Congress, *Annual Report of the Librarian of Congress for the Fiscal Year Ending June 30, 1934*, p. 4). This was a step in the right direction but the position was apparently only a staff or advisory one, with no authority to enforce close administrative coordination. The latter objective was not achieved in any substantive sense until the amalgamation of the various reference units as the Reference Department in 1939.

[36] "Special Bibliographic Service" (Mimeographed statement issued by the Executive Committee of the Carnegie Corporation of New York, February 21, 1932, outlining Dr. Shapley's proposals for a study to be sponsored by the Corporation; in the files of the Carnegie Corporation, New York City).

of research in any field involved many tasks which others could do for the researcher. Such work as locating and collecting materials, preliminary analysis of data, and ascertaining specific facts could well be delegated to a competent assistant. The resultant saving of his time would enable the research worker himself to concentrate on aspects that needed his special skills and by which the real value of his efforts would ultimately be judged.[37]

What the laboratory technician did for the natural scientist, Shapley thought the librarian could do for the humanist and social scientist. He persuaded the Carnegie Corporation of New York to subsidize the employment in a number of university libraries of special bibliographic assistants, to be exclusively at the disposal of professors engaged in humanities or social science research. He hoped that a successful demonstration would ultimately lead to the establishment in university libraries of full-fledged research departments employing a whole corps of skilled assistants, who could provide for the research men whose work was primarily in the library a service parallel to the efficient aid already available for men doing laboratory research.[38]

After some exploration of the most suitable locales for the "experiment," the Corporation made grants to the University of Pennsylvania Library and to the Cornell University Library for the two "studies of bibliographic service," more frequently called "research librarianships." The administrative arrangements were very much the same at both institutions. Service was limited to faculty members engaged in research — requests arising out of teaching duties continued to be treated in the ordinary way.[39] In both cases also, the research librarians — Henry King at Cornell and Arnold Borden at Pennsylvania — received their assignments by a separate channel and had no connection with the regular reference staff.[40]

The work actually done by the two librarians was also roughly similar. Broadly speaking, it consisted of two types: purely bibliographical assistance (such as location of pertinent materials in other libraries) and the critical survey and digesting of material on a given topic. In the latter case the research librarian's function was to assess the material and to describe its import in a report.[41]

The following assignments were typical of the service rendered. At Pennsylvania, Borden prepared a report on methods used in handling strikes in Australia; identified and located (i.e. in other libraries) materials for a history of American monetary theory; summarized the history of the use of the word "pathology" with illustrative quotations.[42] At Cornell, King compiled an extensive catalog, with locations, of world holdings of manuscripts of the Venerable Bede's *Commentary on the Acts of the Apostles;* prepared biographical sketches of sixty-four early British writers on economics; searched the *Annals of Congress* for material on American constitutional history; prepared a study of King Charles I's theory of government as indicated in his speeches.[43]

As suggested by the above topics, the projects were ordinarily of some magnitude, requiring a month or more of the research librarian's time. In his three years' service at Pennsylvania,

---

[37] Letter from Dr. Shapley to the Carnegie Corporation of New York, March 19, 1932 (In files of the Carnegie Corporation, New York City). See also the account of the genesis of the "research librarian" experiment, by Otto Kinkeldey ("The Research Librarian," *Bulletin of the American Library Association,* XXIX [September, 1935], 599).

[38] Arnold K. Borden, "The Research Librarian Idea," *Library Journal,* LVIII (Feb. 1, 1933), 104.

[39] C. Seymour Thompson, "New Position Established," *Library Journal,* LVII (November 1, 1932), 908; Henry H. King, "The Cornell Experiment," *Special Libraries,* XXV (February, 1934), 34.

[40] "The Research Librarianship," (Mimeographed announcement to the faculty of the University of Pennsylvania, October 1, 1932; in files of Carnegie Corporation, New York City); Cornell University Library, *Librarian's Report for 1932-33,* p. 3.

[41] Letter from Dr. Harlow Shapley to the Carnegie Corporation, June 28, 1933 (In files of Carnegie Corporation, New York City).

[42] Arnold K. Borden, "Libraries and Research," *Dartmouth College Library Bulletin,* II (May, 1936), 113-114.

[43] Kinkeldey, *op. cit.,* p. 34; Cornell University Library, *Librarian's Report for 1932-33,* p. 4; *Librarian's Report for 1933-34,* p. 3.

Borden handled only forty assignments coming from thirty-three different faculty members.[44] The rate at Cornell was roughly similar.

The crux of the "experiment" was the reaction of the faculty members to the work done on their behalf. Both Borden and King reported that the faculty members entered into the arrangement with an attitude of skepticism emanating from doubts as to the trustworthiness and relevance of data which they had not personally gathered. There was also a feeling that such assistance would be somehow unethical, in that the researcher would be gaining credit for work not wholly his own.[45]

Actual experience with the work of the research librarians allayed doubts and brought enthusiastic testimony in favor of the service. Dr. E. P. Cheyney of the University of Pennsylvania confessed that his prior skepticism had proven quite unwarranted:

> It [the assistance furnished by the research librarian] was of the utmost value. I have never habituated myself to obtaining help in such research as I have done, and it was a surprise and satisfaction to find the immense advantage of such trained and intelligent help . . . . I have not the least doubt of the value of such assistance. I was not so sure of it at first. The only difficulty, it seems to me, is on our part, that is, to formulate our problems in such a way as to make his contribution to their solution available.[46]

Dr. M. L. W. Laistner, professor of medieval history at Cornell University, wrote in similar vein: "An experiment of which I, as you know, was at first somewhat skeptical, has worked excellently in practice, mainly because Mr. King happened to be the right type of man."[47]

In fact, the whole "experiment," to judge from the official evaluations made by the faculty members and the library directors in charge, proved to be an almost unqualified success. Dean Richtmeyer of Cornell formally reported that the venture had convinced the Cornell faculty group that such service could be one of the most effective means of facilitating research in the humanities.[48] Of a long series of reports made by faculty members at the University of Pennsylvania on the value of the research librarianship, only one expressed other than whole-hearted approval.[49]

When examined closely so as to ascertain precisely wherein the service offered proved of such value, the statements showed a general agreement on two points. As a general and minimum thing, the service provided a worthwhile saving of time and trouble for the research workers. That is to say, the research librarian was doing work which the faculty members might equally well have done for themselves, but of which they were glad to be relieved.[50]

More important, the work of the research librarian represented an important increment, as well as a saving. A number of statements pointed out that the special bibliographical knowledge of the librarian (i.e. his service *qua* librarian rather than *qua* general assistant) enabled him to bring to light information — such as pertinent material in subject fields outside the scholars' specialties, the resources of other libraries, works in lesser-known foreign languages — which the scholars could not have found for themselves at all![51]

---

[44] Letter from Dr. Harlow Shapley to the Carnegie Corporation, October 7, 1935 (In files of Carnegie Corporation, New York City).

[45] King, *op. cit.*, p. 34; Arnold K. Borden, "After a Year," *Pennsylvania Library Notes*, XIII (July, 1933), 326.

[46] Untitled report by C. S. Thompson of the University of Pennsylvania Library to Dr. Harlow Shapley, June 6, 1933, attached to letter from Dr. Shapley to the Carnegie Corporation, June 28, 1933. The report included a number of statements from University of Pennsylvania faculty members on their experiences in working with the research librarian. (In files of Carnegie Corporation, New York City).

[47] Letter of May 22, 1934 to Dean Richtmeyer of Cornell University (In files of Carnegie Corporation, New York City).

[48] Letter from Dean Richtmeyer to Dr. Harlow Shapley, May 20, 1934 (In files of Carnegie Corporation, New York City).

[49] Untitled report by C. S. Thompson to Dr. Harlow Shapley, June 6, 1933, *op. cit.*, pp. 3-6.

[50] Cf. statement by Dr. Cyril James, *ibid.*, p. 5.

[51] Cf. statements by Dr. Quinn and Dr. Malakis, *ibid.*, p. 3.

No one came forward to controvert the testimony of the faculty members or to deny the conclusions to which they seemed to point, yet strangely enough the demonstration had little effect. At the University of Pennsylvania the position of research librarian was eliminated when the Carnegie Corporation's grants expired. At Cornell, the service did have sufficiently strong faculty support to ensure its continuation at the University's expense.[52] However, the service there was never extended, remaining limited to the assistance possible from the efforts of the single research librarian.[53]

Most disheartening of all was the fact that the whole venture attracted surprisingly little emulation from other university libraries. Dr. Shapley's correspondence with the Carnegie Corporation did indeed indicate that there was a certain amount of interest manifested at the outset, with two or three libraries intimating that plans were afoot to inaugurate similar services, but these plans never materialized.[54]

Just why, in the light of the apparent success of the research librarianships, so little in the way of permanent and wide-spread results should have come from the demonstration is not definitely known. Speculation, however, suggests several answers. It is easy to believe that inertia, conservatism, and skepticism were not to be easily overcome by only a couple of examples of effective service, and those elsewhere and probably unknown to most faculty members and librarians. The timing was certainly poor — the depression decade was no time for expansion of services. Dr. Kinkeldey has suggested another reason: the personnel problem may have seemed insuperable. Most librarians and university administrators, he intimated, simply felt that they could not attract the personnel competent to offer such service.[55]

In addition to such external factors militating against the general adoption of the research librarianship plan, it is likely that certain internal administrative features of its operation proved unacceptable to the library profession. Herman Henkle severely criticized what seemed to him the inordinate length of time spent by the research librarians on each project. To devote, as they actually did, an average of almost two months to each problem meant that the service could reach only a negligible number of faculty members.[56]

Theoretically at least, this objection was not wholly valid, since it was never contemplated in Shapley's original plan that a single research librarian could possibly suffice for the entire faculty. But, practically speaking, it was a criticism which must have suggested itself to many a library director, who saw no hope of obtaining funds for a really comprehensive program of faculty assistance. And to provide the service of a single librarian for only a dozen or so faculty members per year, along the lines actually followed at Cornell and Pennsylvania, must have seemed likely to involve the library staff in charges of showing arbitrary favoritism.[57]

Additional criticism attached itself to the policy of dissociating the research service from the regular work and personnel of the library. The policy tended to make the research librarianship

---

[52] Dean Richtmeyer stated that there was "almost consternation" among the members of the small group using the service when the question of its cessation came up after the expiration of the Carnegie grant. (Letter to Dr. Harlow Shapley, May 30, 1934; in files of Carnegie Corporation, New York City).

[53] Cornell University Library, *Librarian's Report for 1935-36*, p. 3.

[54] Letters from Dr. Harlow Shapley to the Carnegie Corporation, March 19, 1932 and October 23, 1933 (In files of Carnegie Corporation, New York City). Dr. Kinkeldey has stated (in an interview, December 11, 1953) that he received very few inquiries from other libraries about the operation of these services at Cornell after the initial publicity attendant upon the Carnegie grants had diminished.

[55] Interview with Dr. Otto Kinkeldey, December 11, 1953. Dr. Kinkeldey recalled that a principal reason for the retention of the research librarianship at Cornell was the unusual ability of the incumbent, Henry King.

[56] Herman Henkle, "An Interpretation of Research Librarianship," *School and Society*, XLVII (April 16, 1938), 496.

[57] To guard against such charges, the Cornell University Library eventually found it expedient to have requests for the research librarian's assistance made subject to the joint approval of the dean of the graduate college and the director of libraries. (Henry H. King, "Assistance to the Faculty in Library Research: Report from Cornell University," *College and Research Libraries*, IX [July, 1948], 230).

seem exotic instead of indigenous to the whole climate of university library operation, an "extra" to be added only by the grace of subsidy from without the library budget, easily ignored and easily dispensed with when special funds were no longer available.[58]

Strangely enough, no one singled out for criticism the obvious fact that the research librarianships quite ignored the whole principle of subject specialization. Aside from limiting their projects to fields other than natural science, both research librarians acted as complete generalists, assisting in inquiries covering subjects ranging from medieval literature to economics. In a sense, the acceptability of their work to the scholars was a tribute to the value of general library training (and probably to the personal qualifications of the particular librarians), but conceivably the projects took as long as they did because of the research librarians' initial unfamiliarity with the subject matter of the inquiries.

These criticisms did not controvert the essential finding of the "research librarianship experiment" — that the reference librarian could profitably be allotted a larger role in the conduct of academic research, even in fields of investigation formerly thought to be unadaptable to such a cooperative approach. They suggested, however, that to make such research service a regular part of university library facilities, a different form of organization would have had to be adopted — one which could integrate the research service with other library operations, and at the same time associate the work of research librarians more closely with specific groups of scholars.

The "Special Library" in the University

The above conclusion is particularly apposite if reference service is thought of, not only as aid in specific inquiries, but also as a continuous information service, serving to keep the scholar abreast of the current literature in his field. A basic condition for the establishment of such service is the close association of the librarian with a specific group of investigators. This condition could not ordinarily be met in the main university library, but the departmental or collegiate library did provide a favorable environment. Granted sufficient desire and financial support, the latter could offer something akin to special library service.

There was evidence that from about 1930 on, some departmental librarians — few but growing in number — did in fact come to identify themselves as "special librarians," with corresponding implications for the expansion of service. The trend was symbolized by the formation of a college and university library section in the Special Libraries Association in 1934. Walter Hausdorfer, a leader in this movement, maintained, for example, that the School of Business Library at Columbia University "should attempt to build up such services as might be given in a corresponding special library."[59]

The influence of this attitude in the practice of reference work was seen in the reports of a number of departmental and collegiate libraries, notably at Columbia University. The Egleston Library there regularly scanned all periodicals on receipt and furnished to the faculty members of the School of Engineering periodic reports on the new books and articles in the fields of their special interest.[60] The Chemical Library posted abstracts on its bulletin board for the information of the department faculty.[61]

At the Library of the College of Physicians and Surgeons, Walter R. Bett, working under the handicap of limited financial support, made a start toward the inauguration of a bibliographic

---

[58] Cf. Henkle, op. cit., p. 497.

[59] Columbia University Library, "Annual Report of the School of Business Library, 1931-32" (Unpublished report), p. 10.

[60] Columbia University, "Report of the Applied Science Libraries for 1932-33" (Unpublished report), p. 5.

[61] Columbia University Library, "Report of the Chemical Library, 1929-1930" (Unpublished report), p. 3.

service by furnishing occasional abstracts and the part-time services of a translator.[62] His successor in the position, Thomas Fleming, was able to expand the service considerably. Under his direction the Library undertook to furnish a continuing report on the current literature by supplying investigators with "a complete or partial bibliography of articles pertaining to a subject under investigation and . . . information concerning new articles as they appear."[63] This plan, described as a "continuous bibliographic service,"[64] actually combined the dual functions of literature reporting and journal routing. The library staff scanned incoming journals, supplied references to each research man according to his previously indicated special field of interest, and on demand brought together the journals themselves for convenient consultation by the scholar.[65] Thirty-six investigators were supplied with over 5000 references in the first year of operation.[66]

Not surprisingly, most examples of extensive service of this kind came from departmental libraries for the natural sciences, a field where research was recognized to be much less dependent upon individual effort and personal interpretation than in the humanities and social sciences. But the principle of library collaboration in research was also applicable to the latter fields,[67] as shown by a few specific examples. At Princeton University, the Industrial Relations Section maintained what was to all intents and purposes a special library service. In this semi-autonomous research unit, the library staff worked in close cooperation with the investigators, acting as a "clearinghouse of information" and supplying "brief abstracts and summaries" to resident staff and outside investigators. In fact, there was no clear line of demarcation between the library, teaching, and research functions, the three operating in close and continuous collaboration.[68]

Another instance of the movement of non-scientific departmental libraries toward the development of a special library type of service came from the Law Library at Columbia. Its report for 1938 made it clear that the Columbia Law Library was supplying valuable assistance to the faculty in line with a deliberate policy of research service. The extent — and the limitations — of the service were described by Miles Price in the following statement:

> We draw the line at interpreting it [the material] for him [the faculty member] but short of that we do not stop. Without, it is believed, the faculty realizing it, they have taken us very far afield; they have come to accept as a matter of course . . . services they never used to ask for or get . . . and I think they are perfectly right. . . . While the library does not do any interpreting of legal data, that being for the research assistant, we do conceive it as part of our duty to give a research worker what a patent attorney would call "the state of the art" as to what material exists in a given field.[69]

Price's statement may well serve as a sort of bench mark for measuring the development of reference services in general research libraries before the Second World War. It is indicative of the trend, not yet established as the norm but growing in strength, to extend the bounds of assistance, and particularly to orient this assistance more closely to the needs of the research group. These objectives were the common denominators that served to unite all the new departures described in the present chapter. "Chairs," "consultantships," "research librarianships," "special

---

[62] Columbia University Library, "Annual Report of the Librarian of the College of Physicians and Surgeons, 1935-36" (Unpublished report), pp. 3-4.

[63] Columbia University Library, "Annual Report of the Medical Library, July 1, 1939-June 30, 1940" (Unpublished report), p. 1.

[64] Thomas P. Fleming, Estelle Brodman and Seymour Robb, "A Continuous Bibliographic Service in University Libraries," *College and Research Libraries*, VIII (July, 1947), 322-28.

[65] Columbia University Library, "Annual Report of the Medical Library . . . 1939-40," p. 1.

[66] *Ibid*.

[67] Cf. Fleming, Brodman and Robb, *op. cit.*, p. 328.

[68] Princeton University, *Report of the President for the Academic Year 1932-1933*, pp. 89-91; Clarence J. Hicks, *My Life in Industrial Relations; Fifty Years in the Growth of a Profession* (New York: Harper & Brothers, 1941), p. 149.

[69] Columbia University Library, "Annual Report of the Law Librarian; Fiscal Year Ending June 30, 1938" (Unpublished report), pp. 4-5.

libraries in the universities" — all these shared the same aim of providing a service for advanced investigators, shaped specifically to their special requirements, and distinct from that provided for the general readers and students.

These ventures also shared the same basic assumption: that these special requirements were for library assistance that would go further than fact-finding and suggestion of sources. The assumption was only that, for it was never definitely proven that the research men did in fact want and need extensive assistance. But the admission by the scholars that they lacked bibliographical competence, their inability to cope with the growing volume of research literature, the fact that, in Price's words, "they came to accept it as a matter of course," all tended to confirm the supposition.

A final basic premise characteristic of all these new ventures was the belief that librarians, — if not always in *esse*, at least in *posse* — were competent to render extensive assistance, and that such assistance would represent a positive contribution to the work of research. The industrial research librarians had, indeed, already gone far toward demonstrating the truth of this premise, but only for research workers in applied science. The great contribution of these new departures, particularly of the "research librarianship experiment," was to indicate that a special library type of service was also appropriate to the work of scholars in the humanities and social sciences.

All these were theoretical considerations. The ways in which to translate them into a practical program of service found no such agreement. The point at which to draw the line for assistance was a continuing problem which brought a variety of answers. Price, for example, thought it inappropriate to interpret data, but the research librarians at Cornell and Pennsylvania considered critical analyses of material an integral part of their responsibilities. The forms of assistance also received varying emphasis. In the Library of Congress chief stress was laid on guidance in the use of a library so large in resources and so complicated in its bibliographical apparatus as to puzzle even the mature scholar. In institutions such as the Huntington Library and the John Carter Brown Library, the emphasis was on special assistance of a bibliographical and paleographical nature — identification of editions and textual criticism. In the "special" university libraries such as those of the Industrial Relations Section at Princeton and of the College of Physicians and Surgeons at Columbia, the most useful avenue of service was thought to lie in the direction of a continuous reporting on current literature.

There was equally great variety in the forms of administrative organization adopted for the provision of research service. The Library of Congress "consultantships" and the "research librarianships" were merely superimposed on the existing framework. Dependent on the irregular support of outside subsidies, they seemed only *ad hoc* ventures, with no real roots in their parent institutions. The ideal of a close and continuous collaboration between the research service and its scholarly clientele on the one hand, between the service and the rest of the library on the other hand, was more nearly realized in endowed reference libraries such as the Huntington Library and in university "special libraries" such as the Princeton Industrial Relations Section.

All this is to indicate that the mechanics of practice for research service in the general research library were not yet worked out before the Second World War. And only naturally so, for in libraries open to the general public and without the strong financial support of great industrial corporations, it was inevitably more difficult to discover an arrangement whereby a large-scale research service could be provided efficiently, economically, and in harmony with the other functions of the libraries.

But if the problems had not yet been solved, at least the direction was already made clear. Few in number as were these new departures in reference service, they were enough to demonstrate that the librarian could be a working member of the research team, capable of doing for the academic scholar much of the work formerly thought necessarily to devolve on the latter himself. They strongly suggested that in the general research library, as in the industrial library, the development of reference services for research was to proceed in the direction of more, not less, assistance.

Chapter IX

SUMMARY, CONCLUSIONS, AND A REVIEW OF PRESENT TRENDS

To trace the development of reference services in American research libraries is to record the transformation of occasional and casual courtesy into a complex and highly specialized service of steadily increasing scope and importance. In most institutions, it is now taken for granted that one of the library's primary functions is to make available personal assistance for readers seeking information. Indeed, reference service is so much a commonplace of present-day American library practice that many American librarians tend to regard it as an inherent element of librarianship — something that was always done.

Yet a consideration of foreign library practices shows that reference work is still by no means universally regarded as a fundamental part of research library service. Actually, reference service is almost a peculiarly American development.[1] It is not merely the product of a simple and logical unfolding of tendencies inherent in the very structure of research libraries everywhere, but the result of a collocation of particular historical factors distinctive to the American library scene.

The introduction of reference service in American research libraries was due in the first instance to the fact that in America research libraries developed as institutions serving general readers as well as scholars. When the transformation of scholarship changed American colleges into universities, the change was one of addition, not displacement — the newer function of research being merely superimposed on the older function of instruction. The libraries which served these universities took on the same dual character. For the professional scholars they rapidly acquired large collections and built up an intricate bibliographical apparatus. But they also continued to serve inexperienced students, whose needs never ceased to represent a major claim on the libraries' attention.

The other main type of research library prominent in the nineteenth century — the public library — was equally "general," that is to say, heterogeneous in purpose and clientele. Though the interests of the scholars may have been the most prominent in the foundation of public libraries,[2] it is certain that the public library rapidly came to be an institution catering to the community as a whole.

It was the existence of this large body of inexperienced readers that first raised the problem of the library's responsibilities for personal assistance to its users. Traditionally the librarian's role had been that of custodian, collector, and cataloger. It had not been supposed that his functions included personal assistance to readers. Of course, there had always been instances of personal helpfulness by librarians, but these had been made as a matter of simple courtesy rather than of responsibility, much less than of organized service.

In the last quarter of the nineteenth century, however, public librarians, notably Samuel Swett Green, began to realize that a policy of *laissez faire* was insufficient to meet the needs of readers unskilled in the use of the library. But, in championing the "desirableness of personal intercourse

---

[1]Dr. William Warner Bishop, whose extensive experience made him familiar with both American and European research library practices, called "the organization in American libraries of an expert service to readers a peculiarly American development" and "the chief American contribution to librarianship." The context of the statement makes it likely that Bishop had in mind the whole congeries of activities comprehended in "service to readers" rather than reference work alone, but certainly reference work is among the most conspicuous elements in such "expert service." ("Research Libraries," *in Overbibliotekar Wilhelm Munthe Pa Femtiarsdagen 20. Oktober 1933 Fra Fagfeller Og Venner* [Oslo: Grøndahl & Søns Boktrykeri, 1933], p. 18).

[2]According to J. H. Shera, *Foundations of the Public Library; the Origins of the Public Library Movement in New England 1629-1855* (Chicago: University of Chicago Press, 1949), pp. 206-i3.

between librarians and readers," Green acted also out of more than altruistic motives. He realized that such assistance, in rendering the public library more useful to a large proportion of its clientele, would contribute as well to its popularity and support.

The first steps in the direction of personal assistance were, however, tentative enough, being confined largely to guidance in the use of the library and to suggestions for the selection of materials. The activity was quite peripheral to the library's main functions of book acquisition, arrangement and supply, and it enlisted only the part-time service of the chief himself.

As the purveyance of information came increasingly to be regarded as a major function of the public library, consonant with its status as an educational institution, the provision of assistance became accepted as a central responsibility rather than a marginal activity. The work itself took on larger proportions, requiring the full-time service of one or more staff members. After 1890, in at least the larger public libraries, it came to be organized as a separate library department. The term "reference work" replaced the older, vaguer designations of "access to librarians" and "aid to readers," and the work of assistance was regarded as a specialized library function, with its own distinctive techniques and training.

In the university libraries the rate of acceptance was slower. To begin with, the older custodial tradition of librarianship was more deeply imbedded in university library practice. Reflecting the small attention paid to the library in the theories and methods of the "old regime" in American higher education, the college library was until well into the eighties commonly no more than an ill-stocked and little-used storehouse of books, and the librarian only its caretaker. The transformation of American higher education, which made the library "the heart of the university," greatly expanded the use of the library by both faculty and students, and made pertinent for the first time the question of how to facilitate the students' use of the library.

The university librarians, closely associated with the public librarians in the new professional associations, adopted the public library idea of organized assistance by the library staff on behalf of the library clientele. In general, the university libraries followed the same lines as had the public libraries, first providing personal assistance on a part-time and occasional basis, later making the work of the reference librarian a specialized function, eventually giving to that function the status of a separate department. The rate of advance in the university libraries was, however, distinctly slower than it was in the public libraries, mainly because the self-interest of the university librarians was not so directly dependent upon the extension of the library's service.

By the end of the nineteenth century, reference service had become a well-established function in both public and university libraries, though by no means in all of the latter. The service was, however, in both cases oriented almost exclusively toward the inexperienced reader. It had made its way into the research libraries, but had as yet almost nothing to do with their scholarly clientele.

This condition reflected the influence of a number of factors. Primarily it was due to the fact that the research men themselves expressed almost no demand for librarians' assistance. The dominant desires of the scholars were first of all for larger collections, and then for a better bibliographical apparatus. Only in a few scattered instances were there any hints that they might appreciate personal assistance from librarians.

A complementary sentiment was the widespread feeling — among scholars and librarians alike — that the scholars really did not need assistance. The usual supposition of the time was that the scholar was the master of the bibliography of his field, quite able to gather information by himself. This supposition may well have had considerable foundation in fact, for, in the nineteenth century, the volume of scholarly publication, though rapidly increasing, was still small enough to warrant confidence that the specialist would have adequate familiarity with the literature of his subject.

In any case, the librarians themselves firmly believed that, for anyone competent to use it (as the scholar presumably could), the catalog provided a sufficient guide to the information available in the library. There was a naive and exaggerated confidence in the efficacy of the library's bibliographic apparatus. At the very least, even where the fallibility of the catalog was recognized, it was considered the library user's first and greatest resource, reducing to the minimum the necessity for personal intervention by the librarian.

For the inexperienced reader, of course, the catalog was recognized to be too complex a tool to be used without explanation by the librarian, and such interpretation constituted a major activity of the reference librarian. However, for even these readers, the assistance was, in theory, carefully limited to instruction and guidance. The proper goal of reference work, according to the "conservative theory" that represented the views of most reference librarians in the period prior to World War I, was the self-dependence of the reader. This aim would be furthered by instruction in the use of the library; it would, ran the contemporary reasoning, be hindered by too great a measure of assistance.

Though their theory sought to limit assistance to guidance, in practice reference librarians had already found themselves drawn into furnishing quite a different kind of aid — "fact-finding" or "information service." Even at its lowest level, say answering an inquiry on the pronunciation of a word, direct information service represented a really radical extension of the concept of assistance. To show a reader how to use the catalog or a reference book was merely to supplement the conventional bibliographic apparatus. To supply him with the facts themselves meant that the librarian was no longer a guide but an information supplier pure and simple, the library being merely his locale and working tool.

The two forms of assistance also had vastly different implications for the relationship of the librarian to the reader and for the status of the librarian himself. The former type stressed the librarian's function as instructor; the latter emphasized the librarian's role as direct participant in the process of investigation. The former implied a policy of minimal assistance; the latter placed no limits on the participation of the librarian other than those consonant with his competence to pursue the inquiry, the wishes of the inquirer, and the facilities of the library.

Probably few libraries of the time deliberately sought to embark on a program of direct information service. It is likely that reference departments were drawn into such service more or less insensibly by following the line of least effort in the everyday practice of reference work. The library clients themselves often had no wish to develop bibliographical competence or independence, and pressed for direct answers rather than guidance. In any case, reference librarians often found it quicker and easier for themselves to supply information directly to readers than to show them how to find it.

Despite the resistance of conservative theorizers, information service came thus gradually to take a prominent place in the duties of the reference staff. For such service, at least in the more esoteric inquiries, a knowledge of the techniques of library use was insufficient. It also required subject knowledge on the part of the reference librarian, a familiarity with the terminology and methods of specialized fields. These considerations dictated a growing trend toward subject specialization in reference service, at first more evident in the public libraries, but gradually penetrating the university libraries as well. In certain cases, the trend toward subject specialization was reinforced by purely administrative considerations: the inconvenience of separating "circulating" and "reference" materials on the same subject, and, where collections presented difficult problems of form or language, the necessity of recruiting staff with the special knowledge to deal with the materials.

By the end of the First World War, the advent of subject specialization and the elaboration of reference techniques had resulted in a considerable qualitative improvement in the reference services of general research libraries, accompanying, and perhaps occasioned by, a definite increase in the volume and prestige of reference work. However, the service in these libraries still tended to be directed toward inexperienced readers rather than scholars, and the scope of assistance was still largely limited to guidance in the use of the library and the simpler sorts of fact-finding.

Meanwhile the information needs of businessmen and legislators had already set under way the development of a new type of library based on a radical extension of the concept of reference service. The special library, popularized by the success of Charles McCarthy and his fellow legislative librarians, had as its chief feature the purveyance of a thorough and reliable information service to its clientele. Since the interest of the clientele was predominantly in the possession of the facts rather than in the development of personal ability in their ascertainment, the role of guidance was minimized and the librarians became frankly and fully information assistants. The special librarians also broadened the scope of reference work, not only supplying answers to specific inquiries but also anticipating questions by furnishing a continuous reporting service on new developments.

As with the beginning of reference service in general libraries, the first application of the "special library idea" was on behalf of clients — businessmen and government officials — who were unskilled in the use of libraries and in the techniques of information extraction. The presumption was that the special librarian was doing for these clients a task which they could do for themselves only incompletely, or at least with great difficulty. Certainly the mainspring of the legislative library movement was the belief that the legislators were unable to procure by their own means the reliable and extensive information needed for effective legislation.

Later, the special library was presented, not just as a form of "help for the helpless," but on its merits as a straight labor-saving device. The reasoning now was that extensive library assistance was worthwhile in any case where the time saved by the client was more valuable than the time spent by the librarian. On this basis, special libraries were established to serve the growing number of research laboratories established by industrial concerns after the First World War. It was really the first wholehearted attempt to provide reference service for research workers (as differentiated from reference service in research libraries).

Even in these industrial research libraries the development of a policy of extensive assistance for research workers was no overnight occurrence. It was argued by some research workers (and, for that matter, by some librarians as well) that only the research worker himself could properly find the data he needed. However, as the special library staffs came to include personnel of the requisite subject knowledge, it was seen as feasible and efficient for the librarian to supply the research worker with the desired information. In some libraries, the library staff eventually was given major responsibility for the "literature side" of research, furnishing literature surveys, reports on the "state of the art," bibliographies and summaries of the current literature, and, in some instances, even going so far as to suggest opportunities and methods for research. In industrial research libraries of this sort, the librarian became a collaborator in the research process, paving the way for and supplementing the work of the laboratory.

In the general research libraries, assistance on this scale was distinctly uncommon right up through 1940. The principal problem was the heterogeneous nature of the demands upon the library, which made it difficult to differentiate service for the scholars from the much more numerous general readers. In the large university and public libraries, with thousands of such general readers, the service load was often so great as to limit the capacity of the reference departments to offer more than minimal assistance.

To this strong practical argument against a policy of extensive reference service were added the continued support of the familiar assumptions that instruction and guidance were really preferable for students, and that scholars did not want or require more than occasional personal assistance from librarians. However, the prejudice against direct information service as a reference department function notably diminished. There were also positive gains in the quality of the assistance rendered, featuring a steady increase in subject specialization, and a notable development of the tools for reference work by a proliferation of union lists, union catalogs, printed bibliographies, and resources surveys.

However, not until a decade after World War I were there any serious attempts to set up in general research libraries a service catering specifically to scholars, and offering them extensive assistance. Of these ventures in research service, the "research librarianships" at Cornell and at Pennsylvania were perhaps the most notable. They showed that extensive assistance by librarians was practicable and useful even for university scholars working in the humanities and social sciences, though it had been usually thought that the "personal" nature of research in these fields precluded the use of the librarian as "collaborator." As "experiments," the research librarianships were successful; as a model for future ventures in the direction of research service they attracted little emulation, because they presented too many problems from the point of view of financial support and administrative organization.

A less striking but probably more promising approach to the problem of providing adequate reference service for faculty members lay in the development of university departmental libraries along the lines of special libraries. In a few instances, notably in the Industrial Relations Section at Princeton and in the Library of the College of Physicians and Surgeons at Columbia University, departmental librarians, working in close collaboration with research personnel, were able to provide a literature-reporting service that represented a real contribution to the work of research.

Such instances were, however, still definitely atypical of reference services in general research libraries in 1940. The usual pattern was one of "moderate service," the product of a compromise between librarians' genuine desire to be of maximum aid and the limitations imposed by lack of time and inability to secure personnel of the requisite qualifications.

The "moderate service" was seen at its best in the high technical skill by which reference librarians were able to help scholars find elusive facts, verify obscure titles and locate needed materials in libraries elsewhere. However, reference workers in general research libraries continued to be saddled with many responsibilities only indirectly related to informational duties, and they seldom even attempted to carry out such larger tasks as translations, literature searches, or critical bibliographies.

In sum, most public and university librarians clung to the notion that extensive assistance for the research group, if not undesirable, was at least impracticable. This reasoning was probably valid enough for public libraries, where the research workers could not be easily identified, the service load was large, and where in any case it was questionable if any single group of clients had proper claims to special service. In the universities, where the research group was readily distinguishable from the mass of general readers and was considered by long-established academic tradition to warrant unusual service, it was more likely and proper that the librarians should find methods and support for a program of extensive assistance to research. The practical problems had not yet been worked out, but the case for an expanded reference service to university research personnel was plausible enough to indicate that the future development of reference service in university libraries would lie in the direction of greater responsibilities for the reference librarian.

Since 1940: Reference Service and Scientific Research

The full history of reference service since 1940 cannot yet be written. The major changes are still in progress, making it hard to discern their exact shape and dimensions, and many of the details are lacking because reports are not yet available. Nevertheless, the main outlines of the present pattern are clear enough, and since much of the interest of a historical study lies in the relationship of past trends to present situation, a tentative sketch of recent developments is here presented.

On the whole the last dozen years, while bringing many important changes in the practice of reference work, have witnessed an acceleration of previous trends rather than their reversal. In the industrial research libraries, the tendency to have reference librarians assume a major share of the responsibility for the literature work involved in research has become widespread. Functions such as preparing abstracts, making literature surveys, reporting on the "state of the art," and editorial work have now become standard operating procedure in many industrial research libraries. For example, Johnson's survey of services in petroleum libraries indicated that 62.5 per cent of the libraries reporting prepared a regular abstract bulletin, 96 per cent of the group did "some sort of literature searching," and 38 per cent engaged in patent searches.[3]

Undoubtedly the prevalence of the practice of providing extensive library assistance in scientific research reflects the strong support of the scientists themselves for such a policy. For example, both the Bush and Steelman reports on the national situation in scientific research stressed the importance of first-class library service in conserving scientists' time for the laboratory part of their work.[4] Perhaps the best indication of the degree to which the policy of extensive reference service corresponds to the views of the research workers themselves is gained from the fact that textbooks on industrial research now commonly describe such service as an economically necessary part of operating procedure in industrial research. The following statement by David Bendel Hertz exemplified both the characteristic reasoning and the attitude of matter-of-fact acceptance:

> It is inefficient to expect a research worker to obtain all this information [i.e. needed for his work] on his own. In any case, it is barely possible for him today to keep up with current information in his own particular specialty, much less maintain his contacts with other fields. The library and staff who operate it in any efficient research group must maintain or have access to all the sources of information which would be of utility to a worker in a given project. For best results, they should be able to prepare bibliographies and abstracts of pertinent material *rapidly* and to furnish specific literature which the researchers feel would be of additional interest.[5]

Hertz' statement brings out two of the main reasons for the increasing willingness of scientists to allot librarians major responsibility in literature service work. Neither reason is new,[6] but both gained added force from the development of research itself during the Second World War and after. One stems from the fact that scientific research, at least in industry and government, now almost always is a "group project."[7] As Hertz explains, the research worker operating as part of a large research unit can not and does not expect to work alone, but frankly depends upon a whole array of "subsidiary services" for supplies, information, and assistance. Given in addition the general scarcity of personnel qualified to conduct research, a ruling principle of present-day research administration is that the greater the part of the subsidiary services, among them the library's informational service, the more efficient the work of the research organization.[8]

The second reason suggested by Hertz was the enormous increase in the volume of scientific literature. The tremendous impetus given to scientific and industrial research by the Second World War, and by the industrial expansion which followed it, resulted in an unprecedented output of research publications. At the International Conference on Science Abstracting (1949), it was estimated that there were then no less than 40,000 scientific and technical journals, publishing some

---

[3]A. B. Johnson, "Services in Petroleum Libraries," *Special Libraries*, XLI (November, 1950), 312-17, 336. See also in this connection: Barbara Johnston, *Special Library Practice; a Report on a Visit to Special Libraries in England, France, Canada and the United States of America in 1948* (Melbourne: Commonwealth Scientific and Industrial Research Organization, 1949), pp. 56-57; Special Libraries Association, Science and Technology Division, *Technical Libraries; Their Organization and Management*... edited by Lucille Jackson (New York: The Special Libraries Association, 1951), pp. 120-42.

[4]United States, Office of Scientific Research and Development, *Science, the Endless Frontier; a Report to the President*, by Vannevar Bush... (Washington: Government Printing Office, 1945), pp. 112, 115; United States, President's Scientific Research Board, *Science and Public Policy; a Report to the President*, by John R. Steelman, Chairman... (Washington: Government Printing Office, 1947), III, 110-12.

[5]David Bendel Hertz, *The Theory and Practice of Industrial Research* (New York: McGraw-Hill Book Company, 1950), p. 303. For similar sentiments in other textbooks, see C. C. Furnas, editor, *Research in Industry, Its Organization and Management, Prepared and Published for Industrial Research Institute, Inc.* (New York: D. Van Nostrand Company, 1948), pp. 364-68; Charles E. K. Mees and John A. Leermakers, *The Organization of Industrial Scientific Research* (2d ed.; New York: McGraw-Hill Book Company, 1950), pp. 284-85.

[6]Cf. *Supra*, pp. 63-64, 67-68.

[7]Hertz, *op. cit.*, p. 303.

[8]*Ibid.*, p. 306.

1,850,000 articles a year, most of them nowhere indexed or abstracted.[9] The number of journals indexed in *Chemical Abstracts* grew from 2,808 in 1936 to 4,318 in 1946, the increase directly reflecting the establishment of new media of publication.[10] It was becoming obvious that the volume of pertinent literature in any single field, except possibly in the most narrow specializations, was growing to the extent that the individual researcher, however expert and conscientious, could not hope to cope with it unaided. As J. D. Bernal, himself an eminent scientist, logically pointed out: "While the annual increment of new knowledge in the whole field of science and in any particular field is rapidly increasing, the capacity for assimilating knowledge, is for each individual research worker, absolutely limited."[11]

In this task of mastering the literature, past and current, the research worker's traditional aids — the abstracting and indexing services — have proven increasingly deficient. Ranganathan and Sundaram, pointing out the manifest duplication and gaps in the coverage of scientific literature effected by the "bibliographic services," have estimated that, by the aid of these alone, the scientist can identify and locate no more than one-third of all the pertinent material in his subject (with some variation, of course, according to the field of study).[12]

Another hindrance to the satisfaction of the scientist's informational needs has arisen out of the fact that scientific research has increasingly tended to be interdisciplinary in its approach. This has meant that the research worker has had to gain cognizance of the work being done in fields outside his immediate specialty — which is to say, very often in fields beyond the scope of his personal bibliographic competence.

A final difficulty relates to the form of publication itself. A large proportion of the research of the last decade has been issued, not in the form of the relatively accessible journal article, but as "technical reports." Many of these "reports," not the least valuable, are not "published" at all, existing only in manuscript form. Others appear in a variety of nearprint forms, in small editions difficult to identify and locate. In certain areas of science, security regulations impose a further hindrance.

All these changes have meant that the task of tracing and using scientific literature has become considerably more difficult in the last decade. The effect has been to reinforce the demand for an intermediary between the research man and his literature, the task of locating information almost necessarily becoming a specialized function devolving upon specially assigned personnel. The case for a special library type of service for the scientific research worker seemed stronger than ever at the mid-century.

Reference Service in the General Research Library since 1940

Much of the reasoning which seems to point to the use of extensive reference service in conjunction with research sponsored by industry and government is equally applicable to the research sponsored by the universities. The parallel has, indeed, been used as ammunition by some university research men in pressing for a larger measure of library assistance. Henry Gilman, for instance, thought that the non-industrial scientist could greatly profit by such service, which would give him more opportunity for the exercise of his purely creative talents. He looked forward to the time when such "special service" would be a regular service of the university library.[13]

---

[9] International Conference on Science Abstracting, Paris, 1949, ... *Final Report* (Paris: UNESCO, 1949), p. 122.

[10] E. J. Crane, "Periodical List of Periodicals," *Chemical and Engineering News*, XXV (July 21, 1947), 2075.

[11] J. D. Bernal, "Information Service as an Essential in the Progress of Science," *ASLIB Proceedings*, (Twentieth Conference, 1945) p. 20.

[12] S. R. Ranganathan, and C. Sundaram, *Reference Service and Bibliography* ... (Madras: The Madras Library Association, 1940-41), I, pp. 287-88.

[13] Henry Gilman, "What the Scientist Expects of the Librarian," *College and Research Libraries*, VIII (July, 1947), 330.

Such a position is probably — in the case of social scientists and humanists, almost certainly — still a minority opinion. On the basis of an informal survey of faculty attitudes, William H. Carlson has concluded that the "faculty member of the present and immediate future will welcome the assistance of a highly trained and competent subject specialist librarian, but only as an aid in locating the literature."[14] The usual reason given by his respondents was that research is too much a matter of purely personal interpretation to admit of much subdivision in the labor it involves.[15]

This negative view of the feasibility and value of a special library type of service within the university library setting is also shared by a number of librarians. In a recent article, Harry Bauer, of the University of Washington Library, simply takes it for granted that "the librarian needs only to provide the learned publications; the scholar is expected to be able to do the rest."[16] Warner Rice, formerly librarian of the University of Michigan, disparages the librarian's ability to supply reliable abstracts and translations, or to undertake critical judgments on the relevance and value of data. Even if the library schools could turn out specialists of the required competence (something which he thinks they are not presently doing), he argues that the economy of the university research library can not be expected to make regularly available for research assistance the services of many specialists.[17]

Perhaps the norm in university library reference work is best indicated by Talmadge's recent study of the practices and policies of the general reference departments of large university libraries concerning the preparation of bibliographies. In general, the reference librarians replying to his questionnaire reported that the compilation of bibliographies for the personal use of faculty members and students, if rendered at all, was an "extra" which ordinarily could not and should not receive a very high priority in the allocation of the reference staff's time.[18] Almost one-fourth of the libraries questioned did not believe that such service should be rendered to patrons *of any category;* nearly all imposed certain restrictions on their bibliographical service.[19]

Though no equivalent data are available for the policies of public libraries, it is highly probable that a roughly similar policy of fairly limited service continues to prevail in these as well. An official statement of the Enoch Pratt Free Library of Baltimore avers, for instance, that the ideal of finding every answer, while sound in special libraries, is not tenable for public libraries. It suggests that reference assistants "should actually do the work" only when the reader is unable to do so for himself because of lack of education or intelligence, or because he is unable to come to the library in person.[20]

The principal reason given for this limitation is traditional and practical: the number of inquiries is simply too large to permit reference librarians time for more than the minimum of help. Indeed, when as at the Information Division of the New York Public Library, each reference assistant is expected to deal with fifty to sixty inquiries per hour, the necessity for restriction on scope of the service seems clear.[21]

---

[14] William H. Carlson, "The Research Worker and the Library," *College and Research Libraries,* VII (October, 1946), 298.

[15] *Ibid.* For similar opinions by other university research men, see W. B. McDaniel, "The Researcher, the Searcher and Research," *Transactions and Studies of the College of Physicians,* Fourth Series, XV, (1947), 126; Fred A. Mettler, "What a Research Man Wants of a Medical Library," *Bulletin of the Medical Library Association,* n.s. XXXVI (January, 1948), 32; Edward G. Lewis, "A Political Scientist in the Reference Library," *College and Research Libraries,* XIII (April, 1952), 162.

[16] Harry C. Bauer, "Information Wanted," *Library Journal,* LXXVIII (September 15, 1953), 1467.

[17] University of Pennsylvania Library, *Changing Patterns of Scholarship and the Future of Research Libraries; a Symposium in Celebration of the 200th Anniversary of the Establishment of the University of Pennsylvania Library* (Philadelphia: University of Pennsylvania Press, 1951), pp. 106-07.

[18] Robert Louis Talmadge, "Practices and Policies of the Reference Departments of Large University Libraries Concerning the Preparation of Bibliographies" (Unpublished M.S. thesis, University of Illinois, 1951), p. 9.

[19] *Ibid.,* pp. 19-20.

[20] Enoch Pratt Free Library, General Reference Department, *General Reference Department Staff Manual* (Baltimore: The Enoch Pratt Free Library, 1950), p. 42.

[21] J. R. Eastman, "The Information Division of the New York Public Library" (Unpublished paper, 1950; in files of Information Division, New York Public Library).

This is not to say that the situation in the general research libraries has remained wholly static. Among the advances achieved in the last dozen years may be noted the trend toward a more careful and precise formulation of reference policy,[22] and the introduction of principles of scientific management in the administration of reference work.[23]

The most promising advances in reference service in the university libraries have taken place outside the general reference departments. The tendency of certain departmental, collegiate, and institute libraries to assume the pattern of service characteristic of special libraries has grown much more common. The trend has been fostered to no little extent by the fact that in many cases these libraries have not been dependent on the regular (and limited) university funds. Since 1941 government, industry, and foundations have contributed large sums for long-term, semi-autonomous research projects. Supported by foundation grants, a dozen industrial relations libraries have appeared on university campuses, all patterned after the Princeton Industrial Section, and giving the same kind of extensive service in close collaboration with the faculty members.[24] In the Johns Hopkins University Applied Physics Laboratory, which operates under a contract with the United States Navy Bureau of Ordnance, the librarian maintains a regular reporting service on current literature for the benefit of the laboratory staff.[25] For the Engineering Experiment Station of the Georgia Institute of Technology, a Technical Information Division prepared literature surveys, advised on patent procedures, assisted in quality control of technical publications, and edited papers for publication.[26]

The trend toward the establishment of special library-like units within the framework, if on the periphery, of the general research library, has gone furthest at the Library of Congress, where a number of sub-divisions of the Reference Department, operating under defense research contracts, provide a broad range of reference services to a limited clientele. Many of these units operate under security restrictions which prevent the full publication of their activities, but the Office of Naval Research Project, as described by Luther Evans, may be taken as typical of the usual scope of operations. This unit, supported by special funds from the Office of Naval Research, abstracted and published for limited circulation the reports of work in progress submitted by naval research contractors, provided a staff of science specialists to answer specific inquiries received from Navy offices, and was to try to work out a high-speed bibliographic service to keep research workers informed about the latest developments in their field.[27] The *Report of the Librarian of Congress* for 1951-1952 lists the following units which may be considered as being really special libraries operating within the framework of the general research library: Air Information Division, Air Research Division, Census Library Project, Technical Information Division, Legislative Reference Service, SIPRE Bibliographic Project, and Civil Defense Information Service.

The fact that governmental agencies have chosen to contract for such services with general libraries such as the Library of Congress rather than establish their own special libraries is particularly interesting, since it gives rise to the supposition that these agencies consider the special

[22] E.g. Enoch Pratt Free Library, *op. cit.*; University of Illinois Library, *Staff Manual,* edited by the Staff Manual Committee of the Librarians' Association of the University of Illinois Library (2d ed.; Urbana: University of Illinois Library, 1948), pp. 68-70; U. S. Armed Forces Medical Library, "Library Manual Section R-R-I: Policies for Reference Service" (Mimeographed statement, 1951), pp. 1-3.

[23] Ralph Shaw, "Cuts Unnecessary Work," *Library Journal,* LXXI (April 15, 1946), 575.

[24] Frederick H. Harbison and Shirley H. Harper, "Industrial Relations — A Case Study of Specialized Communications Involving Several Groups," *American Documentation,* IV (Fall [October], 1953), 155-162.

[25] Saul Herner, "Improving the Internal Information Services in Scientific Research Organizations," *Special Libraries,* XLIV (January, 1953), 15-19.

[26] Gerald A. Rosselot, "The Administration of Small Research Laboratories," in *Conference on the Administration of Research, 1948* ("Technical Bulletin of the School of Engineering, Pennsylvania State College," Number 30), 65. It is instructive to note that "these research facilities were somewhat gingerly utilized by the research men whom (sic) the facilities were first established. However, their advantages and value in assistance in many routine and other matters have now been quite readily realized and have been gratefully accepted by the scientist." *(Ibid.)*

[27] Luther H. Evans, "The Library of Congress and its Service to Science and Technology," *College and Research Libraries,* VIII (July, 1947), 321.

library operating within the framework of a large general library to be the most effective way of meeting the informational needs of the research worker.

If this supposition is true, the explanation would seem to lie in the currently strong trend toward inter-disciplinary research, which must draw on a wide range of resources and staff skills for most effective library service. The 1947 survey of the use of the reference department of the Detroit Public Library has lent substance to this belief. It showed that the very firms large enough to maintain their own special libraries were those that made the heaviest demands upon the public library, because their activities impinged on so many fields that their own highly specialized collections and staff did not suffice to their purpose.[28]

These findings led the Detroit Public Library to plan the establishment of a new department called the Industrial Research Service, designed to supply subscribers, (i.e. industrial corporations) with a comprehensive information service which would include: digests and reports; translations; publication of an "information journal" describing pertinent acquisitions; a regular abstracts bulletin for certain specified subjects; a record of printed materials in the area; and a directory of individuals and organizations in a position to supply special information.[29]

The ambitious Detroit plan has not yet been carried out, but a very similar program of research service has been actually underway at the John Crerar Library since 1948.[30] The organizational plan here has been to establish a new department — the Research Information Service — parallel with the existing departments of Technology, Business, and Medicine but working in close coordination with these.[31] The range of service rendered by the Research Information Service follows the familiar special library pattern: literature searches, continuing reports and abstracts on current scientific literature, translations, and detailed reports on "the state of the art" in a given field.[32] The financial arrangement adopted is to provide these services to any company or individual requesting them on a metered basis, the charges taking into account both the staff time consumed and a percentage for general overhead.[33]

The fact that the research services, as projected for the Detroit Public Library and as actually in operation in the John Crerar Library, call for the payment of fees by their clients may seem to place these ventures in the same category as the long-established practice in many public libraries of arranging to have "extra" service, such as translations, furnished at a fee.[34] However, the latter practice was only loosely identified with the public library, the library's part being often confined to suggesting appropriate persons able to perform the task. Such service was quite unadvertised and was often offered with a specific disclaimer of the library's responsibility for the performance of the service. The Detroit and John Crerar Library plans are well publicized, full-scale ventures, definitely a part of the libraries' operations. The implication of these plans clearly is that extensive service of a special library character is now regarded as a perfectly proper service

---

[28] Mabel Conat, "Detroit P. L. Surveys Reference Use," *Library Journal*, LXXII (November 15, 1947), 1570-71; Charles M. Mohrhardt, "Detroit Projects New Research Plan," *Library Journal*, LXII (September 1, 1947), 1156.

[29] Mohrhardt, *op. cit.*, 1155-59, 1166; Detroit Public Library, *Industrial Research Service for the Metropolitan Detroit Area, a Plan for Industry-Public Library Cooperation*, prepared by Charles M. Mohrhardt and Herman H. Henkle under the direction of the Detroit Public Library for the Ford Motor Company (Detroit: Detroit Public Library, 1947), pp. 11-16.

[30] Mr. Charles Mohrhardt, associate director of the Detroit Public Library, states that the pressure of other administrative problems has so far prevented the Library from putting its plans for the Industrial Research Service into effect. However, the Library still hopes to do so as soon as it can. (Interview, February 4, 1954).

[31] In fact, it was originally hoped that much of the bibliographical work necessary to a given project would be done by the existing departments, with perhaps only the final analysis and evaluation of findings being left to the specialists brought in for the new service. (Herman H. Henkle, "Libraries Can Give Industry Research Aid," *Library Journal*, LXXIII [November 15, 1948], 1633-34). However, according to its director, the John Crerar Library has found that the regular library staff has been too taken up with routine work to be able to contribute much help to the Research Information Service. (Interview with Herman Henkle, January 7, 1954).

[32] Herman Henkle, "Crerar's R.I.S. Explained," *Library Journal*, LXXIV (January 15, 1949), 93-95.

[33] John Crerar Library, *For Economy in Research* (Chicago: Research Information Service, The John Crerar Library, 1953?), p. 10.

[34] E.g. Enoch Pratt Free Library, *op. cit.*, p. 46.

responsibility of the public library, in other words that the public library can and should make arrangements to play a more dynamic role in the activities of industrial research. They suggest that only the present limitations on income prevent the provision of such extensive assistance as a regular, freely available part of the public library's services to its community.

These considerations, when seen in conjunction with the trend for departmental libraries in universities to offer service of a special library character, reinforce the belief that there is really no essential cleavage between the reference service of general libraries and the presently more highly developed "information service" of special libraries.

The contrary, it is true, has been maintained. The fact that special libraries are often in the charge of personnel without formal library training, together with the lingering influence of the old stereotype of the librarian as "custodian of books," has led some observers to claim that "documentalists" and "information officers" in special libraries constitute a profession separate from librarianship. For example, at a recent international conference on "documentation," Lorphèvre drew what purports to be the essential distinction between librarians and "documentalists" in the following statement: "A la différence du bibliothécaire qui conserve des livres et des périodiques, le documentaliste a surtout pour mission de réunir des documents — dans le sens plus large du mot — de *diffuser* cette documentation au moyen de bulletins analytiques, d'aperçus généraux des progrès d'une technique déterminée et de prévenir les desiderata en publiant des revues."[35]

However, when "documentalists" such as Lorphèvre dismiss librarianship as being the business of "preserving books and periodicals," they are only beating a horse already dead at the hands of Green and Dewey. The "documentalists" are undoubtedly justified in claiming to give unusual emphasis to such services as literature reporting, but to treat of these as new functions quite outside the scope of general libraries is to misread the whole history of librarianship. An important objective of the present study has been, in fact, to show that such services have developed as the gradual and logical extension of the program of personal assistance long established as a regular part of the functions of American research libraries.

In the light of this historical trend for the amplification of reference services, it is difficult to escape the conviction that the future is likely to see an expansion in scope of reference work in general research libraries along the lines already followed in special libraries. In the final analysis, the development of reference service depends ultimately, not only on the demonstrable efficacy of certain techniques or forms of organization, but also on the whole philosophy of library service dominating the choice of administrative measures. In this sense, the most compelling reason supporting the likelihood of an expanded reference service stems from the fact that such a development fits in with the whole tradition and character of American library practice.

Certainly in theory a plausible case might be made for the reduction of service to the level usual in European research libraries.[36] But almost every aspect of the operation of American research libraries — the admirable physical accommodations, the close and careful classification, the detailed cataloging, the speedy loan service, the multiplication of printed bibliographies — reflects the influence of a dominant and long-established regard for the reader's convenience and interests, a concern which goes far beyond the mere supply of materials. Out of this same concern, reference service has already become a well-intrenched and steadily growing function in American research library operation. The whole tradition of American librarianship — compounded out of librarians' ideals of service, the steadily rising level of competence in the profession, and the demands of the research workers themselves — points to a development making the reference librarian a full partner in research.

[35]Journées d'Etude Organisées par la Bibliothèque de Liège, *Les Problèmes de la Documentation dans les Bibliothèques Universitaires* (Liège: Association des Amis de l'Université de Liège, 1950), p. 64.

[36]In this connection, see the remarks of Crane Brinton and Keyes Metcalf, in University of Pennsylvania Library, *op. cit.*, pp. 7, 31-32.

A SELECTED BIBLIOGRAPHY

Prefatory Note: - Since the sources used for the present study have been fully cited in the footnotes for each chapter, the entire list is not repeated in this section. The following selected bibliography presents a listing of the material found to have been most useful. The subject-headings roughly correspond to the order in which the subject-matter of the dissertation has been presented.

The bibliography does not include individual library reports, since these are most useful when consulted as a series. The series of reports which have contributed most to the present study are those for the Astor Library; the Baltimore Department of Legislative Reference; the Boston Public Library; the University of California (Berkeley) Library; the University of Chicago Library; the Cincinnati Public Library; the Cleveland Public Library; the Columbia University Library; the Cornell University Library; the Detroit Public Library; the Enoch Pratt Free Library; the Harvard University Library; the Henry E. Huntington Library and Art Gallery; the University of Illinois Library; the John Carter Brown Library; the John Crerar Library; the Johns Hopkins University Library; the Library of Congress; the Lenox Library; the Los Angeles Public Library; the University of Michigan Library; the University of Minnesota Library; the New York Public Library; the New York State Library; the Newberry Library; the Northwestern University Library; the University of Pennsylvania Library; the Princeton University Library; the Providence Public Library; the Stanford University Library; the Wisconsin Free Library Commission (Legislative Reference Department); the Worcester Free Public Library; the Yale University Library. The dates covered by the reports consulted vary; for most of these institutions the present author has examined all the reports available from 1875 through 1940.

Separate mention should also be made here of the files of correspondence and reports on the "research librarianships," and of personal interviews with a number of librarians (see section on acknowledgments). Both these sources provided important primary material.

Definitions: Research, Research Libraries and Reference Service

Child, William B. "Reference Work at the Columbia College Library," *Library Journal*, XVI (October, 1891), 298.

Hutchins, Margaret. Introduction to Reference Work. Chicago: American Library Association, 1944.

Kroeger, Alice Bertha. Guide to the Study and Use of Reference Books; a Manual for Librarians, Teachers and Students. Boston: Houghton, Mifflin Co., 1902.

Ogg, Frederic Austin. Research in the Humanistic and Social Sciences; Report of a Survey Conducted for the American Council of Learned Societies. New York: The Century Co., 1928.

Pennsylvania. University. Library. Changing Patterns of Scholarship and the Future of Research Libraries; a Symposium in Celebration of the 200th Anniversary of the Establishment of the University of Pennsylvania Library. Philadelphia: University of Pennsylvania Press, 1951.

Rothstein, Samuel. "The Development of the Concept of Reference Service in American Libraries, 1850-1900," *Library Quarterly*, XXIII (January, 1953), 1-15.

Shyrock, Richard H. American Medical Research Past and Present. New York: The Commonwealth Fund, 1947.

Stewart, James D. (ed.). The Reference Librarian in University, Municipal and Specialised Libraries. London: Grafton and Co., 1951.

U. S. National Resources Committee. Science Committee. Research — a National Resource; Report of the Science Committee to the National Resources Committee. 3 vols. Washington: Government Printing Office, 1938-41.

Wyer, James Ingersoll. Reference Work; a Text-book for Students of Library Work and Librarians. Chicago: American Library Association, 1930.

Nineteenth-Century American Scholarship and the Rise of Research

Adams, Herbert Baxter. Historical Scholarship in the United States, 1876-1901; as Revealed in the Correspondence of Herbert B. Adams. Edited by W. Stull Holt. The Johns Hopkins University Studies in Historical and Political Science, Series LVI, No. 4. Baltimore: The Johns Hopkins Press, 1938.

Adams, Herbert Baxter. The Study of History in American Colleges and Universities. United States Bureau of Education, Circular of Information No. 2. Washington: Government Printing Office, 1887.

Bestor, Arthur E., Jr. "The Transformation of American Scholarship, 1875-1917," *Library Quarterly,* **XXIII** (July, 1953), 164-79.

Burgess, John William. Reminiscences of an American Scholar; the Beginnings of Columbia University. New York: Columbia University Press, 1934.

Butler, Nicholas Murray. Across the Busy Years; Recollections and Reflections. 2 vols. New York: Charles Scribner's Sons, 1939.

Curti, Merle. The Growth of American Thought. 2d ed. New York: Harper and Brothers, 1951.

Dunlap, Leslie Whittaker. American Historical Societies, 1790-1860. Madison, Wis.: Privately Printed, 1944.

Franklin, Fabian. The Life of Daniel Coit Gilman. New York: Dodd, Mead and Company, 1910.

Gilman, Daniel Coit. The Launching of a University and Other Papers; a Sheaf of Rembrances. New York: Dodd, Mead and Company, 1906.

Gilman, Daniel Coit. University Problems in the United States. New York: The Century Co., 1898.

Howe, M. A. De Wolfe. The Life and Letters of George Bancroft. 2 vols. New York: Charles Scribner's Sons, 1908.

Kraus, Michael. A History of American History. New York: Farrar and Rinehart, 1937.

Long, Orie William. Literary Pioneers; Early American Explorers of European Culture. Cambridge: Harvard University Press, 1935.

Thwing, Charles Franklin. The American and the German University; One Hundred Years of History. New York: The Macmillan Company, 1928.

Ticknor, George. Life, Letters, and Journals of George Ticknor. 2 vols. Boston: Houghton, Mifflin Co., 1900.

U. S. National Resources Committee. Science Committee. Research — a National Resource; Report of the Science Committee to the National Resources Committee. 3 vols. Washington: Government Printing Office, 1938-41.

Walz, J. A. German Influence in American Education and Culture. Philadelphia Carl Schurz Memorial Foundation, 1936.

White, Andrew Dickson. Autobiography of Andrew Dickson White. 2 vols. New York: The Century Co., 1905.

White, Andrew Dickson. "Scientific and Industrial Education in the United States," *Popular Science Monthly*, V (June, 1874), 170-91.

The Development of Research Libraries in the Nineteenth Century

Adams, Herbert Baxter. Seminary Libraries and Historical Extension. Johns Hopkins University Studies in Historical and Political Science, Fifth Series, XI. Baltimore: 1887.

Brough, Kenneth James. Scholar's Workshop; Evolving Conceptions of Library Service. Urbana: University of Illinois Press, 1953.

Carlton, W. N. C. "College Libraries in the Mid-Nineteenth Century," *Library Journal*, XXXII (November, 1907), 479-86.

Fletcher, William Isaac. Public Libraries in America. "Columbian Knowledge Series," No. II. Boston: Roberts Brothers, 1894.

Lovett, Robert W. "The Undergraduate and the Harvard Library, 1877-1937," *Harvard Library Bulletin*, I (Spring, 1947), 221-37.

Mearns, David C. The Story up to Now; the Library of Congress, 1800-1946. Washington: [Government Printing Office], 1947.

Rhees, William J. Manual of Public Libraries, Institutions, and Societies in the United States and British Provinces of North America. Philadelphia: J. B. Lippincott and Co., 1859.

Shera, Jesse Hauk. Foundations of the Public Library; the Origins of the Public Library Movement in New England, 1629-1855. Chicago: University of Chicago Press, 1949.

U. S. Bureau of Education. Public Libraries in the United States of America; Their History, Condition and Management. Special Report, Part I. Washington: Government Printing Office, 1876.

U. S. Bureau of Education. Statistics of Public Libraries in the United States and Canada, by Weston Flint, Statistician of the Bureau of Education. United States Bureau of Education, Circular of Information No. 7. Washington: Government Printing Office, 1893.

The Genesis of Reference Service

Brough, Kenneth James. Scholar's Workshop; Evolving Conceptions of Library Service. Urbana: University of Illinois Press, 1953.

Carney, Frank. "The Harvard Library under Justin Winsor," *Harvard Library Notes*, No. 29 (March, 1939), 245-52.

Columbia University. School of Library Service. School of Library Economy, 1887-1889; Documents for a History. New York: School of Library Service, Columbia University, 1937.

Crunden, Frederick M. "Reports on Aids and Guides, August '83 to June '85," *Library Journal*, XI (Milwaukee Conference Number, 1886), 309-330.

Foster, William E. "Assistance to Readers," in Papers Prepared for the World's Library Congress Held at the Columbian Exposition. Edited by Melvil Dewey. Reprint of Chapter IX of Part II of the Report of the U. S. Commissioner of Education for 1892-93. Washington: Government Printing Office, 1896. Pp. 982-93.

Foster, William E. "The Information Desk at the Providence Public Library," *Library Journal*, XVI (September, 1891), 271-72.

Foster, William E. "Report on Aids and Guides to Readers, 1883," *Library Journal*, VIII (Buffalo Conference Number, 1883), 233-45.

Green, Samuel Swett. "Personal Relations between Librarians and Readers," *Library Journal*, I (October, 1876), 74-81.

Green, Samuel Swett. The Public Library Movement in the United States, 1853-1893. Boston: Boston Book Co., 1913.

Johnston, William Dawson. "Dr. Spofford and the Library of Congress, 1860-1897," in Ainsworth Rand Spofford, 1825-1908; a Memorial Meeting at the Library of Congress on Thursday, November 12, 1908, at Four O'Clock, the Librarian of Congress Presiding. New York: Printed for the District of Columbia Library Association by the Webster Press, 1909. Pp. 22-35.

Kaplan, Louis. "The Early History of Reference Service in the United States," *Library Review*, Number 83 (Autumn, 1947), 286-90.

Kaplan, Louis. The Growth of Reference Service in the United States from 1876 to 1893. *ACRL Monographs*, No. 2. Chicago: Association of College and Reference Libraries, 1952.

Lane, William Coolidge. "The Harvard College Library, 1877-1928," in The Development of Harvard University since the Inauguration of President Eliot, 1869-1929. Edited by Samuel Eliot Morison. Cambridge: Harvard University Press, 1930. Pp. 608-31.

"Massachusetts Library Club," *Library Journal*, XIX (November, 1894), 382-84.

Mearns, David C. The Story up to Now; the Library of Congress, 1800-1946. Washington: [Government Printing Office], 1947.

"Proceedings of the Conference of Librarians, London...1877,...Sixth Sitting..." *Library Journal*, II (1877), 272-82.

"Reference Work in Libraries," *Library Journal*, XVI (October, 1891), 297-300.

Rothstein, Samuel. "The Development of the Concept of Reference Service in American Libraries, 1850-1900," *Library Quarterly*, XXIII (January, 1953), 1-15.

U. S. Bureau of Education. Public Libraries in the United States of America; Their History, Condition and Management. Special Report, Part I. Washington: Government Printing Office, 1876.

U. S. Congress. Joint Committee on the Library of Congress. Report under S. C. R. 26, Relative to the Condition, Organization, and Management of the Library of Congress; with Hearings; March 3, 1897. Senate Report 1573, 54th Cong., 2d Sess. [Washington: Government Printing Office], 1897.

Utley, George Burwell. The Librarians' Conference of 1853; a Chapter in American Library History. Edited by Gilbert H. Doane. Chicago: American Library Association, 1951.

Ware, Henry. "The Harvard College Library, No. 2," *Harvard Register*, II (October, 1880), 201-04.

Winsor, Justin. "The Development of the Library; Address at the Dedication of the Orrington Lunt Library, Northwestern University, Evanston, Illinois," *Library Journal*, XIX (November, 1894), 370-75.

Reference Service in General Research Libraries Before World War I:
Theories of Reference Service

Ahern, Mary Eileen and others. "Reference Work with the General Public," *Public Libraries*, IX (February, 1904), 55-65.

Andrews, Clement W. "The Use of Books," *Library Journal*, XXXII (June, 1907), 249-53.

Austen, Willard. "Educational Value of Reference Room Training for Students," *Bulletin of the American Library Association*, I (July, 1907), 274-77.

Billings, John Shaw. "Some Library Problems of Tomorrow: Address of the President," *Library Journal*, XXVII (Boston and Magnolia Conference Number, 1902), 1-9.

Bishop, William Warner. "The Amount of Help to be Given to Readers," *Bulletin of the American Library Association*, II (September, 1908), 327-32.

Bishop, William Warner. "The Theory of Reference Work," *Bulletin of the American Library Association*, IX (July, 1915), 134-39.

Briggs, Walter B. "Reference Work in Public and College Libraries; a Comparison and a Contrast," *Library Journal*, XXXII (November, 1907), 492-95.

Dana, John Cotton. "Misdirection of Effort in Reference Work," *Public Libraries*, XVI (March, 1911), 108-09.

Daniels, Joseph F. "The Indeterminate Functions of a College Library," *Library Journal*, XXXII (November, 1907), 487-92.

Dewey, Melvil. "The Faculty Library," *The Library*, Second Series, II (July 1, 1901), 238-41.

Hicks, Frederick Charles. "Department Libraries," *Columbia University Quarterly*, XIII (March, 1911), 183-95.

Singleton, M. E. "Reference Teaching in the Pioneer Library Schools, 1883-1903," Unpublished Master's thesis, School of Library Service, Columbia University, 1942.

Spofford, Ainsworth Rand. A Book for All Readers; Designed as an Aid to the Collection, Use, and Preservation of Books, and the Formation of Public and Private Libraries. 2d ed. New York: G. P. Putnam's Sons, 1900.

Van Valkenburg, Agnes. "How Far Should We Help the Public in Reference Work?" *Massachusetts Library Club Bulletin*, V (July-October, 1915), 102-08.

Wyer, James Ingersoll. Reference Work; a Text-book for Students of Library Work and Librarians. Chicago: American Library Association, 1930.

Reference Service in the General Research Library Before World War I:
Organization and Practice

Brough, Kenneth James. Scholar's Workshop; Evolving Conceptions of Library Service. Urbana: University of Illinois Press, 1953.

Billings, John Shaw. "The New York Public Library," *Century*, LXXXI (April, 1911), 839-52.

Foster, William E. The First Fifty Years of the Providence Public Library, 1878-1928. Providence: The Providence Public Library, the Akerman-Standard Company, Printers, 1928.

Hirshberg, Herbert S. "Four Library Buildings," *Bulletin of the American Library Association*, XXVII (December 15, 1933), 732-37.

McMullen, Charles Haynes. "The Administration of the University of Chicago Libraries, 1892-1928." Unpublished Ph.D. dissertation, Graduate Library School, University of Chicago, 1949.

Metcalf, Keyes D. "Departmental Organization in Libraries," in Current Issues in Library Administration. Edited by Carleton B. Joeckel. Chicago: University of Chicago Press, 1938. Pp. 90-110.

Mudge, Isadore Gilbert. "History of the Columbia University Reference Department." Unpublished manuscript, 1941.

Thompson, Madeline Cord. "History of the Reference Department of the University of Illinois Library." Unpublished Master's thesis, Library School, University of Illinois, 1942.

Vitz, Carl P. P. "Cleveland Experience with Departmentalized Reference Work," *Bulletin of the American Library Association*, IX (Berkeley Conference Number, 1915), 169-74.

Special Libraries and the Concept of Amplified Reference Service

Cutter, W. P. "The Technical Library's Field of Service," *Special Libraries*, VI (November, 1915), 150-52.

Dana, John Cotton. Libraries; Addresses and Essays. White Plains, N. Y.: The H. W. Wilson Company, 1916.

Dana, John Cotton. "The President's Opening Remarks," *Special Libraries*, I (January, 1910), 4-5.

Dudgeon, Matthew S. "The Scope and Purposes of Special Libraries," *Special Libraries*, III (June, 1912), 129-33.

Handy, Daniel N. "The Earning Power of Special Libraries," *Special Libraries*, II (January, 1911), 5-6.

Handy, Daniel N. "Special Libraries Association — Its Origin, Growth, and Possible Future;" *Bulletin of the American Library Association*, XX (October, 1926), 333-38.

Johnson, Ethel M. "The Special Library and Some of Its Problems," *Special Libraries*, VI (December, 1915), 157-61.

Johnston, R. H. "The Man and the Book," *Special Libraries*, VI (December, 1915), 162-63.

Johnston, R. H. "Special Libraries — a Report on Fifty Representative Libraries," *Library Journal*, XXXIX (April, 1914), 280-84.

Krause, Louise B. "The Value of a Library in an Engineering Office," *Engineering Record*, LXIX (April 25, 1914), 479-80.

Lapp, John A. "The Growth of a Big Idea," *Special Libraries*, IX (June, 1918), 157-59.

Marion, Guy E. "Interpreting the Library Movement," *Special Libraries*, X (September, 1919), 154-57.

Marion, Guy E. "Résumé of the Association's Activities, 1910-1915," *Special Libraries*, VI (November, 1915), 143-46.

"What is a Special Library?" *Special Libraries*, III (September, 1912), 143-49.

Williamson, C. C. "The Public Official and the Special Library," *Special Libraries*, VII (September, 1916), 112-19.

Legislative and Municipal Reference Work

American Bar Association. Report of the Special Committee on Legislative Drafting, to be Presented at the Meeting of the American Bar Association at Montreal, Canada, September 1-3, 1913. The Association? 1913?

Bailey, Louis J. "Legislative Reference Service," *Special Libraries,* XXI (January, 1930), 7-9.

Brigham, Herbert O. "The Legislative Reference Movement," *Special Libraries,* XV (December, 1924), 240-41.

Brigham, Herbert O. "The Special Libraries Association — a Historical Sketch," *Library Journal,* LIV (April 15, 1929), 337-40.

Brindley, John. "The Legislative Reference Movement," *Iowa Journal of History and Politics,* VII (January, 1909), 132-41.

Bruncken, Ernest. "The Legislative Reference Bureau," *News Notes of California Libraries,* II, Supplement (February, 1907), 96-105.

Commons, John R. Myself. New York: The Macmillan Company, 1934.

Commons, John R. "One Way to Get Sane Legislation," *American Monthly Review of Reviews,* XXXII (December, 1905), 722-23.

Fitzpatrick, Edward A. McCarthy of Wisconsin. New York: Columbia University Press, 1944.

Kaiser, John Boynton. Law, Legislative, and Municipal Reference Libraries; an Introductory Manual and Bibliographical Guide. "Useful Reference Series," No. 9. Boston: Boston Book Company, 1914.

Kohlstedt, Donald Winston. "Municipal Reference Library Services." Unpublished Master's thesis, Library School, University of Illinois, 1935.

Laurent, Eleanore V. Legislative Reference Work in the United States. Chicago: Council of State Governments, 1939.

Leek, J. H. Legislative Reference Work: a Comparative Study. Ph.D. dissertation, University of Pennsylvania. Philadelphia: n.p., 1925.

"Legislative Reference Bureau," *The [Chicago] City Club Bulletin,* II (December 9, 1908), 195-206.

Lowrie, S. Gale. "The Function of the Legislative Reference Bureau," *Library Journal,* XXXIX (April, 1914), 273-79.

McCarthy, Charles. The Wisconsin Idea. New York: The Macmillan Company, 1912.

Mowry, Don E. "Municipal Reference Libraries," *City Hall,* X (October, 1908), 131-33.

Mowry, Don E. "Reference Libraries in Cities — Baltimore as a Type," *Public Libraries,* XII (December, 1907), 387-89.

Nebraska. Legislative Reference Bureau. Legislative Reference Service for a State. Bulletin No. 1, revised. Lincoln: 1926.

Rex, Frederick. "The Municipal Reference Library as a Public Utility," *Special Libraries,* VIII (February, 1917), 23-37.

U. S. Congress. Senate. Committee on the Library. Legislative Drafting Bureau and Reference Division. Senate Report 1271, to accompany S.8337, 62d Cong., 2d Sess. Washington: Government Printing Office, 1913.

Wallis, Mary S. "The Library Side of the Department of Legislative Reference, Baltimore," *Special Libraries,* I (December, 1910), 73-75.

Wisconsin. Free Library Commission. Legislative Reference Department. Circular of Information, No. 6. 2d ed. Madison: 1911.

The Development of Industrial Research in the Twentieth Century

Angell, James Rowland. The Development of Research in the United States. Reprint and Circular Series of the National Research Council, No. 6. Washington: National Research Council, 1919.

Fleming, A. P. M. and Pearce, J. G. Research in Industry, the Basis of Economic Progress. London: Sir Isaac Pitman and Sons, Ltd., 1922.

Hale, George Ellery and others. The National Importance of Scientific and Industrial Research. Bulletin of the National Research Council, No. 1. Washington: National Research Council, 1919.

Jewett, Frank B. Industrial Research. Reprint and Circular Series of the National Research Council, No. 4. Washington: National Research Council, 1918.

Mees, Charles E. K. The Organization of Industrial Scientific Research. New York: McGraw-Hill Book Co., 1920.

National Research Council. Industrial Research Laboratories of the United States. (title varies) Bulletins of the National Research Council, Nos. 2, 16, 60, 81, 91, 102, 104. Washington: National Research Council, 1920-40.

Perazich, George and Field, Philip. Industrial Research and Changing Technology. National Research Project, Report No. M-4. Philadelphia: Work Projects Administration, 1940.

Reese, Charles L. Informational Needs in Science and Technology. Reprint and Circular Series of the National Research Council, No. 33. Washington: National Research Council, 1922.

U. S. National Resources Committee. Science Committee. Research — a National Resource; Report of the Science Committee to the National Resources Committee. 3 vols. Washington: Government Printing Office, 1938-41.

U. S. Office of Scientific Research and Development. Science, the Endless Frontier; a Report to the President, by Vannevar Bush. Washington: Government Printing Office, 1945.

Reference Service for Industrial Research Personnel

Brown, Delbert F. "Petroleum Libraries; Their Present Situation and the Outlook for the Future," *Special Libraries,* XXVIII (January, 1937), 3-7.

Cole, Betty Joy. "The Library vs. the Laboratory as a Basis for Research," *Journal of Chemical Education,* XXI (July, 1944), 319-21.

Cole, Betty Joy. "The Special Library Profession and What It Offers; 4: Chemical Libraries," *Special Libraries,* XXV (December, 1934), 271-77.

Connolly, Arthur. "Library Versus Laboratory Research," *Journal of Chemical Education,* XX (November, 1943), 531-33.

Davies, A. Catherine. "The Role of the Technical Librarian in the Paper Industry," *Paper Trade Journal,* CXV (October 29, 1942), Technical Section, 32-36.

Dean, J. A. "Shell Company of California, Information Service," *Special Libraries,* XVII (June, 1926), 229-30.

Dexter, Gregory. "The Library as an Engineering Tool," *Mechanical Engineering*, LIX (November, 1937), 845-49.

Ferguson, William C. "A Plan for Organized Research and Analytical Chemistry in Successful Chemical Manufacturing," *Journal of Industrial and Engineering Chemistry*, IV (December, 1912), 905-08.

Greenman, E. D. "The Chemist and His Library," *Special Libraries*, IX (November, 1918), 194-95.

Hamor, William A. and Bass, Lawrence W. "Bibliochresis: the Pilot of Research," *Science*, LXXI (April 11, 1930), 375-78.

Hosmer, Helen R. "Library of the Research Labratory (sic) of the General Electric Company at Schenectady, New York," *Special Libraries*, IV (September-October, 1913), 169-71.

Joaness, Edith. "A Fifty-year Old Technical Library," *Special Libraries*, XXX (October, 1939), 254-57.

Kenney, A. W. "The du Pont Experimental Station Library; a Chemical Special Library," *Special Libraries*, XVII (March, 1926), 99-103.

Kenney, A. W. "The Library Chemist," *Catalyst*, XI (June-July, 1926), 12-13.

Key, Mary Elizabeth. "The Technical Department Library of Aluminum Company of America," *Special Libraries*, XIX (February, 1928), 39-41.

Keyes, D. B. "An Informational Service for a Chemical Manufacturing Concern," *Chemical and Metallurgical Engineering*, XXVII (July 12, 1922), 54-58.

Leighty, J. A. "What the Research Worker Expects of the Librarian," *Special Libraries*, XXXI (July-August, 1940), 264-65.

Lewton, Lucy O. "Delimiting the Library Field," *Proceedings of the Special Libraries Association*, I (Thirtieth Annual Conference, 1938), P43-45.

Little, Arthur D. "Industrial Research in America," *Electrical Review and Western Electrician*, LXIV (February 28, 1914), 439-41.

Mann, Margaret. "Research and Reference in the Special Library," *Bulletin of the American Library Association*, XVIII (August, 1924), 185-90.

Marion, Guy E. "The Library as an Adjunct to Industrial Laboratories," *Library Journal*, XXXV (September, 1910), 400-04.

Mitchill, Alma C. "Disseminating Information," *Special Libraries*, XXIX (February, 1938), 45-48.

Morley, Linda H. "The Adaptation of Policies and Methods to Special Libraries of Different Types," *Special Libraries*, XXIII (July-August, 1932), 296-99.

Morley, Linda H. "Report of Professional Standards Committee," *Special Libraries*, XXXI (July-August, 1940), 215-17.

Reissmann, Gertrude. "The Kodak Park Library," *Special Libraries*, X (May, 1919), 94-97.

Shorb, Lura and Beck, Lewis W. "Opportunities for Chemists in Literature Service Work," *Journal of Chemical Education*, XXI (July, 1944), 315-18.

Smith, Julian F. "The Functions of a Research Library in the Dyestuffs Industry," *Special Libraries*, X (May, 1919), 100-02.

Smith, Julian F. and Smith, Irene F. "Information Service in Industrial Research Laboratories," *Industrial and Engineering Chemistry*, XXIV (August, 1932), 949-53.

Soule, Byron A. "Finding the Literature," *Journal of Chemical Education*, XXI (July, 1944), 333-35.

Wood, Dana M. "Use of the Library by the Engineer," *Special Libraries*, XVI (April, 1925), 112-17.

Reference Service in the General Research Libraries, 1917-1940

American Library Association. A Survey of Libraries in the United States. 4 vols. Chicago: American Library Association, 1926-27.

Bay, J. Christian. "Sources of Reference Work," *Bulletin of the Medical Library Association,* n.s. XIV (July, 1924), 10-15.

Bishop, William Warner. "Research Libraries in America," in *Overbibliotekar Wilhelm Munthe Pa Femtiarsdagen 20. Oktober 1933 Fra Fagfeller Og Venner.* Oslo: Grøndahl & Søns Boktrykeri, 1933. Pp. 13-19.

Bostwick, Arthur E. The American Public Library. 4th ed. revised and enlarged. New York: D. Appleton and Company, 1929.

Ellsworth, Ralph E. "Colorado University's Divisional Reading Room Plan: Description and Evaluation," *College and Research Libraries,* II (March, 1941), 103-09, 192.

Flexner, Abraham. Universities: American, English, German. New York: Oxford University Press, 1930.

Flexner, J. M. Circulation Work in Public Libraries. Chicago: American Library Association, 1927.

Hausdorfer, Walter. Professional School and Departmental Libraries; Sponsored by the University and College Departmental Librarians Group. New York: Special Libraries Association, 1939.

Hering, Hollis W. "The Research Library and the Research Librarian," *Special Libraries,* XXII (January, 1931), 7-11.

Hurt, Peyton. "Staff Specialization; a Possible Substitute for Departmentalization," *Bulletin of the American Library Association,* XXIX (July, 1935), 417-21.

Hutchins, Margaret. Introduction to Reference Work. Chicago: American Library Association, 1944.

Learned, William S. The American Public Library and the Diffusion of Knowledge. New York: Harcourt, Brace and Company, 1924.

McCombs, Charles F. The Reference Department. "Manual of Library Economy," XXII. Chicago: American Library Association, 1929.

McDiarmid, Erret W. and McDiarmid, John. The Administration of the American Public Library. Urbana: The American Library Association and the University of Illinois Press, 1943.

Minneapolis. Public Library. Minneapolis Public Library; Fifty Years of Service, 1889-1939. Minneapolis Public Library? 1939.

Mitchell, Sidney B. "Libraries and Scholarship," in The Library of Tomorrow; a Symposium. Edited by Emily Miller Danton. Chicago: American Library Association, 1939. Pp. 68-77.

Mudge, Isadore Gilbert. "History of the Columbia University Reference Department." Unpublished manuscript, 1941.

Palmer, Foster M. "The Reference Section in the Harvard College Library," *Harvard Library Bulletin,* VII (Winter, 1953), 55-72.

Shores, Louis. "The Practice of Reference," *College and Research Libraries,* III (December, 1941), 9-17.

Vormelker, Rose. "The Business Information Bureau," *Special Libraries,* XXIII (July-August, 1932), 300-01.

Vormelker, Rose. "The Librarian's Responsibility," *Special Libraries,* XXXIII (October, 1942), 281-83.

White, Carl M. "Trends in the Use of University Libraries," in College and University Library Service; Papers Presented at the 1937 Midwinter Meeting of the American Library Association. Edited by A. F. Kuhlman. Chicago: American Library Association, 1938. Pp. 15-39.

Warren, Althea. "Departmental Organization of a Public Library by Subject," in Current Issues in Library Administration. Edited by Carleton B. Joeckel. Chicago: University of Chicago Press, 1938. Pp. 111-34.

Winslow, Amy. "Experience in Departmentalization," *Bulletin of the American Library Association,* XXVII (December 15, 1933), 684-87.

Wyer, James Ingersoll. Reference Work; a Text-book for Students of Library Work and Librarians. Chicago: American Library Association, 1930.

Yenawine, Wayne S. "Wanted: a Functional Reference Room," *Library Journal,* LXII (March 15, 1937), 237-39.

Research Service in the General Libraries Before World War II

Baker, John C. "The Place of the Baker Library in the Harvard Business School," *Special Libraries,* XXVI (September, 1935), 199-201.

Borden, Arnold K. "After a Year," *Pennsylvania Library Notes,* XIII (July, 1933), 323-27.

Borden, Arnold K. "Creating Services," *Library Journal,* LVI (January 1, 1931), 23.

[Borden, Arnold K.] "Libraries and Research," *Dartmouth College Library Bulletin,* II (May, 1936), 113-14.

Borden, Arnold K. "The Research Librarian Idea," *Library Journal,* LVIII (February 1, 1933), 104-06.

Coulter, Edith M. "The University Librarian: His Preparation, Position, and Relation to the Academic Department of the University," *Bulletin of the American Library Association,* XVI (May, 1922), 271-75.

Fleming, Thomas P., Brodman, Estelle, and Robb, Seymour. "A Continuous Bibliographic Service in University Libraries," *College and Research Libraries,* VIII (July, 1947), 322-28.

Gabler, Anthony. "The Huntington Library from a Reference Angle," *Bulletin of the American Library Association,* XXVII (December 15, 1933), 687-89.

Henkle, Herman H. "An Interpretation of Research Librarianship," *School and Society,* XLVII (April 16, 1938), 494-99.

Henry, William E. Five Objectives of a University Library. Seattle? University of Washington, 1927.

Hicks, Clarence J. My Life in Industrial Relations; Fifty Years in the Growth of a Profession. New York: Harper and Brothers, 1941.

Hurt, Peyton. "The Need of College and University Instruction in Use of the Library," *Library Quarterly,* IV (July, 1934), 436-48.

Jameson, R. D. "Consultant Service and the College Library," *College and Research Libraries,* III (June, 1942), 230-34.

John Crerar Library. The John Crerar Library, 1895-1944; a Historical Report Prepared under the Authority of the Board Of Directors by the Librarian, J. Christian Bay. Chicago: The John Crerar Library, 1945.

Kaiser, John Boynton. "Newer Functions of University Libraries," *Library Journal*, LI (March 1, 1926), 217-21.

King, Henry H. "Assistance to the Faculty in Library Research; Report from Cornell University," *College and Research Libraries*, IX (July, 1948), 227-30.

King, Henry H. "The Cornell Experiment," *Special Libraries*, XXV (February, 1934), 33-34.

Kinkeldey, Otto. "The Research Librarian," *Bulletin of the American Library Association*, XXIX (September, 1935), 598-99.

MacLeish, Archibald. "The Reorganization of the Library of Congress, 1939-44," *Library Quarterly*, XIV (October, 1944), 1-39.

Noé, A. C. "The University Library and Research," *Library Quarterly*, IV (April, 1934), 300-05.

Putnam, Herbert. "American Libraries in Relation to Study and Research," *Library Journal*, LIV (September, 1929), 693-98.

Putnam, Herbert. "Consultants at the National Library," *Library Quarterly*, I (January, 1931), 18-21.

Putnam, Herbert. "The Future of the Library of Congress," in The Library of Tomorrow; a Symposium. Edited by Emily Miller Danton. Chicago: American Library Association, 1939. Pp. 179-91.

Putnam, Herbert. "Interpretive Service in a Library for Research," in *Overbibliotekar Wilhelm Munthe Pa Femtiarsdagen 20. Oktober 1933 Fra Fagfeller Og Venner*. Oslo: Grøndahl & Søns Boktrykeri, 1933. Pp. 211-13.

Putnam, Herbert. "The National Library; Some Recent Developments," *Bulletin of the American Library Association*, XXII (September, 1928), 346-55.

U. S. Office of Education. Survey of Land-Grant Colleges and Universities. Directed by Arthur J. Klein. Bulletin, 1930, No. 9. 2 vols. Washington: Government Printing Office, 1930.

Wildes, Karl L. "What the College or Institution Expects of its Departmental Libraries," *Special Libraries*, XXVII (February, 1936), 53-55.

Wright, Louis B. "Encouragement of Research at the Huntington Library," *Library Journal*, LIX (September 1, 1934), 639-42.

Wright, Louis B. "More Than a Library," *American Scholar*, II (May, 1933), 366-70.

Wroth, Lawrence C. The First Century of the John Carter Brown Library; a History with a Guide to the Collections. Providence: Associates of the John Carter Brown Library, 1946.

Zahm, Albert F. "The Division of Aeronautics of the Library of Congress," *Mechanical Engineering*, LII (September, 1930), 845-46.

Reference Service and Research since 1940

Bernal, J. D. "Information Service as an Essential in the Progress of Science," *ASLIB Proceedings*, (Twentieth Conference, 1945), 20-24.

Brandes, Julian. "Recent Trends in Library Reference Services," *School and Society*, LXX (September, 1949), 193-95.

Bush, George P. and Hattery, Lowell H. (eds.) Scientific Research: Its Administration and Organization. Washington: The American University Press, 1950.

Carlson, William H. "The Research Worker and the Library," *College and Research Libraries,* VII (October, 1946), 291-300.

Conat, Mabel. "Detroit P. L. Surveys Reference Use," *Library Journal,* LXXII (November 15, 1947), 1569-72.

Conat, Mabel. "Modern Trends in Reference Service," *Ontario Library Review,* XXXI (February, 1947), 76-80.

Detroit. Public Library. Industrial Research Service for the Metropolitan Detroit Area; a Plan for Industry-Public Library Cooperation. Prepared by Charles M. Mohrhardt and Herman H. Henkle under the Direction of the Detroit Public Library for the Ford Motor Company. [Detroit] Detroit Public Library, 1947.

Enoch Pratt Free Library. General Reference Department. General Reference Department Staff Manual. Prepared by Mary N. Barton and Ellen F. Watson. Baltimore: [Enoch Pratt Free Library], 1950.

Evans, Luther H. "The Library of Congress and Its Service to Science and Technology," *College and Research Libraries,* VIII (July, 1947), 315-21.

Furnas, C. C. (ed.) Research in Industry; Its Organization and Management, Prepared and Published for Industrial Research Institute, Inc. New York: D. Van Nostrand Company, 1948.

Gilman, Henry. "What the Scientist Expects of the Librarian," *College and Research Libraries,* VIII (July, 1947), 329-32.

Harbison, Frederick H. and Harper, Shirley H. "Industrial Relations — a Case Study of Specialized Communications Involving Several Groups," *American Documentation,* IV (Fall [October] 1953), 155-62.

Herner, Saul. "Improving the Internal Information Services in Scientific Research Organizations," *Special Libraries,* XLIV (January, 1953), 15-19.

Henkle, Herman H. "Crerar's R. I. S. Explained," *Library Journal,* LXXIV (January 15, 1949), 93-96.

Henkle, Herman H. "The John Crerar Library; a Public Special Library of Science, Technology, and Medicine," *Illinois Libraries,* XXX (April, 1948), 175-77.

Henkle, Herman H. "Libraries Can Give Industry Research Aid," *Library Journal,* LXXIII (November 15, 1948), 1629-34.

Hertz, David Bendel. The Theory and Practice of Industrial Research. New York: McGraw-Hill Book Company, 1950.

Hewitt, William F. "The Academic Literature-Science Unit," *Information,* III (Spring, 1949), 29-31.

Johnson, A. B. "Services in Petroleum Libraries," *Special Libraries,* XLI (November, 1950), 312-17, 336.

John Crerar Library. For Economy in Research. Chicago: Research Information Service, John Crerar Library, 1953?

Journées d'Etude Organisées par la Bibliothèque de l'Université de Liège. Les Problèmes de la Documentation dans les Bibliothèques Universitaires. Liège: Association des Amis de l'Université de Liège, 1950.

Mees, Charles E. K. and Leermakers, John A. The Organization of Industrial Scientific Research. 2d ed. New York: McGraw-Hill Book Company, 1950.

Mohrhardt, Charles M. "Detroit Projects New Research Plan," *Library Journal,* LXII (September 1, 1947), 1155-59, 1166.

Pennsylvania. University. Library. Changing Patterns of Scholarship and the Future of Research Libraries; a Symposium in Celebration of the 200th Anniversary of the Establishment of the University of Pennsylvania Library. Philadelphia: University of Pennsylvania Press, 1951.

Phelps, Rose Bernice. "The Effects of Organizational Patterns on Reference Service in Three Typical Metropolitan Libraries: Boston, St. Louis, and Los Angeles." Unpublished Ph.D. dissertation, University of Chicago, Graduate Library School, 1943.

Ranganathan, S. R. and Sundaram, C. Reference Service and Bibliography. 2 vols. Madras: The Madras Library Association, 1940-41.

Shera, Jesse H. "Emergence of a New Institutional Structure for the Dissemination of Specialized Information," *American Documentation,* IV (Fall [October], 1953), 163-73.

Shera, Jesse H. and Egan, Margaret E. "Documentation in the United States," *American Documentation,* I (Winter [January] 1950), 8-12.

Special Libraries Association. Science-Technology Division. Technical Libraries; Their Organization and Management. Lucille Jackson, editor. New York: Special Libraries Association, 1951.

Talmadge, Robert Louis. "Practices and Policies of the Reference Departments of Large University Libraries Concerning the Preparation of Bibliographies." Unpublished Master's thesis, Library School, University of Illinois, 1951.

U. S. Office of Scientific Research and Development. Science, the Endless Frontier; a Report to the President by Vannevar Bush. Washington: Government Printing Office, 1945.

U. S. President's Scientific Research Board. Science and Public Policy; a Report to the President by John R. Steelman, Chairman. 5 vols. Washington: Government Printing Office, 1947.

ACRL MONOGRAPHS issued to July, 1955

No. 14 -- Rothstein, Samuel, THE DEVELOPMENT OF REFERENCE SERVICES THROUGH ACADEMIC TRADITIONS, PUBLIC LIBRARY PRACTICE AND SPECIAL LIBRAR-IANSHIP (Issued June, 1955) ....$2.75 (paper), $3.25 (cloth)

No. 13 -- LIBRARY-INSTRUCTIONAL INTEGRATION AT THE COLLEGE LEVEL: Report of the 40th Conference of Eastern College Librarians held at Columbia University, Nov. 27, 1954 (Issued April, 1955) $1.00

No. 12 -- Esterquest, Ralph T., LIBRARY COOPERATION IN THE BRITISH ISLES (Issued March, 1955)... 70¢

No. 11 -- Proceedings (illustrated) of the 1954 LIBRARY BUILDING PLANS INSTITUTE conducted by the ACRL BUILDINGS COMMITTEE at Madison, Wisconsin, January 30-31, 1954. Edited by Howard Rovelstad. Includes EVALUATION OF COMPACT BOOK STORAGE SYSTEMS by Robert H. Muller (Issued Spring, 1954) $2.35

No. 10 -- Proceedings (illustrated) of the 1953 LIBRARY BUILDING PLANS INSTITUTE conducted by the ACRL BUILDINGS COMMITTEE at Chicago, February 1 & 2, 1953. Edited by Donald C. Davidson. To which is added a COLLEGE AND UNIVERSITY LIBRARY BUILDINGS BIBLIOGRAPHY, 1945-53, compiled by Mrs. Edna Hanley Byers (Issued Fall, 1953)... $2.25

No. 9 -- A RECOMMENDED LIST OF BASIC PERIODICALS IN ENGINEERING AND THE ENGINEERING SCIENCES (with separate subject lists) prepared by a Special Committee of the PURE AND APPLIED SCIENCE SECTION of the ACRL, under the Chairmanship of William H. Hyde. (July, 1953)........................... 75¢

No. 8 -- Kinney, Mary R., BIBLIOGRAPHICAL STYLE MANUALS: A Guide to Their Use in Documentation and Research (June, 1953)................................ 60¢

Nos. 5, 6, & 7 (Issued under one cover, January, 1953)
No. 5, Jackson, Ellen P., ADMINISTRATION OF THE GOVERNMENT DOCUMENTS COLLECTION; No. 6, Stevens, Rolland E., CHARACTERISTICS OF SUBJECT LITERATURES; No. 7, Broadus, Robert N., THE RESEARCH LITERATURE OF THE FIELD OF SPEECH .... 65¢

No. 4 -- Proceedings (illustrated) of the 1952 LIBRARY BUILDING PLANS INSTITUTE conducted by the ACRL BUILDINGS COMMITTEE at Ohio State University, April 25 and 26, 1952. Edited by David Jolly. (Issued Fall, 1952) $1.75

No. 3 -- Herner, Saul, & Heatwole, M. K., THE ESTABLISHMENT OF STAFF REQUIRE-MENTS IN A SMALL RESEARCH LIBRARY (Issued May, 1952)............... 50¢

No. 2 -- Kaplan, Louis, THE GROWTH OF REFERENCE SERVICE IN THE UNITED STATES FROM 1876 to 1893 (Issued February, 1952) .... 25¢

No. 1 -- Kraus, Joe W., WILLIAM BEER AND THE NEW ORLEANS LIBRARIES, 1891-1927 (Issued January, 1952) .... 35¢

Among the subjects being considered for forthcoming numbers are:
Audio-Visual Aids, College and University Library Bylaws, The College Library's Role in Building Habits of Book Ownership, Friends of the Library Organizations, Library Resources, Rare Books, Reference Service, Scientific Periodicals, Subject Divisional Reading Rooms, and more about College and University Library Buildings.

ACRL MONOGRAPHS are separately priced to be sold at cost. There is no annual subscription rate. Frequency of issue is irregular, and individual numbers vary greatly in size and price. STANDING ORDERS on an "Until forbid" basis should always be placed to insure that every number is received promptly as published. Standing orders are billed at least once annually. BEGINNING WITH ISSUE NO. 12 THERE WILL BE A 10% DISCOUNT FOR STANDING ORDERS. If desired, payment (or deposit) may be made in advance for numbers not yet published. Advance payments in the amount of $5.00 are suggested. Orders for SEPARATE COPIES totaling less than $1.00 must be paid for in advance (send cash, stamps, or check; no billing). All checks must be payable to the order of the ASSOCIATION OF COLLEGE AND REFERENCE LIBRARIES.

ALL ORDERS -- WHETHER SINGLE COPY OR STANDING -- SHOULD BE ADDRESSED ONLY AS FOLLOWS (no dealer discount; please order direct):

ACRL MONOGRAPHS
c/o American Library Association
50 E. Huron Street
Chicago 11, Illinois

DATE DUE

AUG 0 1982		
12-12-86		
IL: 2169551		
(DUE: 1-12-87)		
6/10/88		
IL: 472-88		
(Due: 7/11/88) ✓		